The Edinburgh Anthology of Scottish Literature
Concise Edition

The Edinburgh Anthology of Scottish Literature

Concise Edition

Edited by Robert Irvine

Kennedy & Boyd

Kennedy & Boyd
an imprint of
Zeticula
57 St Vincent Crescent
Glasgow
G3 8NQ
Scotland.

http://www.kennedyandboyd.co.uk
admin@kennedyandboyd.co.uk

First published in 2009
Copyright © Zeticula 2009
Introduction and notes © Robert Irvine 2009.
Cover image: Edinburgh from Arthur's Seat; engraving by William Miller
 after H. W. Williams

ISBN-13 978-1-84921-005-8 Paperback

Acknowledgements

Many thanks are due to Anne Mason for her help in producing this volume.

A grant from Edinburgh University's School of Languages, Literatures and Cultures supported the preparation of some of these texts.

A note on the texts

All texts here are based on their first editions, with the exception of Fragments of Ancient Poetry which is based on its second edition. Obvious errors have been silently amended; a few significant changes in later editions are identified in footnotes.

Contents

Introduction

The texts assembled in this volume are drawn from a period in which Scottish writing enjoyed unparalleled success and influence across the western world. The national epic of 'Ossian', the poetry of Robert Burns, and the poems and novels of Walter Scott were celebrated and imitated all across Europe and the English-speaking world, building on Scotland's established reputation for the historical and philosophical writing of the Scottish Enlightenment. No other European nation of comparable size has ever had this level of international impact. This introduction will sketch some of the issues raised by this remarkable flourishing.

Eighteenth- and early nineteenth-century Scotland was a country going through a historical process we can most conveniently label 'modernisation'. The 'modern' in this sense might be thought of in terms of three developments: the centralisation of political power in a bureaucratic state; the development of a capitalist economy, with banks, joint-stock companies and so on; and the emergence of a public sphere of information exchange and debate mediated by print. By the end of the century, Edinburgh boasted a particularly innovative publishing industry, and Glasgow had become a commercial powerhouse, first as a major centre of trade across the North Atlantic, principally in tobacco, and then, from the end of the eighteenth century, as a centre of industrial production. In the realm of politics, Scotland's 'modernisation' took a slightly unusual form. Certainly, power was increasingly consolidated in a centralised state in this period. The last Jacobite rebellion provides a particularly acute instance of this. In 1745–6, a largely Highland army waged a civil war to restore the (Catholic) Stuart dynasty to the throne, from which it had been excluded by the (Protestant) House of Hanover since 1714. This rebellion was mostly Highland, and indeed only possible, because Highland clan chiefs were able to raise private armies from their dependents, a type of military service long since abolished in the lowlands. The defeat of the Jacobites meant the final destruction of this last vestige of feudal autonomy. Government soldiers imposed government rule across the Highlands, reducing those chiefs who remained to mere landowners on the lowland model. But of course the state that asserted this power was not Scottish, but British; the Jacobites themselves wanted to restore the Stuarts to the throne of England and Ireland, as well as to that of Scotland. Scotland had lost its court, and the aristocratic literary culture that went with it, in 1603, when James VI of Scotland went to London to become James I of England as well. Scotland remained an independent kingdom, albeit one whose king was permanently somewhere else, until 1707. Then, a variety of political and economic pressures persuaded the Scottish parliament to enter a union with the English parliament, dissolving Scotland's political sovereignty in that of a new state, Great Britain.

Scottish aristocrats (the big landowners who inherited political power as dukes or earls) had no remaining reason to make Edinburgh, rather than London, the base of their political operations. Their absence meant that much of Scottish life was governed by the smaller landowners in the countryside, and the business, ecclesiastical and legal elites in the cities. This ruling class was vigorous in the pursuit of those types of modernisation, economic and cultural, open to it in the absence of a state. More than this: it was also highly conscious of this modernisation as constituting a radical break with the past. Its writers and thinkers, in the movement we now celebrate as the Scottish Enlightenment, developed concepts to explain how a society based on trade and manufactures differed from earlier types of society. Economic activity, they speculated, is more than one social practice among others. As its material basis, that which allows it to survive, a society's type of economy determines the nature of many of its other institutions. Modern Britain's foundation in trade required, not only banks and stock-exchanges, but a set of laws protecting property defined in terms of money, and a parliamentary system to make them. As long as its economy had been primarily agricultural, and property meant land, a different type of legal and political system had been required, the one that the historians retrospectively named 'feudal'. In the earliest, 'primitive' or 'savage' ages of humankind, the Scottish historians envisioned hunter-gathers organised in tribes of the kind encountered in North America. Because it thought of human history as progressing though a series of distinct stages, we refer to this model as the 'stadial' theory of history.

A commercial society also required a distinctly modern set of social relations. In particular, it required a means whereby those who had become wealthy through trade could be integrated into the country's elite, one broader than, but incorporating, the old ruling class, whose power was based on their possession of land. Taking their cue from Joseph Addison and Richard Steele's campaign for the reformation of manners in the *Spectator* (1711–12, 1714), some of Scotland's self-consciously modernising elite promoted a model of sociability named 'polite' to this end. This can be defined in terms of its rejection of violence: not just the physical violence associated with a feudal ruling class, but violent attachment to a political party or a religious denomination. Polite 'manners' (the latter term having a broader meaning than today, to signify something like 'cultural norms') were accordingly those thought to mitigate the threat of civil conflict that had torn Britain apart in the previous century (and briefly recurred in 1745–6). Print culture was central to the promotion of this agenda. The nation was to be united, not by a dynasty or a religion, but through the peaceful exchange of ideas through books and journals on the model of a conversation. This meant that polite writing had to avoid reference to sex and the body, to avoid alienating female readers, as well as political and religious controversy. So, for example, the satire of Alexander Pope and Jonathan Swift, often ferociously partisan and sometimes bawdy, was excluded from the canon of the polite: this type of writing largely vanished in English from the 1740s onwards. But the polite encoded its own politics: the vast majority of the population who owned no property, and thus did not have the leisure to take part, were excluded from the conversation.

The new historical thinking also postulated what had been lost in the shift to the modern. While they emphasised that political and legal institutions changed to fit the developing economic basis of a society, the enlightenment philosophers were also deeply interested in what they thought did *not* change in the course of history: the underlying structures of the human mind and the nature of perception, both physical and moral. Morality, they thought, was produced by sympathetic instincts, feelings embedded in our human nature, rather than a civilizing education. The very containment of passion required by modern sociability might erode these instincts. Earlier, more 'primitive' forms of social organisation might accordingly allow more direct, more spontaneous expression of 'natural' feeling than is possible in modern society. And this meant that less-developed societies might retain a higher capacity for poetry than commercial ones. For poetry, on this view, was the sincere expression of individual feeling (as it was to be for Wordsworth) rather than a mode of social criticism (as it had been for Pope). At the same time, this definition includes under 'poetry' types of expression that are not, originally, written down at all, such as ballads transmitted by word-of-mouth.

This understanding of the place of poetry in history was a major factor in the astonishing success, in the 1760s, of the works of 'Ossian', as 'collected' and published by James Macpherson. Presented as translations of ancient Gaelic verse, composed by a Highland bard in the third century, their authenticity was soon called into doubt, most vociferously by Samuel Johnson. Today it is accepted that, at least in the initial volume, *Fragments of Ancient Poetry* (1760; extracted in this anthology), Macpherson did draw on traditional Gaelic ballads which he and his contacts collected in the Highlands. These ballads were first composed perhaps a thousand years later than Macpherson claimed, however, and were certainly not the remains of a single epic poem composed by a single poet as he assumed. Hugh Blair, in the essay extracted in this volume, provided an influential explanation of the origins of Ossian's poetry in terms of the stadial theory of history. But Macpherson's 'translations', re-creations and inventions were shaped from the start by his knowledge of what a polite eighteenth-century readership would expect of a 'primitive' bard; anticipating the critical response, not only of academics like Blair, but of the periodical journals like the *Gentleman's Magazine* or the *Scots Magazine* which set the standard of polite taste in literature.

A large part of that anticipation meant distancing these works from the actually-existing Highland culture in which Macpherson claimed to have found them. By locating them in the third century, he can insist that Fingal and his heroes lived before the coming of Christianity to Scotland, and before the establishment of the clan system in the Highlands. They are thus not immediately identifiable with the often Catholic Highland warriors who invaded lowland Scotland and England in a Jacobite rebellion that was only 15 years in the past when *Fragments* was published. Fingal's people, indeed, do not even identify themselves as *Scottish*: their distant historical period is prior to the establishment of the rival kingdoms of England and Scotland. Rather, they are Celts on the island of Britain who have escaped Roman conquest. To that extent, they can be understood as the original free *Britons*, providing a reassuringly ancient and heroic precedent for the political identity of Macpherson's modern readers.

Yet if the Preface and footnotes to *Fragments of Ancient Poetry* insist on the difference between the tribe of Fingal and the eighteenth-century clans, the poems themselves might now seem to us haunted by the recent historical experience of the Highlands. Ossian mourns the absolute defeat of his people, the destruction of tribal continuity, the end of a family line; a mourning that makes perfect sense as a response to the brutal collective punishment of the rebel clans by the government army, the execution of their chiefs and government appropriation of their estates, the banning of plaid and bagpipes and weaponry. To all this Macpherson had a personal connection, as the nephew of a clan chief and leader in the rebellion who spent nine years in hiding after 1746 before escaping to exile in France. But Fragments mounts no resistance to the forcible integration of his homeland into modern Britain; rather, it is complicit in it. Stripped of their political structures, the Highlands become available to lowland investors as an economic opportunity; stripped of their political associations, they become available to Macpherson's readers as a landscape of pure feeling, where no historical reality will obstruct the pleasurable indulgence of melancholy and the sublime. This is what Blair means when he calls the works of Ossian 'the Poetry of the Heart'.

In 'Ossian', the Enlightenment's postulation of a primitive 'other' as the location of sincere feeling found its perfect confirmation. In Robert Burns, a polite readership found something very similar. Since the labouring poor were by definition excluded from the 'polite', they too could be understood as a repository of natural feeling undiluted by the necessary accommodations of modern society, making them imaginable as an origin for poetry. In the framing material of his first published collection, the Kilmarnock *Poems* of 1786, Burns to a certain extent collaborates in this view of his place as a poet. Some of the poems, too, lend themselves to this kind of reading. Henry Mackenzie's influential review of the Kilmarnock edition in *The Lounger* (a periodical modelled on *The Spectator*) selects for praise the sentimental moralising of, for example, 'The Cotter's Saturday Night', 'To a Mouse', and 'To a Mountain Daisy'. In such poems, the poverty and hard labour of the rural poor act to confirm the naturalness of the conventional piety and domestic morality to which they apparently adhere. These poems thus tend to confirm rather than challenge the values of their propertied readers. Indeed the first of these, dedicated to Burns's lawyer friend Robert Aiken, includes a moment of recognition of this mechanism at work. The poem's description of a labouring family will also, the first stanza tells us, imagine 'what Aiken in a *Cottage* would have been' (l.8), suggesting that the poem reflects the virtues of its propertied reader as much as the life of the people he is reading about. As in Macpherson, the effect is to empty a scene of human suffering of its political meaning. The social difference between the subject of the poetry and its reader generates the pleasures of sympathetic identification rather than the discomfort of political critique.

However, most of Burns's poetry resists this sort of genteel appropriation of labouring-class experience. His use of Scots itself defies the imposition of a standardised, polite English as the only acceptable medium of literary expression. He also revels in satire, that Augustan genre excluded from the improving agenda of polite culture. In the verse epistles, indeed, Burns goes beyond a commitment to an older, politically and socially critical ideal of poetry. If 'A Cotter's Saturday Night' offers up the manners of his own rank for the cultural consumption of the polite, the 'Epistles to Lapraik', for example, do the reverse, appropriating the modes of polite culture for the use of the labouring poor themselves. Here the tenant-farmer poet addresses, not a property-owning audience above him, but one on his own level, and the discursive ideal is the enlightenment one of mutually-improving conversation, with poetry serving as a medium for this specific type of sociability. The politics of such poems lies not in any overt criticism of the ruling class, but in the cultural autonomy from that class that they implicitly assert. In the first 'Epistle to Lapraik', Burns stakes his claim to a poetic vocation on 'Nature' and 'the Heart', rather than on any literary training, just as he had on the Kilmarnock edition's title-page, and in its preface. But there it had served to gratify the Hugh Blairs and Henry Mackenzies of the period in their desire to find untutored inspiration in a son of the soil; in the verse epistles it expresses indifference to the literary expectations of such 'Critic-folk', his 'learned foes', made possible by an alternative readership among the poet's social peers.

That the new modes of modern print culture might be taken over by those ranks they had been designed to exclude had always been a possibility. In England, it had been assumed that their general illiteracy, as well as their lack of access to books, sealed off the Enlightenment from the poor. In Scotland, where the Presbyterian church had established a network of parish schools, basic literacy was more common; but here it was assumed that the reading of the poor would restrict itself to the Bible and other religious materials. The 1790s proved these assumptions to be quite wrong, in the context of the 1789 revolution in France. The British government was horrified at the extent to which sympathy with the French Revolution energised many British working people and revealed a passion for reading and ideas among them that it had previously been safe to deny or ignore. Thomas Paine's defence of the Revolution, *Rights of Man*, sold perhaps 200,000 copies in the two years after its publication in 1791. Even more worrying than this number was the means of its distribution. Radicals had formed themselves into local 'Constitutional Societies' and 'Corresponding Societies' in which to discuss political ideas and, as the latter title suggests, these were in touch with one another, by letter, on a national level. It was through this network that Paine's book was dispersed, allowing many people to read it, or hear it read, who could not afford to buy it. The nation as a conversation held through the medium of print, grounded on a common 'human nature': the ideal of polite sociability, which had evolved to efface the difference between one group of propertied people and another, had now been seized by many among the propertyless majority. What had been understood as a way of evading political difference was revealed as a political weapon. Literacy itself was now a political issue.

The government response in Scotland was particularly ruthless. Thomas Muir, himself a lawyer, was found guilty of circulating, reading out and encouraging others to read 'seditious' texts such as *Rights of Man* in August 1793, and sentenced to 14 years transportation to the penal colony of Botany Bay in Australia. Over the next seven months, the Scottish courts sentenced another four men to transportation for similar 'crimes'. The 'Treason Trials' which followed in London, in contrast, led only to acquittals. It is in this context that one must read Burns's poems of the 1790s: both their anger and despair, and the fact that they generally evoke the French Revolution indirectly, by reference to the Scottish or American wars of independence, rather than explicitly. Many, such as the Washington 'Ode', were not published until long after Burns's death in 1795. Such caution on Burns's part suggests more generally the way in which the new political context had changed the meaning of writing from the lower ranks for propertied audiences. Where before it could be enjoyed for its artless sentiment, divorced from politics, now it was to be scrutinised for signs of resistance to the political status quo.

The British response to the French Revolution also shaped the context in which the work of women writers was received. Polite culture had a quite specific role for propertied women. Their presence in social life was deemed an important way of moderating the political and religious passions of their menfolk. By extension, women's writing had gained a certain amount of cultural authority, although the price for this was a severe narrowing of its subject matter to the moral and domestic. The threat from France was quickly translated by reactionary writers into a threat to the private life of the family and the sexual regulation that supported it (although in fact the Revolution itself was not at all radical in this respect); and so, in the 1790s, the woman writer's role in defending domestic morality assumed a new, and overtly political, importance.

It is striking, then, that Joanna Baillie's remarkable, decades-long project, *A Series of Plays: in which it is attempted to delineate the stronger passions of the mind* claims its literary authority in other ways, by placing itself in relation to genres gendered masculine. The systematic exploration of the psychology of feeling announced on the title page of the 1798 volume, and explained in the 'Introductory Discourse', is a clear continuation of Scottish Enlightenment concerns. In that discourse, the people among whom our 'human nature' is to be 'discovered by stronger and more unequivocal marks' than elsewhere has broadened to encompass all of 'the middling and lower classes of society' and not only the uneducated primitive or ploughman. Still, this could have seemed politically radical in the ideologically-saturated atmosphere of the 1790s, as not before. It could no longer be assumed that crediting the lower classes with a specific claim to 'human nature' did no more than make their songs and poems available for the aesthetic appreciation of their superiors; it could also ground a demand on their part for political rights. When William Wordsworth made an almost identical claim in the 'Preface' to *Lyrical Ballads* two years later it was certainly interpreted in this way. But no one seems to have mistaken Baillie for a dangerous subversive. Her interest in natural feeling is contained within the terms of enlightenment science, rather than, as in Wordsworth, part of a wider social critique. It also helps that the plays themselves so clearly evoke an icon of English national culture, William Shakespeare. Wordsworth's claim to be writing in 'the real language of men' is not realised in his actual verse any more than Baillie's, but it does provide an impetus to formal experiment. Baillie's enlightenment interest in human psychology is realised in a five-act structure, iambic pentameter, and a linguistic register, all borrowed from two hundred years before. In this respect, Baillie is engaged in recovering and reinventing 'ancient' poetic forms within an enlightenment context just as much as Macpherson, but rather than raiding the cultural resources of the rural poor, she appropriates the body of texts at the pinnacle of the English literary canon.

Yet Baillie's plays cannot simply evade the politics of their time. *De Monfort's* anti-hero is an aristocrat who is incapable of containing his own passion for the sake of polite sociability; and the passion that cannot be contained is hatred for a fellow-aristocrat who is a consummate performer in this regard. The hero of the play is Jane de Monfort, the anti-hero's sister. She perfectly embodies conventional feminine moral authority: devoted to the family, self-sacrificing, and defined entirely by the good effect she has on others. To that extent Jane is a familiar conservative ideal. Yet the breakdown of social order with which she is faced does not come from the democratic demands of the lower orders, but from the unconstrained rage of a male member of the aristocracy. If this is a play about its own time and place (and its German setting serves to safely distance it from events in Britain), it suggests that the danger to British society comes not from the French Republic or its British sympathisers, but from the immoderate reaction to them on the part of the ruling class. To that extent, *De Monfort* might be thought of as using an enlightenment conception of human psychology to diagnose a pathology of reaction: the emphasis on unexamined emotion as the basis for a natural social order that Edmund Burke argues for in his *Reflections on the Revolution in France* (1790).

Some of the ideological heat went out of the 'Revolution Controversy' as the threat from France receded. But the years of economic crisis that followed the final defeat of Napoleon in 1815, and the ongoing social revolution caused by industrialisation, made clear that there was no simple return to the pre-1789 status quo. The 1790s revealed as a fantasy the Addisonian idea that politics could be isolated from other aspects of polite society; the decades that followed undermined the Enlightenment's faith that incremental economic change could be trusted to bring social benefits without political management. Thomas Carlyle's essay, 'Signs of the Times', is an attack on that faith, and an assertion of the moral necessity of politics as a creative force in human history. What 'Signs of the Times' calls 'machinery' is, among other things, that version of history that imagines individuals to be the effects, rather than the causes, of social change. In place of the Scottish Enlightenment's conception that legal and political systems are the products of a society's *material* basis, Carlyle (following the German philosopher Hegel, among others) sees human society, including its technology, as the realisation of *ideas*, the expression of great creative concepts forged in the souls of heroic individuals. Even the French Revolution was an example of this, 'an Idea: a Dynamic, not a Mechanic force'. This return of historical agency to the individual is of course potentially politically radical. But Carlyle preaches it in a rhetoric that recalls the Presbyterian pulpit that had he renounced for print culture, with a blizzard of historical examples taking the place of quotation from the bible; and there is a hint that Carlyle wants to close down a radical interpretation of his text, when he writes that 'it is towards a higher freedom than mere freedom from oppression by his fellow-mortal, that man dimly aims'. But as the history of the Enlightenment itself had shown, no text can wholly determine the use that is made of it, or by whom.

FRAGMENTS

OF

ANCIENT POETRY,

Collected in the HIGHLANDS of SCOTLAND,

AND

Translated from the GALIC or ERSE Language.
The SECOND EDITION.

Vos quoque qui fortes animas, belloque peremtas
Laudibus in longum vates dimittitis aevum,
Plurima securi fudistis carmina Bardi.

LUCAN[1]

EDINBURGH
Printed for G. HAMILTON and J. BALFOUR
MDCCLX

PREFACE

The Public may depend on the following fragments as genuine remains of ancient Scottish poetry. The date of their composition cannot be exactly ascertained. Tradition, in the country where they were written, refers them to an æra of the most remote antiquity; and this tradition is supported by the spirit and strain of the poems themselves; which abound in those ideas, and paint those manners, that belong to the most early state of society. The diction too, in the original, is very obsolete; and differs widely from the style of such poems as have been written in the same language two or three centuries ago. They were certainly composed before the establishment of clanship in the northern part of Scotland, which is itself very ancient; for had clans been then formed and known, they must have made a considerable figure in the work of a Highland Bard; whereas there is not the least mention of them in these poems. It is remarkable that there are found in them no allusions to the Christian religion or worship; indeed, few traces of religion of any kind. One circumstance seems to prove them to be coeval with the very infancy of Christianity in Scotland. In a fragment of the same poems, which the translator has seen, a Culdee or Monk is represented as desirous to take down in writing from the mouth of Oscian, who is the principal personage in several of the following fragments, his warlike atchievements and those of his family. But Oscian treats the Monk and his religion with disdain, telling him, that the deeds of such great men were subjects too high to be recorded by him, or by any of his religion: A full proof that Christianity was not as yet established in the country.

Though the poems now published appear as detached pieces in this collection, there is ground to believe that most of them were originally episodes of a greater work which related to the wars of Fingal. Concerning this hero innumerable traditions remain, to this day, in the Highlands of Scotland. The story of Oscian, his son, is so generally known, that to describe one in whom the race of a great family ends, it has passed into a proverb; "Oscian the last of the heroes."

---

1 These lines are from the *Pharsalia,* an epic poem of the Civil War between Caesar and Pompey by the Roman poet Marcus Annaeus Lucanus (A.D. 39–65): 'You too, ye Bards! whom sacred Raptures fire, / To chaunt your Heroes to your Country's Lyre; / Who consecrate in your immortal Strain, / Brave Patriot Souls in righteous Battle slain; / Securely now the tuneful Task renew, / And noblest Themes in deathless Songs pursue' (a contemporary translation by Nicholas Rowe).

There can be no doubt that these poems are to be ascribed to the Bards; a race of men well known to have continued throughout many ages in Ireland and the north of Scotland. Every chief or great man had in his family a Bard or poet, whose office it was to record in verse, the illustrious actions of that family. By the succession of these Bards, such poems were handed down from race to race; some in manuscript, but more by oral tradition. And tradition, in a country so free of intermixture with foreigners, and among a people so strongly attached to the memory of their ancestors, has preserved many of them in a great measure incorrupted to this day.

They are not set to music, or sung. The versification in the original is simple; and to such as understand the language, very smooth and beautiful. Rhyme is seldom used: but the cadence, and the length of the line varied, so as to suit the sense. The translation is extremely literal. Even the arrangement of the words in the original has been imitated; to which must be imputed some inversions in the style, that otherwise would not have been chosen.

Of the poetical merit of these fragments nothing shall here be said. Let the public judge, and pronounce. It is believed, that, by a careful inquiry, many more remains of ancient genius, no less valuable than those now given to the world, might be found in the same country where these have been collected. In particular there is reason to hope that one work of considerable length, and which deserves to be styled an heroic poem, might be recovered and translated, if encouragement were given to such an undertaking. The subject is, an invasion of Ireland by Swarthan King of Lochlyn; which is the name of Denmark in the Erse language. Cuchulaid, the General or Chief of the Irish tribes, upon intelligence of the invasion, assembles his forces; councils are held; and battles fought. But after several unsuccessful engagements, the Irish are forced to submit. At length, Fingal King of Scotland, called in this poem, "The Desert of the hills," arrives with his ships to assist Cuchulaid. He expels the Danes from the country; and returns home victorious. This poem is held to be of greater antiquity than any of the rest that are preserved: And the author speaks of himself as present in the expedition of Fingal. The three last poems in the collection are fragments which the translator obtained of this Epic poem; and tho' very imperfect, they were judged not unworthy of being inserted. If the whole were recovered, it might serve to throw considerable light upon the Scottish and Irish antiquities.

FRAGMENT I.
SHILRIC, VINVELA.

VINVELA
My love is a son of the hill. He pursues the flying deer. His gray dogs are panting around him; his bow-string sounds in the wind. Whether by the fount of the rock, or by the stream of the mountain thou liest; when the rushes are nodding with the wind, and the mist is flying over thee, let me approach my love unperceived, and see him from the rock. Lovely I saw thee first by the aged oak of Branno; thou wert returning tall from the chace; the fairest among thy friends.

SHILRIC
What voice is that I hear? that voice like the summer-wind. — I sit not by the nodding rushes; I hear not the fount of the rock. Afar, Vinvela, afar I go to the wars of Fingal. My dogs attend me no more. No more I tread the hill. No more from on high I see thee, fair moving by the stream of the plain; bright as the bow of heaven; as the moon on the western wave.

2

Then thou art gone, O Shilric! and I am alone on the hill. The deer are seen on the brow; void of fear they graze along. No more they dread the wind; no more the rustling tree. The hunter is far removed; he is in the field of graves. Strangers! sons of the waves! spare my lovely Shilric.

SHILRIC

If fall I must in the field, raise high my grave, Vinvela. Grey stones, and heaped-up earth, shall mark me to future times. When the hunter shall sit by the mound, and produce his food at noon, "Some warrior rests here," he will say; and my fame shall live in his praise. Remember me, Vinvela, when low on earth I lie!

VINVELA

Yes! — I will remember thee — indeed my Shilric will fall. What shall I do, my love! when thou art gone for ever? Through these hills I will go at noon: I will go through the silent heath. There I will see the place of thy rest, returning from the chace. Indeed, my Shilric will fall; but I will remember him.

II.

I sit by the mossy fountain; on top of the hill of winds. One tree is rustling above me. Dark waves roll over the heath. The lake is troubled below. The deer descend from the hill. No hunter at a distance is seen; no whistling cow-herd is nigh. It is mid-day: but all is silent. Sad are my thoughts alone. Didst thou but appear, O my love, a wanderer on the heath! thy hair floating on the wind behind thee; thy bosom heaving on the sight; thine eyes full of tears for thy friends, whom the mist of the hill had concealed! Thee I would comfort, my love, and bring thee to thy father's house.

But is it she that there appears, like a beam of light on the heath? bright as the moon in autumn, as the sun in the summer-storm, comest thou lovely maid over rocks, over mountains to me? — She speaks: but how weak her voice! like the breeze in the reeds of the pool. Hark!

Returnest thou safe from the war? Where are thy friends, my love? I heard of thy death on the hill; I heard and mourned thee, Shilric!

Yes, my fair, I return; but I alone of my race. Thou shalt see them no more: their graves I raised on the plain. But why art thou on the desert hill? why on the heath, alone?

Alone I am, O Shilric! alone in the winter-house. With grief for thee I expired. Shilric, I am pale in the tomb.

She fleets, she sails away; as grey mist before the wind! — and, wilt thou not stay, my love? Stay and behold my tears? fair thou appearest, my love! fair thou wast, when alive!

By the mossy fountain I will sit; on the top of the hill of winds. When mid-day is silent around, converse, O my love, with me! come on the wings of the gale! on the blast of the mountain, come! Let me hear thy voice, as thou passest, when mid-day is silent around.

III.

Evening is grey on the hills. The north wind resounds through the woods. White clouds rise on the sky: the thin-wavering snow descends. The river howls afar, along its winding course. Sad, by a hollow rock, the grey-hair'd Carryl sat. Dry fern waves over his head; his seat is an aged birch. Clear to the roaring winds he lifts his voice of woe.

Tossed on the wavy ocean is He, the hope of the isles; Malcolm, the support of the poor; foe to the proud in arms! Why hast thou left us behind? why live we to mourn thy fate? We might have heard, with thee, the voice of the deep; have seen the oozy rock.

Sad on the sea-beat shore thy spouse looketh for thy return. The time of thy promise is come; the night is gathering around. But no white sail is on the sea; no voice but the blustering winds. Low is the soul of the war! Wet are the locks of youth! By the foot of some rock thou liest; washed by the waves as they come. Why, ye winds, did ye bear him on the desert rock? Why, ye waves, did ye roll over him?

But, Oh! what voice is that? Who rides on that meteor of fire! Green are his airy limbs. It is he! it is the ghost of Malcolm! — Rest, lovely soul, rest on the rock; and let me hear thy voice — He is gone, like a dream of the night. I see him through the trees. Daughter of Reynold! he is gone. Thy spouse shall return no more. No more shall his hounds come from the hill, forerunners of their master. No more from the distant rock shall his voice greet thine ear. Silent is he in the deep, unhappy daughter of Reynold!

I will sit by the stream of the plain. Ye rocks! hang over my head. Hear my voice, ye trees! as ye bend on the shaggy hill. My voice shall preserve the praise of him, the hope of the isles.

IV.
CONNAL, CRIMORA.

CRIMORA.

Who cometh from the hill, like a cloud tinged with the beam of the west? Whose voice is that, loud as the wind, but pleasant as the harp of Carryl? It is my love in the light of steel; but sad is his darkened brow. Live the mighty race of Fingal? or what disturbs my Connal?

CONNAL.

They live. I saw them return from the chace, like a stream of light. The sun was on their shields: Like a ridge of fire they descended the hill. Loud is the voice of the youth; the war, my love, is near. To-morrow the enormous Dargo comes to try the force of our race. The race of Fingal he defies; the race of battle and wounds.

CRIMORA.

Connal, I saw his sails like grey mist on the sable wave. They slowly came to land. Connal, many are the warriors of Dargo!

CONNAL.

Bring me thy father's shield; the iron shield of Rinval; that shield like the full moon when it is darkened in the sky.

CRIMORA.

That shield I bring, O Connal; but it did not defend my father. By the spear of Gauror he fell. Thou mayst fall, O Connal!

CONNAL.

Fall indeed I may: But raise my tomb, Crimora. Some stones, a mound of earth, shall keep my memory. Bend thy red eye over my tomb, and beat thy breast of sighs. Though fair thou art, my love, as the light; more pleasant than the gale of the hill; yet I will not stay. Raise my tomb, Crimora.

Then give me those arms of light; that sword, and that spear of steel. I shall meet Dargo with thee, and aid my lovely Connal. Farewell, ye rocks of Ardven! ye deer! and ye streams of the hill! — We shall return no more. Our tombs are distant far.

V.

Autumn is dark on the mountains; grey mist rests on the hills. The whirlwind is heard on the heath. Dark rolls the river thro' the narrow plain. A tree stands alone on the hill, and marks the grave of Connal. The leaves whirl round with the wind, and strew the grave of the dead. At times are seen here the ghosts of the deceased, when the musing hunter alone stalks slowly over the heath. Appear in thy armour of light, thou ghost of the mighty Connal! Shine, near thy tomb, Crimora! like a moon-beam from a cloud.

Who can reach the source of thy race, O Connal? and who recount thy Fathers? Thy family grew like an oak on the mountain, which meeteth the wind with its lofty head. But now it is torn from the earth. Who shall supply the place of Connal?

Here was the din of arms; and here the groans of the dying. Mournful are the wars of Fingal! O Connal! it was here thou didst fall. Thine arm was like a storm; thy sword, a beam of the sky; thy height, a rock on the plain; thine eyes, a furnace of fire. Louder than a storm was thy voice, when thou confoundedst the field. Warriors fell by thy sword, as the thistle by the staff of a boy.

Dargo the mighty came on, like a cloud of thunder. His brows were contracted and dark. His eyes like two caves in a rock. Bright rose their swords on each side; dire was the clang of their steel.

The daughter of Rinval was near; Crimora, bright in the armour of man; her hair loose behind, her bow in her hand. She followed the youth to the war, Connal her much-beloved. She drew the string on Dargo; but erring pierced her Connal. He falls like an oak on the plain; like a rock from the shaggy hill. What shall she do, hapless maid! — He bleeds; her Connal dies. All the night long she cries, and all the day, O Connal, my love, and my friend! With grief the sad mourner died.

Earth here incloseth the loveliest pair on the hill. The grass grows between the stones of their tomb; I sit in the mournful shade. The wind sighs through the grass; and their memory rushes on my mind. Undisturbed you now sleep together; in the tomb of the mountain you rest alone.

VI.

Son of the noble Fingal, Oscian, Prince of men! what tears run down the cheeks of age? what shades thy mighty soul?

Memory, son of Alpin, memory wounds the aged. Of former times are my thoughts; my thoughts are of the noble Fingal. The race of the king return into my mind, and wound me with remembrance.

One day, returned from the sport of the mountains, from pursuing the sons of the hill, we covered this heath with our youth. Fingal the mighty was here, and Oscur, my son, great in war. Fair on our sight from the sea, at once, a virgin came. Her breast was like the snow of one night. Her cheek like the bud of the rose. Mild was her blue rolling eye: but sorrow was big in her heart.

Fingal renowned in war! she cries, sons of the king, preserve me! Speak secure, replies the king, daughter of beauty, speak: our ear is open to all: our swords redress the injured. I fly from Ullin, she cries, from Ullin famous in war. I fly from the embrace of him who would debase my blood. Cremor, the friend of men, was my father; Cremor the Prince of Inverne.

Fingal's younger sons arose; Carryl expert in the bow; Fillan beloved of the fair; and Fergus first in the race. — Who from the farthest Lochlyn? who to the seas of Molochasquir? who dares hurt the maid whom the sons of Fingal guard? Daughter of beauty, rest secure; rest in peace, thou fairest of women.

Far in the blue distance of the deep, some spot appeared like the back of the ridge-wave. But soon the ship increased on our sight. The hand of Ullin drew her to land. The mountains trembled as he moved. The hills shook at his steps. Dire rattled his armour around him. Death and destruction were in his eyes. His stature like the oak of Morven. He moved in the lightning of steel.

Our warriors fell before him, like the field before the reapers. Fingal's three sons he bound. He plunged his sword into the fair-one's breast. She fell as a wreath of snow before the sun in spring. Her bosom heaved in death; her soul came forth in blood.

Oscur my son came down; the mighty in battle descended. His armour rattled as thunder; and the lightning of his eyes was terrible. There, was the clashing of swords; there, was the voice of steel. They struck and they thrust; they digged for death with their swords. But death was distant far, and delayed to come. The sun began to decline; and the cow-herd thought of home. Then Oscur's keen steel found the heart of Ullin. He fell like a mountain-oak covered over with glistering frost: He shone like a rock on the plain. — Here the daughter of beauty lieth; and here the bravest of men. Here one day ended the fair and the valiant. Here rest the pursuer and the pursued.

Son of Alpin, the woes of the aged are many: their tears are for the past. This raised my sorrow, warrior; memory awaked my grief. Oscur my son was brave, but Oscur is now no more. Thou hast heard of my grief, O son of Alpin; forgive the tears of the aged.

VII.[2]

Why openest thou afresh the spring of my grief, O son of Alpin, inquiring how Oscur fell? My eyes are blind with tears; but memory beams on my heart. How can I relate the mournful death of the head of the people! Prince of the warriors, Oscur, my son, shall I see thee no more!

He fell as the moon in a storm; as the sun from the midst of his course, when clouds rise from the waste of the waves, when the blackness of the storm inwraps the rocks of Ardanidder. I, like an ancient oak on Morven, I moulder alone in my place. The blast hath lopped my branches away; and I tremble at the wings of the north. Prince of the warriors, Oscur, my son! shall I see thee no more!

Dermid and Oscur were one: They reaped the battle together. Their friendship was strong as their steel; and death walked between them to the field. They came on the foe like two rocks falling from the brow of Ardven. Their swords were stained with the blood of the valiant: warriors fainted at their names. Who was a match for Oscur, but Dermid? and who for Dermid, but Oscur!

They killed mighty Dargo in the field; Dargo before invincible. His daughter was fair as the morn; mild as the beam of night. Her eyes, like two stars in a shower: her breath, the gale of spring: her breasts, as the new-fallen snow floating on the moving heath. The warriors saw her, and loved; their souls were fixed on the maid. Each loved her, as his fame; each must possess her or die. But her soul was fixed on Oscur; my son was the youth of her love. She forgot the blood of her father; and loved the hand that slew him.

Son of Oscian, said Dermid, I love; O Oscur, I love this maid. But her soul cleaveth unto thee; and nothing can heal Dermid. Here, pierce this bosom, Oscur; relieve me,

2 This fragment was the one originally shown by Macpherson to John Home, famous as the playwright of *Douglas* (1756), in 1759: Home strongly encouraged publishing this collection.

my friend, with thy sword.

My sword, son of Morny, shall never be stained with the blood of Dermid.

Who then is worthy to slay me, O Oscur son of Oscian? Let not my life pass away unknown. Let none but Oscur slay me. Send me with honour to the grave, and let my death be renowned.

Dermid, make use of thy sword; son of Morny, wield thy steel. Would that I fell with thee! that my death came from the hand of Diarmid!

They fought by the brook of the mountain, by the streams of Branno. Blood tinged the silvery stream, and crudled round the mossy stones. Dermid the graceful fell; fell, and smiled in death.

And fallest thou, son of Morny; fallest thou by Oscur's hand! Dermid invincible in war, thus do I see thee fall! — He went, and returned to the maid whom he loved; returned, but she perceived his grief.

Why that gloom, son of Oscur? what shades thy mighty soul?

Though once renowned for the bow, O maid, I have lost my fame. Fixed on a tree by the brook of the hill, is the shield of Gormur the brave, whom in battle I slew. I have wasted the day in vain, nor could my arrow pierce it.

Let me try, son of Oscian, the skill of Dargo's daughter. My hands were taught the bow: my father delighted in my skill.

She went. He stood behind the shield. Her arrow flew and pierced his breast.[3]

Blessed be that hand of snow; and blessed be thy bow of yew! I fall resolved on death: and who but the daughter of Dargo was worthy to slay me? Lay me in the earth, my fair-one; lay me by the side of Dermid.

Oscur! I have the blood, the soul of the mighty Dargo. Well pleased I can meet death. My sorrow I can end thus. — She pierced her white bosom with steel. She fell; she trembled; and died.

By the brook of the hill their graves are laid; a birch's unequal shade covers their tomb. Often on their green earthen tombs the branchy sons of the mountain feed, when mid-day is all in flames, and silence is over all the hills.

VIII.

By the side of a rock on the hill, beneath the aged trees, old Oscian sat on the moss; the last of the race of Fingal. Sightless are his aged eyes; his beard is waving in the wind. Dull through the leafless trees he heard the voice of the north. Sorrow revived in his soul: he began and lamented the dead.

How hast thou fallen like an oak, with all thy branches round thee! Where is Fingal the King? where is Oscur my son? where are all my race? Alas! in the earth they lie. I feel their tombs with my hands. I hear the river below murmuring hoarsely over the stones. What dost thou, O river, to me? Thou bringest back the memory of the past.

The race of Fingal stood on thy banks, like a wood in a fertile soil. Keen were their spears of steel. Hardy was he who dared to encounter their rage. Fillan the great was there. Thou Oscur wert there, my son! Fingal himself was there, strong in the grey locks of years. Full rose his sinewy limbs; and wide his shoulders spread. The unhappy met with his arm, when the pride of his wrath arose.

---

3 Nothing was held by the ancient Highlanders more essential to their glory, than to die by the hand of some person worthy or renowned. This was the occasion of Oscur's contriving to be slain by his mistress, now that he was weary of life. In those early times, suicide was utterly unknown among that people, and no traces of it are found in the old poetry. Whence the translator suspects the account that follows of the daughter of Dargo killing herself, to be the interpolation of some later Bard. [Macpherson's note]

The son of Morny came; Gaul, the tallest of men. He stood on the hill like an oak; his voice was like the streams of the hill. Why reigneth alone, he cries, the son of the mighty Corval? Fingal is not strong to save: he is no support for the people. I am strong as a storm in the ocean; as a whirlwind on the hill. Yield, son of Corval; Fingal, yield to me. He came like a rock from the hill, resounding in his arms.

Oscur stood forth to meet him; my son would meet the foe. But Fingal came in his strength, and smiled at the vaunter's boast. They threw their arms round each other; they struggled on the plain. The earth is ploughed with their heels. Their bones crack as the boat on the ocean, when it leaps from wave to wave. Long did they toil; with night, they fell on the sounding plain; as two oaks, with their branches mingled, fall crashing from the hill. The tall son of Morny is bound; the aged overcame.

Fair with her locks of gold, her smooth neck, and her breasts of snow; fair, as the spirits of the hill when at silent noon they glide along the heath; fair, as the rain-bow of heaven; came Minvane the maid. Fingal! she softly saith, loose me my brother Gaul. Loose me the hope of my race, the terror of all but Fingal. Can I, replies the King, can I deny the lovely daughter of the hill? Take thy brother, O Minvane, thou fairer than snow of the north!

Such, Fingal! were thy words; but thy words I hear no more. Sightless I sit by thy tomb. I hear the wind in the wood; but no more I hear my friends. The cry of the hunter is over. The voice of war is ceased.

* * * * *

XIV.[4]

Cuchulaid sat by the wall; by the tree of the rustling leaf.[5] His spear leaned against the mossy rock. His shield lay by him on the grass. Whilst he thought on the mighty Carbre whom he slew in battle, the scout of the ocean came, Moran the son of Fithil.

Rise, Cuchulaid, rise! I see the ships of Garve. Many are the foe, Cuchulaid; many the sons of Lochlyn.

Moran! thou ever tremblest; thy fears increase the foe. They are the ships of the Desert of hills arrived to assist Cuchulaid.

I saw their chief, says Moran, tall as a rock of ice. His spear is like that fir; his shield like the rising moon. He sat upon a rock on the shore, as a grey cloud upon the hill. Many, mighty man! I said, are our heroes; Garve, well art thou named,[6] many are the sons of our king.

He answered like a wave on the rock; who is like me here? The valiant live not with me; they go to the earth from my hand. The king of the Desert of hills alone can fight with Garve. Once we wrestled on the hill. Our heels overturned the wood. Rocks fell from their place, and rivulets changed their course. Three days we strove together; heroes stood at a distance, and feared. On the fourth, the King saith that I fell; but Garve saith, he stood. Let Cuchulaid yield to him that is strong as a storm.

No. I will never yield to man. Cuchulaid will conquer or die. Go, Moran, take my spear; strike the shield of Caithbait with hangs before the gate. It never rings in peace. My heroes shall hear on the hill. —

---

4 This is the opening of the epic poem mentioned in the preface. The two following fragments [not given here] are parts of some episodes of the same work. [Macpherson's note. These three fragments, with an advertisement for the forthcoming publication of this epic, close the 1760 volume.]

5 The aspen or poplar tree. [Macpherson's note]

6 Garve signifies a man of great size. [Macpherson's note]

A

CRITICAL DISSERTATION

ON THE

POEMS OF OSSIAN,

THE

SON OF FINGAL.

LONDON:
printed for T. BECKET and P. A. DE HONDT, at *Tully's–*
Head, in the *Strand*. MDCCLXIII.

Advertisement.

The Substance of the following Dissertation was delivered by the Author in the Course of his Lectures on Rhetorick and Belles-Lettres, in the University of Edinburgh. At the Desire of several of his Hearers, he has enlarged, and given it to the Publick, in its present Form.[1]

In this Dissertation, it is proposed, to make some Observations on the ancient Poetry of Nations, particularly the Runic and the Celtic;[2] *to point out those characters of Antiquity, which the Works of Ossian bear; to give an Idea of the Spirit and Strain of his Poetry; and after applying the Rules of Criticism to Fingal, as an Epic Poem, to examine the Merit of Ossian's Compositions in general, with Regard to Description, Imagery, and Sentiment.*

AMONG the monuments remaining of the ancient state of nations, few are more valuable than their poems or songs. History, when it treats of remote and dark ages, is seldom very instructive. The beginnings of society, in every country, are involved in fabulous confusion; and though they were not, they would furnish few events worth recording. But, in every period of society, human manners are a curious spectacle; and the most natural pictures of ancient manners are exhibited in the ancient poems of nations. These present to us, what is much more valuable than the history of such transactions as a rude age can afford, the history of human imagination and passion. They make us acquainted with the notions and feelings of our fellow-creatures in the most artless ages; discovering what objects they admired, and what pleasures they pursued, before those refinements of society had taken place, which enlarge indeed, and diversify the transactions, but disguise the manners of mankind.

Besides this merit, which ancient poems have with philosophical observers of human nature, they have another with persons of taste. They promise some of the highest beauties of poetical writing. Irregular and unpolished we may expect the productions

---

1   The author is Hugh Blair (1718–1800), minister and professor of Rhetoric and Belles-Lettres at Edinburgh. The *Dissertation* appeared after the publication of the coherent epic *Fingal* in 1761-2, promised in the Preface to *Fragments of Ancient Poetry* and advertised at the end of that volume: I have omitted the sections which deal specifically and in depth with *Fingal*. The 'present Form' of the *Dissertation* was the same quarto format as *Fingal* and indeed the later *Works of Ossian* (1765) which included a second epic, *Temora*. As books were usually bought unbound, this allowed purchasers to have the criticism bound in one volume with the poems, and most copies of the *Dissertation* in libraries are found like this.

2   By 'Runic' Blair refers to old Germanic and Scandinavian literatures. I have omitted the sections which develop the comparison between these and Ossian.

of uncultivated ages to be; but abounding, at the same time, with that enthusiasm, that vehemence and fire, which are the soul of poetry. For many circumstances of those times which we call barbarous, are favourable to the poetical spirit. That state, in which human nature shoots wild and free, though unfit for other improvements, certainly encourages the high exertions of fancy and passion.

In the infancy of societies, men live scattered and dispersed, in the midst of solitary rural scenes, where the beauties of nature are their chief entertainment. They meet with many objects, to them new and strange; their wonder and surprize are frequently excited; and by the sudden changes of fortune occurring in their unsettled state of life, their passions are raised to the utmost. Their passions have nothing to restrain them: their imagination has nothing to check it. They display themselves to one another without disguise: and converse and act in the uncovered simplicity of nature. As their feelings are strong, so their language, of itself, assumes a poetical turn. Prone to exaggerate, they describe every thing in the strongest colours; which of course renders their speech picturesque and figurative. Figurative language owes its rise chiefly to two causes; to the want of proper names for objects, and to the influence of imagination and passion over the form of expression. Both these causes concur in the infancy of society. Figures are commonly considered as artificial modes of speech, devised by orators and poets, after the world had advanced to a refined state. The contrary of this is the truth. Men never have used so many figures of style, as in those rude ages when, besides the power of a warm imagination to suggest lively images, the want of proper and precise terms for the ideas they would express, obliged them to have recourse to circumlocution, metaphor, comparison, and all those substituted forms of expression, which give a poetical air to language. An American chief, at this day, harangues at the head of his tribe, in a more bold metaphorical style, than a modern European would adventure to use in an Epic poem.

In the progress of society, the genius and manners of men undergo a change more favourable to accuracy than to sprightliness and sublimity. As the world advances, the understanding gains ground upon the imagination; the understanding is more exercised; the imagination, less. Fewer objects occur that are new or surprizing. Men apply themselves to trace the causes of things; they correct and refine one another; they subdue or disguise their passions; they form their exterior manners upon one uniform standard of politeness and civility. Human nature is pruned according to method and rule. Language advances from sterility to copiousness, and at the same time, from fervour and enthusiasm, to correctness and precision. Style becomes more chaste; but less animated. The progress of the world in this respect resembles the progress of age in man. The powers of imagination are most vigorous and predominant in youth; those of the understanding ripen more slowly, and often attain not their maturity, till the imagination begin to flag. Hence, poetry, which is the child of imagination, is frequently most glowing and animated in the first ages of society. As the ideas of our youth are remembered with a peculiar pleasure on account of their liveliness and vivacity; so the most ancient poems have often proved the greatest favourites of nations.

Poetry has been said to be more ancient than prose: and however paradoxical such an assertion may seem, yet, in a qualified sense, it is true. Men certainly never conversed with one another in regular numbers; but even their ordinary language would, in ancient times, for the reasons before assigned, approach to a poetical style; and the first compositions transmitted to posterity, beyond doubt, were, in a literal sense, poems; that is, compositions in which imagination had the chief hand, formed into some kind of numbers, and pronounced with a musical modulation or tone. Music or song has been found coæval with society among the most barbarous nations. The only subjects which could prompt men, in their first rude state, to utter their thoughts in compositions of any length, were such as naturally assumed the tone of poetry; praises of their gods, or of their ancestors; commemorations of their own warlike exploits; or lamentations over their misfortunes. And before writing was invented, no other compositions, except songs and poems, could take such hold of the imagination and memory, as to be preserved by oral tradition, and handed down from one race to another.

Hence we may expect to find poems among the antiquities of all nations. It is probable too, that an extensive search would discover a certain degree of resemblance among all the most ancient poetical productions, from whatever country they have proceeded. In a similar state of manners, similar objects and passions operating upon the imaginations of men, will stamp their productions with the same general character. Some diversity will, no doubt, be occasioned by climate and genius. But mankind never bear such resembling features, as they do in the beginnings of society. Its subsequent revolutions give rise to the principal distinctions among nations; and divert, into channels widely separated, that current of human genius and manners, which descends originally from one spring. What we have been long accustomed to call the oriental vein of poetry, because some of the earliest poetical productions have come to us from the East, is probably no more oriental than occidental; it is characteristical of an age rather than a country; and belongs, in some measure, to all nations at a certain period. Of this the works of Ossian seem to furnish a remarkable proof.

*****

Now when we consider a college or order of men [the Bards], who, cultivating poetry throughout a long series of ages, had their imaginations continually employed on the ideas of heroism; who had all the poems and panegyricks, which were composed by their predecessors, handed down to them with care; who rivalled and endeavoured to outstrip those who had gone before them, each in the celebration of his particular hero; is it not natural to think, that at length the character of a hero would appear in their songs with the highest lustre, and be adorned with qualities truly noble? Some of the qualities indeed which distinguish a Fingal, moderation, humanity, and clemency, would not probably be the first ideas of heroism occurring to a barbarous people: But no sooner had such ideas begun to dawn on the minds of poets, than, as the human mind easily opens to the native representations of human perfection, they would be seized and embraced; they would enter into their panegyricks; they would afford materials for succeeding bards to work upon, and improve; they would contribute not a little to exalt the publick manners. For such songs as these, familiar to the Celtic warriors from their childhood, and throughout their whole life, both in war and in peace, their principal entertainment, must have had a very considerable influence in propagating among them real manners nearly approaching to the poetical; and in forming even such a hero as Fingal. Especially when we consider that among their limited objects of ambition, among the few advantages which in a savage state, man could obtain over man, the chief was Fame, and that Immortality which they expected to receive from their virtues and exploits, in the songs of the bards.

*****

The compositions of Ossian are so strongly marked with characters of antiquity, that although there were no external proof to support that antiquity, hardly any reader of judgment and taste, could hesitate in referring them to a very remote æra. There are four great stages through which men successively pass in the progress of society.

The first and earliest is the life of hunters; pasturage succeeds to this, as the ideas of property begin to take root; next agriculture; and lastly, commerce.[3] Throughout Ossian's poems, we plainly find ourselves in the first of these periods of society; during which, hunting was the chief employment of men, and their principal method of their procuring subsistence. Pasturage was not indeed wholly unknown; for we hear of dividing the herd in the case of divorce; but the allusions to herds and to cattle are not many; and of agriculture, we find no traces. No cities appear to have been built in the territories of Fingal. No arts are mentioned except that of navigation and working in iron.[4] Every thing presents to us the most simple and unimproved manners. At their feasts, the heroes prepared their own repast; they sat round the light of the burning oak; the winds lifted their locks, and whistled through their open halls. Whatever was beyond the necessities of life was known to them only as the spoil of the Roman province; "the gold of the stranger; the lights of the stranger; the steeds of the stranger, the children of the rein."

*****

The manner of composition bears all the marks of the greatest antiquity. No artful transitions; nor full and extended connection of parts; such as we find among the poets of later times, when order and regularity of composition were more studied and known; but a style always rapid and vehement; in narration concise even to abruptness, and leaving several circumstances to be supplied by the reader's imagination. The language has all that figurative cast, which, as I before shewed, partly a glowing and undisciplined imagination, partly the sterility of language and the want of proper terms, have always introduced into the early speech of nations; and in several respects, it carries a remarkable resemblance to the style of the Old Testament. It deserves particular notice, that as one of the most genuine and decisive characters of antiquity, that very few general terms or abstract ideas, are to be met with in the whole collection of Ossian's works. The ideas of men, at first, were all particular. They had not words to express general conceptions. These were the consequence of more profound reflection, and longer acquaintance with the arts of thought and of speech.[5] Ossian, accordingly, almost never expresses himself in the abstract. His ideas extended little farther than to the objects he saw around him. A public, a community, the universe, were conceptions beyond his sphere. Even a mountain, a sea, or a lake, which he has occasion to mention, though only in a simile, are for the most part particularized; it is the hill of Cromla, the storm of the sea of Malmor, or the reeds of the lake of Lego. A mode of expression, which whilst it is characteristical of ancient ages, is at the same time highly favourable to descriptive poetry. For the same reasons, personification is a poetical figure not very common with Ossian. Inanimate objects, such as winds, trees, flowers, he sometimes personifies with great beauty. But the personifications which are so familiar to later poets of Fame, Time, Terror, Virtue, and the rest of that class, were unknown to our Celtic bard. These were modes of conception too abstract for his age.

3   This 'four-stages' model of history is an influential one in Scottish thinking of the period: it appears, for example, in Book V of Adam Smith's *Wealth of Nations* (1776) and received fuller treatment in Smith's *Lectures on Jurisprudence* (delivered in the University of Glasgow in 1763–4).
4   Blair adds a footnote here giving evidence for these claims.
5   That human knowledge derives in the first place from our encounters with particular things, from which the mind by a secondary operation constructs general or abstract ideas, is fundamental to the empirical philosophy underpinning much enlightenment thought, especially in its crucial formulation by John Locke in *An Essay Concerning Human Understanding* (1690): see especially Book III, 'Of Words', chapter iii, 'Of General Terms'.

12

*****

Assuming it, then, as we well may, for certain, that the poems now under consideration, are genuine venerable monuments of very remote antiquity; I proceed to make some remarks upon their general spirit and strain. The two great characteristics of Ossian's poetry are, tenderness and sublimity. It breathes nothing of the gay and chearful kind; an air of solemnity and seriousness is diffused over the whole. Ossian is perhaps the only poet who never relaxes, or lets himself down into the light and amusing strain; which I readily admit to be no small disadvantage to him, with the bulk of readers. He moves perpetually in the high region of the grand and the pathetick. One key note is struck at the beginning, and supported to the end; nor is any ornament introduced, but what is perfectly concordant with the general tone or melody. The events recorded, are all serious and grave; the scenery throughout, wild and romantic. The extended heath by the sea shore; the mountain shaded with mist; the torrent rushing through a solitary valley; the scattered oaks, and the tombs of warriors overgrown with moss; all produce a solemn attention in the mind, and prepare it for great and extraordinary events. We find not in Ossian, an imagination that sports itself, and dresses out gay trifles to please the fancy. His poetry, more perhaps than that of any other writer, deserves to be styled, *The Poetry of the Heart.* It is a heart penetrated with noble sentiments, and with sublime and tender passions; a heart that glows, and kindles the fancy; a heart that is full, and pours itself forth. Ossian did not write, like modern poets, to please readers and critics. He sung from the love of poetry and song. His delight was to think of the heroes among whom he had flourished; to recall the affecting incidents of his life; to dwell upon his past wars and loves and friendships; till, as he expresses it himself, "the light of his soul arose; the days of other years rose before him;" and under this true poetic inspiration, giving vent to his genius, no wonder we should often hear, and acknowledge in his strains, the powerful and ever-pleasing voice of nature.

– Arte, natura potentior omni. –
Est Deus in nobis, agitante calescimus illo. [Ovid, *Fasti*, 6.][6]

It is necessary here to observe, that the beauties of Ossian's writings cannot be felt by those who have given them only a single or hasty perusal. His manner is so different from that of the poets, to whom we are most accustomed; his style is so concise, and so much crowded with imagery; the mind is kept at such a stretch in accompanying the author; that an ordinary reader is at first apt to be dazzled and fatigued, rather than pleased. His poems require to be taken up at intervals, and to be frequently reviewed; and then it is impossible but his beauties must open to every reader who is capable of sensibility. Those who have the highest degree of it, will relish them the most.

As Homer is of all the great poets, the one whose manner, and whose times come the nearest to Ossian's, we are naturally led to run a parallel in some instances between the Greek and the Celtic bard. For though Homer lived more than a thousand years before Ossian, it is not from the age of the world, but from the state of society, that we are to judge of resembling times. The Greek has, in several points, a manifest superiority. He introduces a greater variety of incidents; he possesses a larger compass of ideas; has more diversity in his characters; and a much deeper knowledge of human nature. It was not to be expected, that in any of these particulars, Ossian could equal Homer. For Homer lived in a country where society was much further advanced; he had beheld

---

6   The last line reads, 'There is a god within us. It is when he stirs us that our bosom warms'; and the next line continues 'it is his impulse that sows the seeds of inspiration' (ll.5-6) in J.G. Frazer's 1931 translation of the unfinished poetic calendar of the Roman year by Ovid (43 B.C.-17/18 A.D.). The first line here adapts 1.302-3 of the tenth satire of Juvenal (c.60-c.130 A.D.): 'quid enim puero conferre potest plus / custode et cura natura potentior omni' ('For Nature is a better Guardian far, / Than Sawcy Pedants, or dull Tutors are' [Dryden's translation ll.466-7]).

many more objects; cities built and flourishing; laws instituted; order, discipline, and arts begun. His field of observation was larger and more splendid; his knowledge, of course, more extensive; his mind also, it shall be granted, more penetrating. But if Ossian's ideas and objects be less diversified than those of Homer, they are all, however, of the kind fittest for poetry: The bravery and generosity of heroes, the tenderness of lovers, the attachment of friends, parents, and children. In a rude age and country, though the events that happen be few, the undissipated mind broods over them more; they strike the imagination, and fire the passions in a higher degree; and of consequence become happier materials to a poetical genius, than the same events when scattered through the wide circle of more varied action, and cultivated life.

Homer is more cheerful and sprightly than Ossian. You discern in him all the Greek vivacity; whereas Ossian uniformly maintains the gravity and solemnity of a Celtic hero. This too is in a great measure to be accounted for from the different situations in which they lived, partly personal, and partly national. Ossian had survived all his friends,[7] and was disposed to melancholy by the incidents of his life. But besides this, chearfulness is one of the many blessings which we owe to formed society. The solitary wild state is always a serious one. Bating the sudden and violent bursts of mirth, which sometimes break forth at their dances and feasts; the savage American tribes have been noted by all travellers for their gravity and taciturnity. Somewhat of this taciturnity may be also remarked in Ossian. On all occasions he is frugal of his words; and never gives you more of an image or description, than is just sufficient to place it before you in one clear point of view. . . .

---

7   See *Fragments* VI–VIII.

POEMS,

CHIEFLY IN THE

SCOTTISH DIALECT,

BY

ROBERT BURNS.

THE Simple Bard, unbroke by rules of Art,
He pours his wild effusions of the heart:
And if inspir'd, 'tis Nature's pow'rs inspire;
Her's all the melting thrill, and her's the kindling fire.
                                      ANONYMOUS

KILMARNOCK:
PRINTED BY JOHN WILSON.
MDCCLXXXVI.[1]

PREFACE.

THE following trifles are not the production of a Poet, who, with all the advantages of learned art, and perhaps amid the elegancies and idlenesses of upper life, looks for a rural theme, with an eye to Theocrites or Virgil.[2] To the Author of this, these and other celebrated names their countrymen are, in their original languages, 'A fountain shut up, and a book sealed.' Unacquainted with the necessary requisites for commencing Poet by rule, he sings the sentiments and manners, he felt and saw in himself and his rustic compeers around him, in his and their native language. Though a Rhymer from his earliest years, at least from the earliest impulses of the softer passions, it was not till very lately, that the applause, perhaps the partiality, of Friendship, wakened his vanity so far as to make him think any thing of his was worth showing; and none of the following works were ever composed with a view to the press. To amuse himself with the little creations of his own fancy, amid the toil and fatigues of a laborious life; to transcribe the various feelings, the loves, the griefs, the hopes, the fears, in his own breast; to find some kind of counterpoise to the struggles of a world, always an alien scene, a task uncouth to the poetical mind; these were his motives for courting the Muses, and in these he found Poetry to be it's own reward.

Now that he appears in the public character of an Author, he does it with fear and trembling. So dear is fame to the rhyming tribe, that even he, an obscure, nameless Bard, shrinks aghast, at the thought of being branded as 'An impertinent blockhead, obtruding his nonsense on the world; and because he can make a shift to jingle a few doggerel, Scotch rhymes together, looks upon himself as a Poet of no small consequence forsooth.'

It is an observation of the celebrated Poet,[3] whose divine Elegies do honor to our

---

1   This volume, Burns's first, is usually referred to as the 'Kilmarnock edition': later, enlarged editions of the *Poems* were published in Edinburgh. The epigraph is Burns's own.

2   Virgil: Publius Vergilius Maro (70–19 B.C.), whose poems describing the routines of rural life, the *Georgics*, were an important model and source of legitimacy for descriptive poetry in the eighteenth century. Theocritus (c.300–c.260 B.C.), Greek pastoral poet.

3   Shenstone [Burns's note. William Shenstone (1714–63), nature-poet and essayist.]

language, our nation, and our species, that 'Humility has depressed many a genius to a hermit, but never raised one to fame.' If any Critic catches at the word *genius*, the Author tells him, once for all, that he certainly looks upon himself as possest of some poetic abilities, otherwise his publishing in the manner he has done, would be a manoeuvre below the worst character, which, he hopes, his worst enemy will never give him: but to the genius of a Ramsay, or the glorious dawnings of the poor, unfortunate Ferguson,[4] he, with equal unaffected sincerity, declares, that, even in his highest pulse of vanity, he has not the most distant pretentions. These two justly admired Scotch Poets he has often had in his eye in the following pieces; but rather with a view to kindle at their flame, than for servile imitation.

To his Subscribers, the Author returns his most sincere thanks.[5] Not the mercenary bow over a counter, but the heart-throbbing gratitude of the Bard, conscious how much he is indebted to Benevolence and Friendship, for gratifying him, if he deserves it, in that dearest wish of every poetic bosom — to be distinguished. He begs his readers, particularly the Learned and Polite, who may honor him with a perusal, that they will make every allowance for Education and Circumstances of Life: but, if after a fair, candid, and impartial criticism, he shall stand convicted of Dulness and Nonsense, let him be done by, as he would in that case do by others — let him be condemned, without mercy, to contempt and oblivion.

---

4   Allan Ramsay (1684–1758), the most successful of the post-Union revivalists of poetry in Scots; Robert Fergusson (1750–74), vivid lyricist of the urban (Edinburgh) scene who died in poverty. Burns arranged and paid for a stone to mark Fergusson's grave on his first visit to Edinburgh in 1786–7.
5   Publication by Subscription involved getting potential readers to promise in advance to purchase a copy once it appeared, reducing the financial risk to both publisher and author. In return, a subscriber's name would appear in a list in the front of the volume.

ADDRESS TO THE DEIL.

O Prince, O chief of many throned pow'rs,
That led th' embattl'd Seraphim to war —
           MILTON[1]

O Thou, whatever title suit thee!
Auld Hornie, Satan, Nick, or Clootie,
Wha in yon cavern grim and sootie   who
        Clos'd under hatches,
Spairges about the brunstane cootie,   5   splashes; brimstone dish
        To scaud poor wretches!   scald

Hear me, *auld Hangie*, for a wee,
An' let poor *damned bodies* bee;
I'm sure sma' pleasure it can gie,
        Ev'n to a *deil*,   10
To skelp an' scaud poor dogs like me,   slap and scald
        An' hear us squeel!

Great is thy pow'r, an' great thy fame;
Far ken'd, an' noted is thy name;
An' tho' yon *lowan heugh*'s thy hame,   15   that blazing pit
        Thou travels far;
An' faith! thou's neither lag nor lame,
        Nor blate nor scaur.   bashful; timid

Whyles, ranging like a roaran lion,
For prey, a' holes an' corners tryin;   20
Whyles, on the strong-wing'd Tempest flyin,
        Tirlan the *kirks*;   shaking
Whyles, in the human bosom pryin,
        Unseen thou lurks.

I've heard my rev'rend *Graunie* say,   25
In lanely glens ye like to stray;
Or where auld, ruin'd castles, gray,
        Nod to the moon,
Ye fright the nightly wand'rer's way,
        Wi' eldritch croon.   30   uncanny

When twilight did my *Graunie* summon,
To say her pray'rs, douse, honest woman!   sedate and kindly
Aft 'yont the dyke she's heard you bumman,   often beyond; humming
        Wi' eerie drone,
Or, rustling, thro' the boortries coman,   35   elder-hedges
        Wi' heavy groan.

---

1   Beelzebub's address to Satan in Book I, ll.128–9 of *Paradise Lost* (1667).

Ae dreary, windy, winter night,
The stars shot down wi' sklentan light,   slanting
Wi' you, *mysel*, I gat a fright
              Ayont the lough;   40   beyond
Ye, like a *rash-buss*, stood in sight,   clump of rushes
              Wi' waving sugh: wind

The cudgel in my nieve did shake,   fist
Each bristl'd hair stood like a stake,
When wi' an eldritch, stoor, *quaick, quaick*,   45   tumultuous
              Amang the springs,
Awa ye squatter'd like a *drake*,
              On whistling wings.

Let *Warlocks* grim, an' wither'd *Hags*,
Tell, how wi' you on ragweed nags,   50
They skim the muirs an' dizzy crags,
              Wi' wicked speed;
And in kirk-yards renew their leagues,
              Owre howcket dead.   dug-up

Thence, countra wives, wi' toil an' pain,   55
May plunge an' plunge the *kirn* in vain;   churn
For Oh! the yellow treasure 's taen   taken
              By witching skill;
An' dawtet, twal-pint *Hawkie* 's gane[2]   treasured; twelve
              As yell 's the Bill.   60   dry as the bull

Thence, mystic knots mak great abuse,
On *Young-Guidmen*, fond, keen an' croose;   husbands; cocksure
When the best *wark-lume* i' the house,   tool (or penis) in
              By cantraip wit,   magic
Is instant made no worth a louse,   65
              Just at the bit.   crucial moment

When thowes dissolve the snawy hoord,   thaws; hoard
An' float the jinglan icy boord,
Then, *Water-kelpies* haunt the foord,
              By your direction,   70
An' nighted Trav'llers are allur'd
              To their destruction.

An' aft your moss-traversing *Spunkies*   often; sparks
Decoy the wight that late an' drunk is: fellow
The bleezan, curst, mischievous monkies   75
              Delude his eyes,
Till in some miry slough he sunk is,
              Ne'er mair to rise.

---

2   'Hawkie' is a traditional name for a cow.

When MASONS' mystic *word* an' *grip*,
In storms an' tempests raise you up,   80
Some cock or cat, your rage maun stop,   must
            Or, strange to tell!
The *youngest Brother* ye wad whip
            Aff straught to *H–ll*.

Lang syne in EDEN'S bonie yard,   85   long since
When youthfu' lovers first were pair'd,
An' all the Soul of Love they shar'd,
            The raptur'd hour,
Sweet on the fragrant, flow'ry swaird,
            In shady bow'r.   90

Then you, ye auld, snick-drawing dog!   crafty
Ye cam to Paradise incog,   incognito
An' play'd on man a cursed brogue,   trick
            (Black be your fa'!)   fall
An' gied the infant warld a shog,   95   jolt
            'Maist ruin'd a'.   Almost

D'ye mind that day, when in a bizz,   flurry
Wi' reeket duds, an' reestet gizz,   smoky clothes; scorched wig
Ye did present your smoutie phiz   smutty face
            'Mang better folk,   100   among
An' sklented on the *man of Uzz*[3]   threw
            Your spitefu' joke?

An' how ye gat him i' your thrall,
An' brak him out o' house an' hal',
While scabs an' botches did him gall,   105   tumours
            Wi' bitter claw,
An' lows'd his ill-tongu'd, wicked *Scawl*   let loose; scold (i.e. wife)
            Was worst ava?   of all

But a' your doings to rehears,
Your wily snares an' fechtin fierce,   110   fighting
Sin' that day MICHAEL did you pierce,[4]
            Down to this time,
Wad ding a *Lallan* tongue, or *Erse*,[5]
            In prose or Rhyme.

---

3   The Man of Uz is Job, 'perfect and upright', and very rich: the Book of Job begins when God puts everything of Job's in Satan's power to prove that His servant does not only obey Him because he is rewarded for it. Satan proceeds to visit every kind of devastation on Job's household, family, and body.

4   Vide Milton, Book 6th. [Burns's note. Satan 'first knew pain' when the Archangel Michael cuts him with a sword during the War in Heaven in *Paradise Lost* Book VI ll.325–8].

5   I.e. would defeat both Scots and Gaelic to express.

An' now, auld *Cloots*, I ken ye're thinkan,   115
A certain *Bardie*'s rantin, drinkin,
Some luckless hour will send him linkan,   tripping
        To your black pit;
But faith! he'll turn a corner jinkan,   dodging
        An' cheat you yet.   120

But fare-you-weel, auld *Nickie-ben*!
O wad ye tak a thought an' men'!   mend (your ways)
Ye aiblins might—I dinna ken—   perhaps; don't
        Still hae a *stake* —
I'm wae to think upo' yon den,   125   woe; upon that
        Ev'n for your sake!

THE VISION.
DUAN FIRST.[1]

THE sun had clos'd the *winter-day*,
The Curlers quat their roaring play,
And hunger'd Maukin taen her way,   a hare; taken
     To kail-yards green,   cabbage-patches
While faithless snaws ilk step betray   5 each
     Whare she has been.

The thresher's weary *flingin-tree*,   flail
The lee-lang day had tir'd me;
And when the Day had clos'd his e'e,   eye
     Far i' the West,   10
Ben i' the *Spence*, right pensivelie,   through in; parlour
     I gaed to rest.   went

There, lanely, by the ingle-cheek,   fireplace
I sat and ey'd the spewing reek,   smoke
That fill'd, wi' hoast-provoking smeek, 15 cough-
     The auld, clay biggin;   building
And heard the restless rattons squeak   rats
     About the riggin.   roof

All in this mottie, misty clime,   dusty
I backward mus'd on wasted time,   20
How I had spent my *youthfu' prime*,
     An' done nae-thing,
But stringing blethers up in rhyme   nonsense
     For fools to sing.

Had I to guid advice but harket,   25
I might, by this, hae led a market,
Or strutted in a Bank and clarket
     My *Cash-Account*;
While here, half-mad, half-fed, half-sarket, half-clothed (shirted)
     Is a' th' amount.   30

I started, mutt'ring blockhead! coof!   fool
And heav'd on high my waukit loof,   calloused palm
To swear by a' yon starry roof,   that
     Or some rash aith,
That I, henceforth, wad be *rhyme-proof* 35
     Till my last breath —

When click! the *string* the *snick* did draw;
And jee! the door gaed to the wa';   went; wall

---

1 Duan, a term of Ossian's for the different divisions of a digressive Poem. See his Cath-Loda, Vol. 2 of M'Pherson's translation. [Burns's note. 'Cath-Loda' appears in the 1765 *Works of Ossian*.]

And by my ingle-lowe I saw,
        Now bleezin bright,   40
A tight, outlandish *Hizzie*, braw,
        Come full in sight.

Ye need na doubt, I held my whisht;
The infant aith, half-form'd, was crusht;
I glowr'd as eerie's I'd been dusht,[2]   45
        In some wild glen;
When sweet, like *modest Worth*, she blusht,
        An' stepped ben.

Green, slender, leaf-clad *Holly-boughs*
Were twisted, gracefu', round her brows,   50
I took her for some SCOTTISH MUSE,
        By that same token;
And come to stop those reckless vows,
        Would soon been broken.

A "hair-brain'd, sentimental trace"   55
Was strongly marked in her face;
A wildly-witty, rustic grace
        Shone full upon her;
Her *eye*, ev'n turn'd on empty space,
        Beam'd keen with *Honor*.   60

Down flow'd her robe, a *tartan* sheen,
Till half a leg was scrimply seen;
And such a *leg*! my BESS, I wean,[3]
        Could only peer it;
Sae straught, sae taper, tight and clean—   65
        Nane else came near it.

Her *Mantle* large, of greenish hue,
My gazing wonder chiefly drew;
Deep *lights* and *shades*, bold-mingling, threw
        A lustre grand;   70
And seem'd, to my astonish'd view,
        A *well-known* Land.

Here, rivers in the sea were lost;
There, mountains to the skies were tost:
Here, tumbling billows mark'd the coast,   75
        With surging foam;
There, distant shone, *Art*'s lofty boast,
        The lordly dome.

Glosses (right margin):
- 40 fireplace-glow; blazing
- 41 young woman; fine
- 43 kept quiet
- 45 apprehensive as if
- 48 within
- 62 scarcely
- 63 believe
- 64 match

---

2   Burns translates 'dusht' as 'pushed by a ram, ox, &c.'

3   'My BESS, I wean' in the Kilmarnock edition is replaced by 'my bonny *Jean*' in the Edinburgh edition of the following year, 1787. This refers to Jean Armour, who had twins to Burns in the meantime. He married her in 1788 (after another set of twins).

Here, DOON pour'd down his far-fetch'd floods;
There, well-fed IRWINE stately thuds: 80
Auld hermit AIRE staw thro' his woods,[4]   stole
          On to the shore;
And many a lesser torrent scuds,
          With seeming roar.

Low, in a sandy valley spread,   85
An ancient BOROUGH rear'd her head;[5]
Still, as in *Scottish Story* read,
          She boasts a *Race*
To ev'ry nobler virtue bred,
          And polish'd grace. [6]   90

DUAN SECOND.

With musing-deep, astonish'd stare,
I view'd the heavenly-seeming *Fair*;
A whisp'ring *throb* did witness bear
          Of kindred sweet,
When with an elder Sister's air   95
          She did me greet.

'All hail! *my own* inspired Bard!
'In me thy native Muse regard!
'Nor longer mourn thy fate is hard,
          'Thus poorly low!   100
'I come to give thee such *reward*,
          'As *we* bestow.

'Know, the great *Genius* of this Land,
'Has many a light, aerial band,
'Who, all beneath his high command,   105
          'Harmoniously,
'As *Arts* or *Arms* they understand,
          'Their labors ply.

'They SCOTIA'S Race among them share;
'Some fire the *Sodger* on to dare;   110   soldier
'Some rouse the *Patriot* up to bare
          'Corruption's heart:
'Some teach the *Bard*, a darling care,
          The tuneful art.

---

4   The Doon, Irvine and Ayr are all rivers in Ayrshire; Burns's muse is named after another, the Coyle.

5   I.e. Ayr, a Royal Burgh since 1205.

6   In the Edinburgh Edition of 1787, after Burns's fame had won him access to the highest levels of Scottish society, he added a further seven stanzas at this point, singing the praises of several members of the local gentry.

"'Mong swelling floods of reeking gore,   115
'They ardent, kindling spirits pour;
'Or, mid the venal Senate's roar,
                    'They, sightless, stand,
'To mend the honest *Patriot-lore*,
                    'And grace the hand.   120

'Hence, FULLARTON, the brave and young;
'Hence, DEMPSTER'S truth-prevailing tongue;[7]
'Hence, sweet harmonious BEATTIE sung
                    'His "Minstrel lays;"
'Or tore, with noble ardour stung,   125
                    The *Sceptic's* bays.[8]

'To lower Orders are assign'd
'The humbler ranks of Human-kind,
'The rustic Bard, the lab'ring Hind,
                    'The Artisan;   130
'All chuse, as, various they're inclin'd,
                    'The various man.

'When yellow waves the heavy grain,
'The threat'ning *Storm*, some, strongly, rein;
'Some teach to meliorate the plain   135
                    'With *tillage-skill*;
'And some instruct the Shepherd-train,
                    'Blythe o'er the hill.

'Some hint the Lover's harmless wile;
'Some grace the Maiden's artless smile;   140
'Some soothe the Lab'rer's weary toil,
                    'For humble gains,
'And make his *cottage-scenes* beguile
                    'His cares and pains.

'Some, bounded to a district-space   145
'Explore at large Man's *infant race*,
'To mark the embryotic trace,
                    'Of *rustic Bard*;
'And careful note each op'ning grace,
                    'A guide and guard.   150

---

7   Burns names two prominent Scottish landowners. Colonel William Fullarton (1754–1808) had led troops, partly raised on his Ayrshire estates, in the Second Mysore War (1780–84) in India, and been an actively 'improving' landlord since his return. George Dempster (1732–1818), another agriculturalist, and M.P. for the Fife and Forfar burghs, was a Whig with a reputation for independence and critical of government on issues such the American War and the East India Company.

8   James Beattie (1735 –1803), now best remembered for his influential poem on the education of a poet, *The Minstrel* (1771, 1774), was in his own time also celebrated as the author of *Essay on the Nature and Immutability of Truth* (1770), a scathing (though incoherent) rebuttal of the scepticism of David Hume's *Treatise of Human Nature* (1739–40).

'*Of these am I*—COILA my name;
'And this district as mine I claim,
'Where once the *Campbells*, chiefs of fame,
        'Held ruling pow'r:
'I mark'd thy embryo-tuneful flame,   155
        'Thy natal hour.

'With future hope, I oft would gaze,
'Fond, on thy little, early ways,
'Thy rudely-caroll'd, chiming phrase,
        'In uncouth rhymes,   160
'Fir'd at the simple, artless lays
        'Of other times.

'I saw thee seek the sounding shore,
'Delighted with the dashing roar;
'Or when the *North* his fleecy store   165
        'Drove thro' the sky,
'I saw grim Nature's visage hoar,
        'Struck thy young eye.

'Or when the deep-green-mantl'd Earth,
'Warm-cherish'd ev'ry floweret's birth,   170
'And joy and music pouring forth,
        'In ev'ry grove,
'I saw thee eye the gen'ral mirth
        'With boundless love.

'When ripen'd fields, and azure skies,   175
'Call'd forth the *Reaper's* rustling noise,
'I saw thee leave their ev'ning joys,
        'And lonely stalk,
'To vent thy bosom's swelling rise,
        'In pensive walk.   180

'When *youthful Love*, warm-blushing, strong,
'Keen-shivering shot thy nerves along,
'Those accents, grateful to thy tongue,
        'Th' adored *Name*,
'I taught thee how to pour in song,   185
        'To soothe thy flame.

'I saw thy pulse's maddening play,
'Wild-send thee Pleasure's devious way,
'Misled by Fancy's *meteor-ray*,
        'By Passion driven;   190
'But yet the *light* that led astray,
        'Was *light* from Heaven.

'I taught thy manners-painting strains,
'The *loves*, the *ways*, of simple swains,
'Till now, o'er all my wide domains   195
                    'Thy fame extends;
'And some, the pride of *Coila*'s plains,
                    'Become thy friends.

'Thou canst not learn, nor I can show,
'To paint with *Thomson*'s landscape-glow;   200
'Or wake the bosom-melting throe,
                    'With Shenstone's art;
'Or pour, with *Gray*, the moving flow,
                    'Warm on the heart.[9]

'Yet all beneath th'unrivall'd Rose,   205
'The lowly Daisy sweetly blows;
'Tho' large the forest's Monarch throws
                    'His army shade,
Yet green the juicy Hawthorn grows,
                    'Adown the glade.   210

'Then never murmur nor repine;
'Strive in thy *humble sphere* to shine;
'And trust me, not *Potosi's mine*,[10]
                    'Nor *King's regard*,
'Can give a bliss o'ermatching thine,   215
                    'A *rustic Bard*.

'To give my counsels all in one,
'Thy *tuneful flame* still careful fan;
'Preserve *the dignity of Man*,
                    'With Soul erect;   220
'And trust, the UNIVERSAL PLAN
                    'Will all protect.

'*And wear thou this*' — She solemn said,
And bound the *Holly* round my head:
The polish'd leaves, and berries red,   225
                    Did rustling play;
And, like a passing thought, she fled,
                    In light away.

---

9   Burns acknowledges some of the major poets of the previous generation: James Thomson
     (1700–48), Scottish-born member of Pope's circle and author of the nature-descriptive *The
     Seasons*; for Shenstone see note 3 to 'Preface'; Thomas Gray (1716–71) author of elegies, odes,
     and Bardic verse.
10   Potosi was a silver mine in what is now Bolivia, and a major source of wealth for the Spanish
     Empire.

THE COTTER'S SATURDAY NIGHT.
INSCRIBED TO R. A****, Esq.[1]

Let not Ambition mock their useful toil,
Their homely joys, and destiny obscure;
Nor Grandeur hear, with a disdainful smile,
The short and simple annals of the Poor.

GRAY[2]

I.

My lov'd, my honor'd, much respected friend,
    No mercenary Bard his homage pays;
With honest pride, I scorn each selfish end,
    My dearest meed, a friend's esteem and praise:
To you I sing, in simple Scottish lays,
    The *lowly train* in life's sequester'd scene;
The native feelings strong, the guileless ways,
    What A**** in a *Cottage* would have been;
Ah! tho' his worth unknown, far happier there I ween!

II.

November chill blaws loud wi' angry sugh;   rush of wind
    The short'ning winter-day is near a close;
The miry beasts retreating frae the pleugh;   from the plough
    The black'ning trains o' craws to their repose:
The toil-worn COTTER frae his labor goes,[3]   from
    This night his weekly moil is at an end,
Collects his *spades*, his *mattocks* and his *hoes*,
    Hoping the *morn* in ease and rest to spend,
And weary, o'er the moor, his course does hameward bend.[4]

III.

At length his lonely *Cot* appears in view,
    Beneath the shelter of an aged tree;
The expectant *wee-things*, toddlan, stacher through   totter
    To meet their *Dad*, wi' flichterin noise and glee.   fluttering
His wee-bit ingle, blinkan bonilie,   fireplace
    His clean hearth-stane, his thrifty *Wifie*'s smile,
The *lisping infant*, prattling on his knee,
    Does a' his weary *kiaugh* and care beguile,   anxiety
And makes him quite forget his labor and his toil.

---

1   Robert Aiken (1739–1807), the prosperous Ayr lawyer who gathered almost a quarter of the subscriptions (see note 5 to 'Preface') that made the Kilmarnock edition possible, Aiken was also involved in the case behind 'Holy Willie's Prayer': see below.
2   Thomas Gray, *Elegy written in a Country Church-Yard* (1751) st.8.
3   A cotter is a tenant of a cottage with a small piece of land, originally paying rent in the form of service on a larger farm to which it was attached.
4   Echoes the opening stanza of Gray's *Elegy*: 'The plowman homeward plods his weary way, / And leaves the world to darkness and to me.'

IV.

Belyve, the *elder bairns* come drapping in,   soon; children
    At *Service* out, amang the Farmers roun';
Some ca' the pleugh, some herd, some tentie rin   drive; careful run
    A cannie errand to a neebor toun:
Their eldest hope, their *Jenny*, woman-grown,
    In youthfu' bloom, Love sparkling in her e'e,   eye
Comes hame, perhaps, to shew a braw new gown,   fine
    Or deposite her sair-won penny-fee,   hard-won
To help her *Parents* dear, if they in hardship be.

V.

With joy unfeign'd, *brothers* and *sisters* meet,
    And each for other's weelfare kindly spiers: asks
The social hours, swift-wing'd, unnotic'd fleet;
    Each tells the uncos that he sees or hears.   news
The Parents partial eye their hopeful years;
    Anticipation forward points the view;
The *Mother* wi' her needle and her sheers
    Gars auld claes look amaist as weel's the new;   makes; almost
The *Father* mixes a' wi' admonition due.

VI.

Their Master's and their Mistress's command,
    The *youngkers* a' are warned to obey;
And mind their labors wi' an eydent hand,
    And ne'er, tho' out o' sight, to jauk or play:
'And O! be sure to fear the LORD alway!
    'And mind your *duty*, duely, morn and night!
'Lest in temptation's path ye gang astray,   go
    'Implore his *counsel* and assisting *might*:
'They never sought in vain, that sought the LORD aright.'

VII.

But hark! a rap comes gently to the door;
    Jenny, wha kens the meaning o' the same,
Tells how a neebor lad came o'er the muir,
    To do some errands, and convoy her hame.
The wily Mother sees the *conscious flame*
    Sparkle in *Jenny's* e'e, and flush her cheek,   eye
With heart-struck, anxious care enquires his name,
    While Jenny hafflins is afraid to speak;   nearly
Weel-pleas'd the Mother hears, it's nae wild, worthless *Rake*.[5]

VIII.

With kindly welcome, *Jenny* brings him ben;   within
    A *strappan youth*; he takes the Mother's eye;
Blythe *Jenny* sees the *visit's* no ill-taen;   ill-taken
    The Father cracks of horses, pleughs and kye.   chats; cattle

---

5   I.e. a seducer from the gentry class.

The *Youngster's* artless heart o'erflows wi' joy,
　　But blate and laithfu', scarce can weel behave;　　bashful
The Mother, wi' a woman's wiles, can spy
　　What makes the *youth* sae bashfu' and sae grave;
Weel-pleas'd to think her *bairn's* respected like the lave.　　the rest

IX.

O happy love! where love like this is found!
　　O heart-felt raptures! bliss beyond compare!
I've paced much this weary, *mortal round*,
　　And sage EXPERIENCE bids me this declare—
'If Heaven a draught of heavenly pleasure spare,
　　'One *cordial* in this melancholly *Vale*,
''Tis when a youthful, loving, *modest* Pair,
　　'In other's arms, breathe out the tender tale,
'Beneath the milk-white thorn that scents the ev'ning gale.'

X.

Is there, in human form, that bears a heart—
　　A Wretch! a Villain! lost to love and truth!
That can, with studied, sly, ensnaring art,
　　Betray sweet *Jenny's* unsuspecting youth?
Curse on his perju'd arts! dissembling smooth!
　　Are *Honor, Virtue, Conscience*, all exil'd?
Is there no Pity, no relenting Ruth,
　　Points to the Parents fondling o'er their Child?
Then paints the *ruin'd Maid*, and *their* distraction wild!

XI.

But now the Supper crowns their simple board,
　　The healsome *Porritch*, chief of SCOTIA'S food:
The soupe their *only Hawkie* does afford,　　(their cow)
　　That 'yont the hallan snugly chows her cood:　　beyond; partition
The *Dame* brings forth, in complimental mood,
　　To grace the lad, her weel-hain'd kebbuck, fell;　　hoarded cheese; pungent
And aft he's prest, and aft he ca's it guid;　　often; calls
　　The frugal *Wifie*, garrulous, will tell,
How 'twas a towmond auld, sin' Lint was i' the bell.　　twelvemonth; flax; in flower

XII.

The chearfu' Supper done, wi' serious face,
　　They, round the ingle, form a circle wide;　　fireplace
The Sire turns o'er, with patriarchal grace,
　　The big *ha'-Bible*, ance his *Father's* pride:　　hall (family) Bible
His bonnet rev'rently laid aside,
　　His *lyart haffets* wearing thin and bare;　　grizzled temple-hair
Those strains that once did sweet in ZION glide,
　　He wales a portion with judicious care;　　chooses
'*And let us worship GOD!*' he says with solemn air.

XIII.

They chant their artless notes in simple guise;
  They tune their hearts, by far the noblest aim:
Perhaps *Dundee's* wild-warbling measures rise,
  Or plaintive *Martyrs*, worthy of the name;
Or noble *Elgin* beets the heaven-ward flame,   fans
  The sweetest far of SCOTIA'S holy lays:[6]
Compar'd with these, *Italian trills* are tame;
  The tickl'd ears no heart-felt raptures raise;
Nae unison hae they, with our CREATOR'S praise.

XIV.

The priest-like Father reads the sacred page,
  How *Abram* was the Friend of GOD on high;
Or, *Moses* bade eternal warfare wage,
  With *Amalek's* ungracious progeny;[7]
Or how the *royal Bard* did groaning lye,
  Beneath the stroke of Heaven's avenging ire;[8]
Or *Job's* pathetic plaint, and wailing cry;
  Or rapt *Isaiah's* wild, seraphic fire;
Or other *Holy Seers* that tune the *sacred lyre*.

XV.

Perhaps the *Christian Volume* is the theme;
  How *guiltless blood* for *guilty man* was shed;
How HE, who bore in heaven the second name,
  Had not on Earth whereon to lay His head:
How His first *followers* and *servants* sped;
  The *Precepts sage* they wrote to many a land:
How *he*, who lone in *Patmos* banished,
  Saw in the sun a mighty angel stand;
And heard great *Bab'lon's* doom pronounc'd by Heaven's command.[9]

XVI.

Then kneeling down to HEAVEN'S ETERNAL KING,
  The *Saint*, the *Father*, and the *Husband* prays:
Hope 'springs exulting on triumphant wing,'[10]
  That *thus* they all shall meet in future days:
There, ever bask in *uncreated rays*,

---

6 These are the names of old Common Metre psalm tunes.

7 Amalek, a Duke of Edom, is defeated by Joshua in Exodus 17; but his descendents keep coming back for more, on and off, throughout the first half of the Old Testament.

8 When David (author of the Psalms) gets another man's wife pregnant, and arranges for her husband to die in battle, God punishes him by having the child die (2 Samuel 11–12).

9 It was on Patmos that St John the Divine had the visions recorded in the Book of Revelation. He sees an angel standing in the sun at 19.17; the final pronouncement of Babylon's destruction comes at 18.21.

10 Pope's *Windsor Forest*. [Burns's note. 'See! from the Brake the whirring Pheasant springs, / And mounts exulting on triumphant Wings' (ll. 111–12). The pheasant is shot in the following couplet.]

No more to sigh, or shed the bitter tear,
    Together hymning their CREATOR'S praise
        In *such society*, yet still more dear;
While circling Time moves round in an eternal sphere.

XVII.

Compar'd with *this*, how poor Religion's pride,
        In all the pomp of *method*, and of *art*,
When men display to congregations wide,
        Devotion's ev'ry grace, except the *heart!*
The POWER, incens'd, the Pageant will desert,
        The pompous strain, the sacredotal stole;
But haply, in some *Cottage* far apart,
        May hear, well pleas'd, the language of the *Soul*;
And in His *Book of Life* the Inmates poor enroll.

XVIII.

Then homeward all take off their sev'ral way;
        The youngling *Cottagers* retire to rest:
The Parent-pair their *secret homage* pay,
        And proffer up to Heaven the warm request,
That HE who stills the *raven*'s clam'rous nest,
        And decks the *lily* fair in flow'ry pride,
Would, in the way His *Wisdom* sees the best,
        For them and for their *little ones* provide;
But chiefly, in their hearts with *Grace divine* preside.

XIX.

From scenes like these, old SCOTIA'S grandeur springs,
        That makes her lov'd at home, rever'd abroad:
Princes and lords are but the breath of kings,
        'An honest man 's the noble work of GOD:'[11]
And *certes*, in fair Virtue's heavenly road,
        The *Cottage* leaves the *Palace* far behind:
What is a lordling's pomp? a cumbrous load,
        Disguising oft the *wretch* of human kind;
Studied in arts of Hell, in wickedness refin'd!

XX.

O SCOTIA! my dear, my native soil!
        For whom my warmest wish to heaven is sent!
Long may thy hardy sons of *rustic toil*
        Be blest with health and peace and sweet content!
And O may Heaven their simple lives prevent
        From *Luxury*'s contagion, weak and vile!
Then howe'er *crowns* and *coronets* be rent,
        A *virtuous Populace* may rise the while;

---

11   Another (mis)quote from Pope, which Burns clearly expected his readers to identify, from
the *Essay on Man* Epistle IV: 'A Wit's a feather, and a Chief a rod; / An honest Man's the
noblest work of God' (ll.247–8).

And stand a wall of fire, around their much-lov'd ISLE.

XXI.

O THOU! who pour'd the *patriotic tide*,
    That stream'd thro' great, unhappy WALLACE' heart;
Who dar'd to, nobly, stem tyrannic pride,
    Or *nobly die*, the second glorious part:
(The Patriot's GOD, peculiarly thou art,
    His *friend, inspirer, guardian* and *reward!*)
O never, never SCOTIA'S realm desert,
    But still the *Patriot*, and the *Patriot-Bard*,
In bright succesion raise, her *Ornament* and *Guard*!

TO A MOUSE,

On turning her up in her Nest, with the Plough, November, 1785.

Wee, sleeket, cowran, tim'rous *beastie*,		glossy, cringing
O, what a panic's in thy breastie!		
Thou need na start awa sae hasty,		
Wi' bickering brattle!		scurrying hurry
I wad be laith to rin an' chase thee,	5	
Wi' murd'ring *pattle*!		small spade

I'm truly sorry Man's dominion
Has broken Nature's social union,
An' justifies that ill opinion,
        Which makes thee startle,   10
At me, thy poor, earth-born companion,
        An' *fellow-mortal*!

I doubt na, whyles, but thou may *thieve*;		
What then? poor beastie, thou maun live!		must
A *daimen-icker* in a *thrave*	15	odd ear in a sheaf
'S a sma' request:		
I'll get a blessin wi' the lave,		with the rest
An' never miss't!		

Thy wee-bit *housie*, too, in ruin!		
It's silly wa's the win's are strewin!	20	walls; winds
An' naething, now, to big a new ane,		build
O' foggage green!		tall grass
An' bleak *December's winds* ensuin,		
Baith snell an' keen!		both bitter

Thou saw the fields laid bare an' wast,	25	
An' weary *Winter* comin fast,		
An' cozie here, beneath the blast,		
Thou thought to dwell,		
Till crash! the cruel *coulter* past		plough-blade
Out thro' thy cell.	30	

That wee-bit heap o' leaves an' stibble,		
Has cost thee monie a weary nibble!		
Now thou's turn'd out, for a' thy trouble,		
But house or hald,		refuge
To thole the Winter's *sleety dribble*,	35	endure
An' *cranreuch* cauld!		hoar-frost

But Mousie, thou art no thy-lane,		on your own
In proving *foresight* may be vain:		
The best laid schemes o' *Mice* an' *Men*,		
Gang aft agley,	40	go often awry

An' lae'e us nought but grief an' pain,
          For promis'd joy!

Still, thou art blest, compar'd wi' *me!*
The *present* only toucheth thee:
But Och! I *backward* cast my e'e,
          On prospects drear!
An' *forward*, tho' I canna *see,*
          I *guess* an' *fear!*

leave

45   eye

cannot

TO A MOUNTAIN-DAISY,
On turning one down, with the Plough, in April — 1786.

WEE, modest, crimson-tipped flow'r,
Thou's met me in an evil hour;
For I maun crush amang the stoure   must; dust
         Thy slender stem:
To spare thee now is past my pow'r,   5
         Thou bonie gem.

Alas! it's no thy neebor sweet,
The bonie *Lark*, companion meet!
Bending thee 'mang the dewy weet!   among
         Wi's spreckl'd breast,   10
When upward-springing, blythe, to greet
         The purpling East.

Cauld blew the bitter-biting *North*   cold
Upon thy early, humble birth;
Yet cheerfully thou glinted forth   15
         Amid the storm,
Scarce rear'd above the *Parent-earth*
         Thy tender form.

The flaunting *flow'rs* our Gardens yield,
High-shelt'ring woods and wa's maun shield,   20   walls must
But thou, beneath the random bield   shelter
         O' clod or stane,
Adorns the histie *stibble-field*,   dry
         Unseen, alane.

There, in thy scanty mantle clad,   25
Thy snawie bosom sun-ward spread,
Thou lifts thy unassuming head
         In humble guise;
But now the *share* uptears thy bed,
         And low thou lies!   30

Such is the fate of artless Maid,
Sweet *flow'ret* of the rural shade!
By Love's simplicity betray'd,
         And guileless trust,
Till she, like thee, all soil'd, is laid   35
         Low i' the dust!

Such is the fate of simple Bard,
On Life's rough ocean luckless starr'd!
Unskilful he to note the card
         Of *prudent Lore*,   40

Till billows rage, and gales blow hard,
            And whelm him o'er!

Such fate to *suffering worth* is giv'n,
Who long with wants and woes has striv'n,
By human pride or cunning driv'n   45
            To Mis'ry's brink,
Till wrench'd of ev'ry stay but HEAV'N,
            He, ruin'd, sink!

Ev'n thou who mourn'st the *Daisy*'s fate,
That fate is thine — no distant date;   50
Stern Ruin's *plough-share* drives, elate,
            Full on thy bloom,
Till crush'd beneath the *furrow*'s weight,
            Shall be thy doom!

A DEDICATION TO G**** H*******, Esq. [1]

Expect na, sir, in this narration,		
A fleechin, fleth'rin *Dedication*,		flattering, wheedling
To roose you up, an' ca' you guid,		praise; call
An' sprung o' great an' noble bluid;		
Because ye're surnam'd like *His Grace*,[2]	5	
Perhaps related to the race:		
Then when I'm tir'd — and sae are ye,		
Wi' mony a fulsome, sinfu' lie,		
Set up a face, how I stop short,		make a pretence
For fear your modesty be hurt.	10	

This may do — maun do, Sir, wi' them wha		must
Maun please the Great-folk for a wamefou;		stomach-full
For me! sae laigh I need na bow,		low
For, LORD be thanket, *I can plough*;		
And when I downa yoke a naig,	15	cannot
Then, LORD be thanket, *I can beg*;		
Sae I shall say, an' that's nae flatt'rin,		
It's just *sic Poet* an' *sic Patron*.		such a

The Poet, some guid Angel help him,		
Or else, I fear, some *ill ane* skelp him!	20	slap
He may do weel for a' he's done yet,		
But only — he's no just begun yet.		

The Patron, (sir, ye maun forgie me,		must forgive
I winna lie, come what will o' me)		will not
On ev'ry hand it will allow'd be,	25	
He's just — nae better than he should be.		

I readily and freely grant,		
He downa see a poor man want;		cannot
What's no his ain, he winna tak it;		own; will not
What ance he says, he winna break it;	30	once
Ought he can lend he'll no refus't,		
Till aft his guidness is abus'd;		often
And rascals whyles that do him wrang,		sometimes
Ev'n *that*, he does na mind it lang:		
As Master, Landlord, Husband, Father,[3]	35	
He does na fail his part in either.		

---

1   Gavin Hamilton (1751–1805), landowner, Mauchline solicitor, and fellow freemason; like Aiken, instrumental in getting the Kilmarnock *Poems* published; and one of Burns's best friends until a disagreement over money matters in 1788. See note to 'Holy Willie's Prayer' below.

2   I.e. like the Duke of Hamilton, one of the most powerful noblemen in the region.

3   Hamilton was in one sense Burns's landlord: he had subleased the farm at Mossgiel to Burns and his brother since 1783.

But then, nae thanks to him for a' that;
Nae *godly symptom* ye can ca' that;   call
It's naething but a milder feature,
Of our poor, sinfu', corrupt Nature: 40
Ye'll get the best o' moral works,
'Mang black *Gentoos*, and Pagan *Turks*,   among
Or Hunters wild on *Ponotaxi*,
Wha never heard of Orth–d–xy.[4]
That he's the poor man's friend in need,   45
The GENTLEMAN in word and deed,
It's no thro' terror of D–mn–t–n;
It's just a carnal inclination,
And Och! that's nae r–g–n–r–t–n![5]

Morality, thou deadly bane,   50
Thy tens o' thousands thou hast slain!
Vain is his hope, whase stay an' trust is,
In *moral* Mercy, Truth, and Justice!

No – stretch a point to catch a plack;[6]   farthing
Abuse a Brother to his back;   55
Steal through the *winnock* frae a wh–re,   window from
But point the Rake that taks the *door*;
Be to the Poor like onie whunstane,   any whinstone
And haud their noses to the grunstane;   grindstone
Ply ev'ry art o' *legal* thieving;   60
No matter – stick to *sound believing*.

Learn three-mile pray'rs, an' half-mile graces,
Wi' weel-spread looves, an' lang, wry faces;   palms
Grunt up a solemn, lengthen'd groan,
And damn a' Parties but your own;   65
I'll warrant then, ye're nae Deceiver,
A steady, sturdy, staunch *Believer*.

O ye wha leave the springs o' C–lv–n,
For *gumlie dubs* of your ain delvin!   muddy pools of your own digging
Ye sons of Heresy and Error,   70
Ye'll *some day* squeel in quaking terror!
When Vengeance draws the sword in wrath,
And in the fire throws the *sheath*;
When Ruin, with his sweeping *besom*,   broom
Just frets till Heav'n commission gies him;   75
While o'er the *Harp* pale Misery moans,
And strikes the ever-deep'ning tones,
Still louder shrieks, and heavier groans!

---

4   I.e. the orthodox Calvinism of the Church of Scotland. 'Gentoos' are Hindus, and 'Ponotaxi'
    sounds like a generic South American location.
5   Regeneration: i.e., the work of God within the believer's soul.
6   A traditional expression: 'bend the truth if you can make money out of it'.

Your pardon, Sir, for this digression,
I maist forgat my *Dedication*;   80   almost
But when Divinity comes cross me,
My readers then are sure to lose me.[7]

So, Sir, you see 'twas nae daft vapour;
But I maturely thought it proper,
When a' my works I did review,   85
To *dedicate* them, sir, to YOU:
Because (ye need na tak it ill)
I thought them something like *yoursel*.

Then patronize them wi' your favor,
And your Petitioner shall ever —   90
I had amaist said, *ever pray*,   almost
But that's a word I need na say:
For prayin I hae little skill o't;
I'm baith dead-sweer, an' wretched ill o't;   both quite disinclined
But I'se repeat each poor man's *pray'r*,   95   I shall
That kens or hears about you, Sir —

'May ne'er Misfortune's gowling bark,   howling
'Howl thro' the dwelling o' the CLERK!
'May ne'er his gen'rous, honest heart,
'For that same gen'rous spirit smart!   100
'May K******'s far-honour'd name[8]
'Lang beet his hymeneal flame,   long fan
'Till H*******'s, at least a diz'n,
'Are frae their nuptial labors risen: from
'Five bonie Lasses round their table,   105
'And sev'n braw fellows, stout an' able,   fine
'To serve their King an' Country weel,
'By word, or pen, or pointed steel!
'May Health and Peace, with mutual rays,
'Shine on the ev'ning o' his days;   110
'Till his wee, curlie *John*'s ier-oe,   great-grandchild
'When ebbing life nae mair shall flow,
'The last, sad, mournful rites bestow!'

I will not wind a lang conclusion,
With complimentary effusion;   115
But, whilst your wishes and endeavours
Are blest with Fortune's smiles and favours,
I am, Dear Sir, with zeal most fervent,
Your much indebted, humble servant.

---

7   For the specific context of the anti-clericalism shared by Burns and Hamilton, see also under
    'Holy Willie's Prayer' below.
8   Hamilton's wife Helen Kennedy.

But if, which Pow'rs above prevent,   120
That iron-hearted Carl, *Want*,
Attended, in his grim advances,
By *sad mistakes*, and *black mischances*,
While hopes, and joys, and pleasures fly him,
Make you as poor a dog as I am,   125
Your *humble servant* then no more;
For who would humbly serve the Poor?
But, by a poor man's hopes in Heav'n!
While recollection's pow'r is giv'n,
If, in the vale of humble life,   130
The victim sad of Fortune's strife,
I, through the tender-gushing tear,
Should recognise my *Master dear*,
If friendless, low, we meet together,
Then, sir, your hand — my FRIEND and BROTHER.

EPISTLE TO J. L*****K,
AN OLD SCOTCH BARD.[1]

April 1st, 1785

WHILE briers an' woodbines budding green,
An' Paitricks scraichan loud at e'en,   *corncrakes; evening*
And morning Poossie whiddan seen,   *hare running easily*
        Inspire my Muse,
This freedom, in an *unknown* frien',   5
        I pray excuse.

On Fasteneen we had a rockin,[2]   *spinning party*
To ca' the crack and weave our stockin;   *gossip*
And there was muckle fun and jokin,   *lots of*
        Ye need na doubt;   10
At length we had a hearty yokin,   *took turns*
        At *sang about.*

There was ae *sang*, amang the rest,
Aboon them a' it pleas'd me best,   *above*
That some kind husband had addrest,   15
        To some sweet wife:
It thirl'd the heart-strings thro' the breast,   *pierced*
        A' to the life.

I've scarce heard ought describ'd sae weel,
What gen'rous, manly bosoms feel;   20
Thought I , 'Can this be *Pope*, or *Steele*,
        Or *Beattie's* wark;'[3]
They tald me 'twas an odd kind chiel   *bloke*
        About *Muirkirk.*

It pat me fidgean-fain to hear't,   25   *made me restlessly eager*
An' sae about him there I spier't;   *asked*
Then a' that kent him round declar'd,
        He had *ingine*,   *genius*
That nane excell'd it, few cam near 't ,
        It was sae fine.   30

That set him to a pint of ale,
An' either douse or merry tale,   *sober*
Or rhymes an' sangs he'd made himsel,
        Or witty catches,
'Tween Inverness and Tiviotdale,   35
        He had few matches.

---

1   John Lapraik (1727-1807) went on to publish *Poems on Several Occasions* in 1788 after losing his farm in a bank-crash.
2   Fasteneen is Shrove Tuesday.
3   Alexander Pope (1688-1744), the greatest English poet of his time; Richard Steele (1672–1796), poet, playwright and essayist. For Beattie see note 8 to 'The Vision'.

Then up I gat, an' swoor an aith,
Tho' I should pawn my pleugh an' graith,   tools
Or die a cadger pownie's death,   pedlar's pony's
        At some dyke-back,   40
A *pint* an' *gill* I'd gie them *baith*,   measure of whisky
        To hear your crack.   chat

But first an' foremost, I should tell,
Amaist as soon as I could spell,   almost
I to the *crambo-jingle* fell,   45   doggerel
        Tho' rude and rough,
Yet crooning to a body's sel,   self
        Does weel eneugh.

I am nae *Poet*, in a sense,
But just a *Rhymer* like by chance,   50
An' hae to Learning nae pretence,
        Yet, what the matter?
Whene'er my Muse does on me glance,
        I jingle at her.

Your Critic-folk may cock their nose,   55
And say, 'How can you e'er propose,
'You wha ken hardly *verse* frae *prose*,   from
        'To mak a *sang*?'
Yet by your leaves, my learned foes,
        Ye're maybe wrang.   60

What's a' your jargon o' your Schools,
Your Latin names for horns an' stools;
If honest Nature made you *fools*,
        What sairs your Grammars?   serves
Ye'd better taen up *spades* and *shools*,   65   taken; shovels
        Or *knappin-hammers*.   for breaking stones

A set o' dull, conceited Hashes,   wasters
Confuse their brains in *Colledge-classes*!
They *gang in* Stirks, and *come out* Asses,   go in bullocks
        Plain truth to speak;   70
An' syne they think to climb Parnassus[4]   then
        By dint o' Greek!

Gie me ae spark o' Nature's fire,
That's a' the learning I desire;
Then tho' I drudge thro' dub an' mire   75   mud
        At pleugh or cart,
My Muse, tho' hamely in attire,
        May touch the heart.

---

4   The mythical mountain home of the muses.

O for a spunk o' ALLAN'S glee,   *spark*
Or FERGUSON'S, the bauld an' slee,[5] 80 *bold and sly*
Or bright L*****K'S, my friend to be,
   If I can hit it!
That would be *lear* eneugh for me, *learning*
   If I could get it.

Now, Sir, if ye hae friends enow, 85 *enough*
Tho' *real friends* I b'lieve are few,
Yet, if your catalogue be fow, *full*
   I'se no insist; *I shall*
But gif ye want ae friend that's true, *if*
   I'm on your list. 90

I winna blaw about *mysel*, *will not*
As ill I like my fauts to tell; *fauts*
But friends an' folk that wish me well,
   They sometimes roose me; *praise*
Tho' I maun own, as monie still, 95 *must*
   As far abuse me.

There's ae *wee faut* they whiles lay to me,
I like the lasses — Gude forgie me!
For mony a Plack they wheedle frae me, *farthing; from*
   At dance or fair: 100
Maybe some *ither thing* they gie me
   They weel can spare.

But MAUCHLINE Race or MAUCHLINE Fair,[6]
I should be proud to meet you there;
We'se gie ae nights's discharge to *care*, 105 *we shall*
   If we forgather, *meet up*
An' hae a swap o' *rhymin-ware*,
   Wi' ane anither.

The *four-gill chap*, we'se gar him clatter, *half-pint measure*
An kirs'n him wi' reekin water; 110 *christen; smoking*
Syne we'll sit down an' tak our whitter, *then; draught*
   To chear our heart;
An' faith, we'se be *acquainted* better *we shall*
   Before we part.

Awa ye selfish, warly race, 115 *worldly*
Wha think that havins, sense an' grace, *manners*
Ev'n love an' friendship should give place
   To *catch-the-plack*! *farthing*
I dinna like to see your face, *don't*
   Nor hear your crack. 120

---

5 See note 4 to 'Preface'.
6 Mauchline was the parish where Robert and Gilbert Burns were renting Mossgiel farm at this time.

But ye whom social pleasure charms,
Whose hearts the *tide of kindness* warms,
Who hold your *being* on the terms,
        'Each aid the others,'
Come to my bowl, come to my arms,   125
        My friends, my brothers!

But to conclude my lang epistle,
As my auld pen's worn to the grissle;
Twa lines frae you wad gar me fissle,   from; make; excited
        Who am, most fervent,   130
While I can either sing, or whistle,
        Your friend and servant.

TO THE SAME.[1]

April 21st, 1785.

WHILE new-ca'd kye rowte at the stake,		driven; cattle; bellow
An' pownies reek in pleugh or braik,		smoke; harrow
This hour on e'enin's edge I take,		evening
To own I'm debtor,		
To honest-hearted, auld L*****K,	5	
For his kind *letter*.		
Forjesket sair, with weary legs,		worn out
Rattlin the corn out-owre the rigs,		casting seed-corn
Or dealing thro' amang the naigs		horses
Their ten-hours' bite,	10	
My awkart Muse sair pleads and begs,		obstinate
I would na write.		
The tapetless, ramfeezl'd hizzie,		heedless; exhausted
She's saft at best an' something lazy,		
Quo' she, 'Ye ken we've been sae busy	15	
'This month an' mair,		
'That trouth, my head is grown right dizzie,		
'An' something sair.'		
Her dowf excuses pat me mad;		feeble; made
'Conscience,' says I, 'ye thowless jad!	20	spiritless jade
'I'll write, an' that a hearty blaud,		specimen
'This vera night;		
'So dinna ye affront your trade,		don't
'But rhyme it right.		
'Shall bauld L*****K, the *king o' hearts*,	25	bold
'Tho' mankind were a *pack o' cartes*,		
'Roose you sae weel for your deserts,		praise; well
'In terms sae friendly,		
'Yet ye'll neglect to shaw your parts		
'An' thank him kindly?'	30	
Sae I gat paper in a blink,		
An' down gaed *stumpie* in the ink:		went; [his pen]
Quoth I, 'Before I sleep a wink,		
'I vow I'll close it;		
'An' if ye winna mak it clink,	35	will not
'By Jove I'll prose it!'		

---

1   Usually known as the 'Second Epistle to Lapraik'.

Sae I've begun to scrawl, but whether
In rhyme, or prose, or baith thegither,   *both together*
Or some hotch-potch that's rightly neither,
           Let time mak proof;   40
But I shall scribble down some blether   *nonsense*
           Just clean aff-loof.   *off the cuff*

My worthy friend, ne'er grudge an' carp,
Tho' fortune use you hard an' sharp;
Come, kittle up your *moorlan harp*[2]   45   *tune up*
           Wi' gleesome touch!
Ne'er mind how Fortune *waft* an' *warp*;
           She's but a b–tch.

She's gien me mony a jirt an' fleg,   *given; jerk and scare*
Sin' I could striddle owre a rig;   50
But, by the L – d, tho' I should beg
           Wi' lyart pow,   *grizzled head*
I'll laugh, an' sing, an' shake my leg,
           As lang's I dow!   *dare*

Now comes the *sax an' twentieth* simmer,   55
I've seen the bud upo' the timmer,   *on the wood*
Still persecuted by the limmer   *jade*
           Frae year to year;   *from*
But yet, despite the kittle kimmer,   *fickle wench*
           I, Rob, am here.   60

Do ye envy the *city-gent,*
Behint a kist to lie an' sklent;   *chest; squint greedily*
Or purse-proud, big wi' cent per cent,
           An' muckle wame,   *big belly*
In some bit *Brugh* to represent   65
           A *Baillie*'s name?[3]

Or is't the paughty, feudal *Thane,*   *insolent*
Wi' ruffl'd sark an' glancing cane,   *shirt*
Wha thinks himsel nae *sheep-shank bane,*
           But lordly stalks,   70
While caps and bonnets aff are taen,   *taken*
           As by he walks?

'O *Thou* wha gies us each guid gift!
'Gie me o' *wit* an' *sense* a lift,   *large amount*
'Then turn me, if *Thou* please, *adrift,*   75
           'Thro' Scotland wide;
'Wi' *cits* nor *lairds* I wadna shift,   *change places*
           'In a' their pride!'

---

2   Lapraik's farm was near Muirkirk ('Epistle to Lapraik' l.24), twelve miles further up the
      valley of the River Ayr from Mauchline; as its name suggests, this is an upland area.
3   Brugh: a burgh, a market-town. A baillie is a local magistrate in a burgh.

Were this the *charter* of our state,
'On pain o' *hell* be rich an' great,'   80
Damnation then would be our fate,
                    Beyond remead;
But, thanks to *Heav'n*, that's no the gate   way
                    We learn our *creed.*

For thus the royal *Mandate* ran,   85
When first the human race began,
'The social, friendly, honest man,
                    'Whate'er he be,
''Tis *he* fulfils *great Nature's plan,*
                    And none but *he.'*   90

O *Mandate*, glorious and divine!
The followers o' the ragged Nine,[4]
Poor, thoughtless devils! yet may shine
                    In glorious light,
While sordid sons o' Mammon's line   95
                    Are dark as night!

Tho' here they scrape, an' squeeze, an' growl,
Their worthless nievefu' of a *soul,*   fistful
May in some *future carcase* howl,
                    The forest's fright;   100
Or in some day-detesting *owl*
                    May shun the light.

Then may L*****K and B**** arise,
To reach their native, kindred skies,
And *sing* their pleasures, hopes an' joys,   105
                    In some mild sphere,
Still closer knit in friendship's ties
                    Each passing year!

---

4   'The Nine' are the Muses, goddesses responsible for the various arts.

TAM O' SHANTER: A TALE.[1]

Of Brownyis and of Bogillis full is this Buke.

GAWIN DOUGLAS.[2]

WHEN chapman billies leave the street,		pedlars
And drouthy neebors, neebors meet,		thirsty
As market-days are wearing late,		
And folk begin to tak the gate;		take the road
While we sit bousing at the nappy,	5	ale
An' getting fou and unco happy,		drunk; very
We think na on the lang Scots miles,		
The mosses, waters, slaps and styles,		gap in a dyke
That lie between us and our hame,		
Where sits our sulky, sullen dame,	10	
Gathering her brows like gathering storm,		
Nursing her wrath to keep it warm.		
This truth fand honest *Tam o' Shanter*,		found
As he frae Ayr ae night did canter:		from
(Auld Ayr, wham ne'er a town surpasses,	15	
For honest men and bonny lasses).		
O *Tam*! hadst thou but been sae wise,		
As taen thy ain wife *Kate*'s advice!		taken your own
She tauld thee weel thou was a skellum,		rascal
A blethering, blustering, drunken blellum;	20	blusterer
That frae November till October,		from
Ae market-day thou was nae sober;		
That ilka melder,[3] wi' the miller,		each
Thou sat as lang as thou had siller;		silver
That ev'ry naig was ca'd a shoe on,	25	horse; hammered
The smith and thee gat roaring fou on;		drunk
That at the L—d's house, even on Sunday,		
Thou drank wi' Kirkton Jean till Monday.		
She prophesied that late or soon,		
Thou wad be found, deep drown'd in Doon;	30	
Or catch'd wi' warlocks in the mirk,		
By Alloway's auld, haunted kirk.		
Ah, gentle dames! it gars me greet,		makes me weep
To think how mony counsels sweet,		
How mony lengthen'd sage advices,	35	
The husband frae the wife despises!		from

---

1   First published in the *Edinburgh Herald* 18th March 1791.
2   From Douglas's *Eneados*, his translation of Virgil's *Aeneid* into Scots (completed 1513), book VI, Prologue, l.18.
3   The occasion of getting your corn ground by the miller.

But to our tale: Ae market-night,
Tam had got planted unco right;   *very well*
Fast by an ingle, bleezing finely,   *fireplace*
Wi reaming swats, that drank divinely;   40   *foaming new beer*
And at his elbow, Souter *Johnny*,   *cobbler*
His ancient, trusty, drouthy crony;   *thirsty*
Tam lo'ed him like a vera brither;   *loved*
They had been fou for weeks thegither.   *drunk*
The night drave on wi' sangs and clatter;   45
And ay the ale was growing better:
The landlady and *Tam* grew gracious,
Wi' favours, secret, sweet, and precious:
The Souter tauld his queerest stories;
The landlord's laugh was ready chorus: 50
The storm without might rair and rustle,   *roar*
Tam did na mind the storm a whistle.

Care, mad to see a man sae happy,
E'en drown'd himsel amang the nappy: *ale*
As bees flee hame wi' lades o' treasure,   55   *loads*
The minutes wing'd their way wi' pleasure:
Kings may be blest, but *Tam* was glorious,
O'er a' the ills o' life victorious!

But pleasures are like poppies spread,
You seize the flower, its bloom is shed;   60
Or like the snow falls in the river,
A moment white — then melts for ever;
Or like the borealis race,
That flit ere you can point their place;
Or like the rainbow's lovely form   65
Evanishing amid the storm. —
Nae man can tether time or tide,
The hour approaches *Tam* maun ride;   *must*
That hour, o' night's black arch the key-stane,
That dreary hour he mounts his beast in;   70
And sic a night he taks the road in,   *such*
As ne'er poor sinner was abroad in.

The wind blew as 'twad blawn its last;   *if it would have*
The rattling showers rose on the blast;
The speedy gleams the darkness swallow'd;   75
Loud, deep, and lang, the thunder bellow'd:
That night, a child might understand,
The deil had business on his hand.

Weel mounted on his grey mare, *Meg*,
A better never lifted leg,   80
Tam skelpit on thro' dub and mire,   belted; mud
Despising wind, and rain, and fire;
Whiles holding fast his gude blue bonnet;
Whiles crooning o'er some auld Scots sonnet;
Whiles glowring round wi' prudent cares,   85
Lest bogles catch him unawares: ghosts/goblins
Kirk-Alloway was drawing nigh,
Where ghaists and houlets nightly cry.   owls

By this time he was cross the ford,
Whare, in the snaw, the chapman smoor'd;   90 pedlar; smothered
And past the birks and meikle stane,   birches; big
Whare drunken *Charlie* brak 's neck-bane;   broke his
And thro' the whins, and by the cairn,
Whare hunters fand the murder'd bairn;   found
And near the thorn, aboon the well,   95 above
Whare *Mungo*'s mither hang'd hersel. —
Before him *Doon* pours all his floods;
The doubling storm roars thro' the woods;
The lightnings flash from pole to pole;
Near and more near the thunders roll: 100
When, glimmering thro' the groaning trees,
Kirk-Alloway seem'd in a bleeze;   blaze
Thro' ilka bore the beams were glancing;   every crack
And loud resounded mirth and dancing. —

Inspiring bold *John Barleycorn*!   105
What dangers thou canst make us scorn!
Wi' tippeny, we fear nae evil;   small beer
Wi' usquabae, we'll face the devil! —   whisky
The swats sae ream'd in *Tammie*'s noddle,   beer so foamed
Fair play, he car'd na deils a boddle.   110 did not care for; penny
But *Maggie* stood right sair astonish'd,
Till, by the heel and hand admonish'd,
She ventured forward on the light;
And, wow! *Tam* saw an unco sight!   strange
Warlocks and witches in a dance;   115
Nae cotillion brent new frae *France*,[4]   brand new from
But hornpipes, jigs, strathspeys, and reels,
Put life and mettle in their heels.
A winnock-bunker in the east,   window seat
There sat auld Nick, in shape o' beast;   120
A towzie tyke, black, grim, and large,   shaggy mongrel
To gie them music was his charge:
He screw'd the pipes and gart them skirl,   made
Till roof and rafters a' did dirl. —   shake

---

4   *Cotillion* could name several types of fashionable dance.

Coffins stood round, like open presses,   125   *cupboards*
That shaw'd the dead in their last dresses;   *showed*
And by some devilish cantraip slight   *magic*
Each in its cauld hand held a light. —
By which heroic *Tam* was able
To note upon the haly table,   130   *altar*
A murderer's banes in gibbet airns;   *bones; irons*
Twa span-lang, wee, unchristen'd bairns;
A thief, new-cutted frae a rape,   *from a rope*
Wi' his last gasp his gab did gape;   *mouth*
Five tomahawks, wi' blude red-rusted: 135
Five scymitars, wi' murder crusted;
A garter which a babe had strangled;
A knife, a father's throat had mangled,
Whom his ain son o' life bereft,   *own*
The grey hairs yet stack to the heft;   140
Three Lawyers' tongues, turned inside out,
Wi' lies seamed like a beggar's clout;   *cloth*
Three Priests' hearts, rotten black as muck,
Lay stinking, vile, in every neuk.[5]   *corner*

    As *Tammie* glow'rd, amaz'd, and curious,   145
The mirth and fun grew fast and furious:
The piper loud and louder blew;
The dancers quick and quicker flew;
They reel'd, they set, they cross'd, they cleekit,   *linked arms*
Till ilka carlin swat and reekit,   150   *woman; steamed*
And coost her duddies to the wark,   *cast; clothes*
And linkit at it in her sark!   *tripped; shift*

    Now *Tam*, O *Tam*! had they been queans,
A' plump and strapping in their teens,
Their sarks, instead o' creeshie flannen,   155   *shifts; greasy flannel*
Been snaw-white seventeen hunder linnen!
Thir breeks o' mine, my only pair,   *these trousers*
That ance were plush, o' guid blue hair,   *once*
I wad hae gien them off my hurdies,   *given*
For ae blink o' the bonie burdies!   160

    But wither'd beldams, auld and droll,
Rigwoodie hags wad spean a foal,   *withered; wean*
Louping and flinging on a crummock,   *jumping; stick*
I wonder didna turn thy stomach.

---

5   On the advice of Alexander Fraser Tytler, Edinburgh historian and lawyer, Burns cut lines 141-144 when the poem was republished in an edition of his poems in 1793. He replaced them with this couplet: 'Wi' mair o' horrible and awefu', / Which even to name wad be unlawfu'.'

But *Tam* kent what was what fu' brawlie,	165	full well
There was ae winsome wench and wawlie,		handsome
That night enlisted in the core,		company
(Lang after kend on *Carrick* shore;[6]		
For mony a beast to dead she shot,		
And perish'd mony a bony boat,	170	
And shook baith meikle corn and bear,		much; barley
And kept the country-side in fear:)		
Her cutty sark, o' Paisley harn,		short shift; linen
That while a lassie she had worn,		
In longitude tho' sorely scanty,	175	
It was her best, and she was vauntie. —		vain
Ah! little kend thy reverend grannie,		
That sark she coft for her wee Nannie,		shift; bought
Wi' twa pund Scots ('twas a' her riches),		
Wad ever grac'd a dance of witches!	180	

But here my Muse her wing maun cour;		must fold
Sic flights are far beyond her pow'r;		such
To sing how Nannie lap and flang,		jumped
(A souple jade she was and strang),		
And how *Tam* stood, like ane bewitch'd,	185	
And thought his very een enrich'd;		eyes
Even Satan glowr'd, and fidg'd fu' fain,		twitched with excitement
And hotch'd and blew wi' might and main:		jerked
Till first ae caper, syne anither,		then another
Tam tint his reason a' thegither,	190	lost; altogether
And roars out, 'Weel done, Cutty-sark!'		
And in an instant all was dark:		
And scarcely had he Maggie rallied,		
When out the hellish legion sallied.		

As bees bizz out wi' angry fyke,	195	fuss
When plundering herds assail their byke;		
As open pussie's mortal foes,		a hare's
When, pop! she starts before their nose;		
As eager runs the market-crowd,		
When 'Catch the thief!' resounds aloud;	200	
So Maggie runs, the witches follow,		
Wi' mony an eldritch skreich and hollow.		uncanny

Ah, *Tam*! Ah, *Tam*! thou'll get thy fairin!		reward, deserts
In hell, they'll roast thee like a herrin!		
In vain thy *Kate* awaits thy comin!	205	
Kate soon will be a woefu' woman!		
Now, do thy speedy utmost, Meg,		

---

6   I.e. the coast south of Ayr.

And win the key-stane[7] o' the brig;
There, at them thou thy tail may toss,
A running stream they dare na cross.   210
But ere the keystane she could make,
The fient a tail she had to shake!   The devil a
For Nannie, far before the rest,
Hard upon noble Maggie prest,
And flew at *Tam* wi' furious ettle;   215   purpose
But little wist she Maggie's mettle —
Ae spring brought off her master hale,
But left behind her ain grey tail: own
The carlin claught her by the rump,   old woman
And left poor Maggie scarce a stump.   220

   Now, wha this tale o' truth shall read,
Ilk man and mother's son, take heed: every
Whene'er to drink you are inclin'd,
Or cutty-sarks run in your mind,
Think, ye may buy the joys o'er dear,   225
Remember Tam o' Shanter's mare.

---

7   It is a well known fact that witches, or any evil spirits, have no power to follow a poor
    wight any farther than the middle of the next running stream. — It may be proper likewise to
    mention to the benighted traveller, that when he falls in with *bogles*, whatever danger may be
    in his going forward, there is much more hazard in turning back. [Burns's note]

POEMS AND SONGS PUBLISHED ANONYMOUSLY
OR POSTHUMOUSLY.

Robert Bruce's March to Bannockburn — [1]

SCOTS, wha hae wi' WALLACE bled,	who have with
Scots, wham Bruce has aften led,	
Welcome to your gory bed, —	
Or to victorie. —	

Now 's the day, and now 's the hour;   5
See the front o' battle lour;
See approach proud EDWARD's power,
    Chains and Slaverie.

Wha will be a traitor-knave?
Wha will fill a coward's grave?   10
Be sae base as be a Slave?
    — Let him turn and flie: —

Wha for SCOTLAND's king and law,
Freedom's sword will strongly draw,
FREE-MAN stand, or FREE-MAN fa',   15   fall
    Let him follow me. —

By Oppression's woes and pains!
By your Sons in servile chains!
We will drain our dearest veins,
    But they *shall* be free!   20

Lay the proud Usurpers low!
Tyrants fall in every foe!
LIBERTY's in every blow!
    Let us DO — OR DIE!!!

---

1   First published anonymously in the London *Morning Chronicle*, May 1794. Also known as 'Scots wha hae'; sung to the tune 'Hey tuti tatey'.

Song—For a' that and a' that—[1]

Is there, for honest Poverty
    That hings his head, and a' that;   hangs
The coward-slave, we pass him by,
    We dare be poor for a' that!
For a' that, and a' that,   5
    Our toils obscure and a' that,
The rank is but the guinea's stamp,
    The Man's the gowd for a' that.—   gold

What though on hamely fare we dine,
    Wear hoddin grey,[2] and a' that?   10
Gie fools their silks, and knaves their wine,
    A Man's a Man for a' that.
For a' that, and a' that,
    Their tinsel show, and a' that;
The honest man, tho' e'er sae poor,   15
    Is king o' men for a' that.—

Ye see yon birkie ca'd, a lord,   that fellow called
    Wha struts, and stares, and a' that,
Though hundreds worship at his word,
    He 's but a coof for a' that.   20   fool
For a' that, and a' that,
    His ribband, star and a' that,
The man of independent mind,
    He looks and laughs at a' that.—

A prince can mak a belted knight,   25
    A marquise, duke, and a' that;
But an honest man's aboon his might,   above
    Gude faith, he mauna fa' that!   must not lay claim to
For a' that, and a' that,
    Their dignities and a' that,   30
The pith o' Sense, and pride o' Worth,
    Are higher rank than a' that.—

Then let us pray that come it may,
    As come it will for a' that,
That Sense and Worth, o'er a' the earth   35
    Shall bear the gree, and a' that.
For a' that, and a' that,
    It's comin yet for a' that,
That Man to Man the warld o'er,
    Shall brothers be for a' that.—   40

---

1   First published anonymously in the *Glasgow Magazine*, August 1795 (although the first stanza given here was added later from the MS). Also known as 'A Man's a Man for a' That': strictly speaking, 'For a' that and a' that' is the name of the tune Burns was writing for.
2   Coarse woollen cloth used for work-clothes.

Holy Willie's Prayer[1]

And send the Godly in a pet to pray —
POPE[2]

Argument.

Holy Willie was a rather oldish batchelor Elder in the parish of Mauchline, and much and justly famed for that polemical chattering which ends in tippling Orthodoxy, and for that Spiritualized Bawdry which refines to Liquorish Devotion. — In a Sessional process with a gentleman in Mauchline, a Mr. Gavin Hamilton, Holy Willie, and his priest, father Auld, after full hearing of the Presbytry of Ayr, came off but second best; owing partly to the oratorical powers of Mr. Robt. Aiken, Mr. Hamilton's Counsel; but chiefly to Mr. Hamilton's being one of the most irreproachable and truly respectable characters in the country. — On losing his Process, the Muse overheard him at his devotions as follows —

O THOU that in the heavens does dwell!
Wha, as it pleases best thysel,
Sends ane to heaven and ten to h–ll,
   A' for thy glory!
And no for ony gude or ill   5
   They've done before thee. —

I bless and praise thy matchless might,
When thousands thou hast left in night,
That I am here before thy sight,
   For gifts and grace,   10
A burning and a shining light
   To a' this place. —

What was I, or my generation,
That I should get such exaltation?
I, wha derserv'd most just damnation,   15
   For broken laws
Sax thousand years ere my creation,
   Thro' Adam's cause!

When from my mother's womb I fell,
Thou might hae plunged me in hell,   20
To gnash my gooms, and weep, and wail,
   In burning lakes,
Where damned devils roar and yell
   Chain'd to their stakes. —

---

1 First printed in pamphlet form in 1799 (without the 'Argument' at its head), but written in 1785, at the time of the events alluded to in the poem, and circulated privately. The charges, a vehicle for Rev. Auld's personal animus against Hamilton, were: '1. Unnecessary absence from church two Sabbaths in December and three Sabbaths in January together; 2. Setting out on a journey to Carrick on the third Sabbath in January; 3. Habitual if not total neglect of family worship; 4. Abusive letter to [Mauchline Kirk] Session dated 13th Nov. 1784.' Session appealed to the Synod of Glasgow and Ayr but Hamilton was again exonerated.

2 In Pope's *The Rape of the Lock* canto IV it is the spleen, understood as producing caprice and ill-humour, which has this effect (among various others).

Yet I am here, a chosen sample,   25
To shew thy grace is great and ample:
I'm here, a pillar o' thy temple
        Strong as a rock,
A guide, a ruler and example
        To a' thy flock. —   30

O L—d thou kens what zeal I bear,
When drinkers drink, and swearers swear,
And singin' there, and dancin' here,
        Wi' great an' sma';
For I am keepet by thy fear,   35
        Free frae them a'. —   from

But yet—O L—d—confess I must—
At times I'm fash'd wi' fleshly lust;   troubled with
And sometimes too, in warldly trust
        Vile Self gets in;   40
But thou remembers we are dust,
        Defil'd wi' sin. —

O L—d—yestreen—thou kens—wi' Meg—   yesterday evening
Thy pardon I sincerely beg!
O may't ne'er be a living plague,   45
        To my dishonor!
And I'll ne'er lift a lawless leg
        Again upon her. —

Besides, I farther maun avow,   must
Wi' Leezie's lass, three times—I trow—   50
But L—d, that friday I was fou   drunk
        When I cam near her;
Or else, thou kens, thy servant true
        Wad never steer her. —   afflict

Maybe thou lets this fleshly thorn   55
Buffett thy servant night and morn,
Lest he o'er proud and high should turn,
        That he 's sae gifted;
If sae, thy hand maun e'en be borne   must
        Untill thou lift it. —   60

L—d bless thy Chosen in this place,
For here thou has a chosen race:
But G-d, confound their stubborn face,
        And blast their name,
Wha bring thy rulers to disgrace   65
        And open shame. —

L—d mind Gaun Hamilton's deserts!
He drinks, and swears, and plays at cartes,
Yet has sae mony taking arts
     Wi' Great and Sma',   70
Frae G—d's ain priest the people's hearts   from God's own
     He steals awa.—

And when we chasten'd him therefore,
Thou kens how he bred sic a splore,   such an uproar
And set the warld in a roar   75
     O' laughin at us:
Curse thou his basket and his store,
     Kail and potatoes.—   cabbage

L—d hear my earnest cry and prayer
Against that Presbytry of Ayr!   80
Thy strong right hand, L—d, make it bare
     Upon their heads!
L—d visit them, and dinna spare   don't
     For their misdeeds!

O L—d my G—d, that glib-tongued Aiken!   85
My very heart and flesh are quaking
To think how I sat, sweating, shaking,
     And p—ss'd wi' dread,
While Auld wi' hingin lip gaed sneaking   hanging; went
     And hid his head!   90

L—d, in thy day o' vengeance try him!
L—d visit him that did employ him!
And pass not in thy mercy by them,
     Nor hear their prayer;
But for thy people's sake destroy them,   95
     And dinna spare!   don't

But L—d, remember me and mine
Wi' mercies temporal and divine!
That I for grace and gear may shine,   property
     Excell'd by nane!   100
And a' the glory shall be thine!
     AMEN! AMEN!

Love and Liberty—A Cantata[1]

Recitativo — [1][2]

WHEN lyart leaves bestrow the yird,	grey; earth
Or wavering like the Bauckie-bird,[3]	
Bedim cauld Boreas' blast;[4]	
When hailstanes drive wi' bitter skyte,	sudden blow
And infant Frosts begin to bite,	
In hoary cranreuch drest;	hoar-frost
Ae night at e'en a merry core	company
O' randie, gangrel bodies,	rude vagrant
In Poosie Nansie's[5] held the splore,	carousal
To drink their orra dudies:	spare clothes
Wi' quaffing, and laughing,	
They ranted an' they sang,	
Wi' jumping, an' thumping,	
The vera girdle rang.	griddle (on the fire)
First, niest the fire, in auld, red rags,	next to
Ane sat; weel braced wi' mealy bags	
And knapsack a' in order;	
His doxy lay within his arm;	tart
Wi' USQEBAE an' blankets warm,	whisky
She blinket on her Sodger:	
An' ay he gies the tozie drab	tipsy
The tither skelpan kiss,	Another smacking
While she held up her greedy gab,	mouth
Just like an aumous dish:	alms dish
Ilk smack still, did crack still,	each
Just like a cadger's whip;	pedlar's
Then staggering, an' swaggering,	
He roar'd this ditty up —	

---

1   This series of poems and songs is also known as *The Jolly Beggars*; not Burns's title, but suggestive of the obvious precedent for this kind of work, John Gay's *Beggar's Opera* of 1728. It was written in 1785–6 and published in 1799. For the tunes to the songs, see James Kinsley's edition of the *Poems and Songs* (OUP 1969).

2   *Recitative* is the type of delivery, between speaking and singing, used to fill in the dialogue and narration between songs in eighteenth-century opera.

3   The old Scotch name for the Bat. [Burns's note]

4   Boreas is the North Wind.

5   The Hostess of a noted Caravansary in M—, well known to and much frequented by the lowest orders of Travellers and Pilgrims. [Burns's note: i.e., an inn in Mauchline.]

Air [1]. *Tune, Soldier's joy*

I AM a son of Mars who have been in many wars,
    And show my cuts and scars wherever I come;
This here was for a wench, and that other in a trench,
    When welcoming the French at the sound of the drum.
                [Chorus:] Lal de daudle &c.

My Prenticeship I past where my LEADER breath'd his last,
    When the bloody die was cast on the heights of ABRAM;
And I served out my TRADE when the gallant *game* was play'd,
    And the MORO low was laid at the sound of the drum.

I lastly was with Curtis among the *floating batt'ries*,
    And there I left for witness, an arm and a limb;
Yet let my Country need me, with ELLIOT to head me,
    I'd clatter on my stumps at the sound of a drum.[6]

And now tho' I must beg, with a wooden arm and leg,
    And many a tatter'd rag hanging over my bum,
I'm as happy with my wallet, my bottle, and my Callet,
    As when I us'd in scarlet to follow a drum.

What tho', with hoary locks, I must stand the winter shocks,
    Beneath the woods and rocks oftentimes for a home,
When the tother bag I sell and the tother bottle tell,
    I could meet a troop of HELL at the sound of a drum.

Recitativo — [2]

He ended; and the kebars sheuk,	rafters
Aboon the chorus roar;	above
While frighted rattons backward leuk,	rats
An' seek the benmost bore:	furthest in crack
A fairy FIDDLER frae the neuk,	corner
He skirl'd out, ENCORE.	
But up arose the martial CHUCK,	sweetheart
An' laid the loud uproar —	

---

6   The soldier has fought in some of the campaigns that established Britain's global dominance in the mid-eighteenth century: on the Heights of Abraham (13th September 1759), where Gen. Woolfe's victory over the French (achieved in part by his use of Highland troops) established British control in Canada, but at which Woolfe himself was killed; at the storming of El Moro, the Spanish fortress on Cuba, that secured Havana for British troops in 1762 (the ensuing treaty granted Florida to the UK instead); and in Gibralter, where Gen. Sir George Eliot held out against a three-year Spanish seige, aided by Rear Admiral Roger Curtis's supplies and destruction of the naval batteries bombarding the peninsula in 1782.

Air [2]. *Tune, Sodger laddie*

I ONCE was a Maid, tho' I cannot tell when,
And still my delight is in proper young men:
Some one of a troop of DRAGOONS was my dadie,
No wonder I'm fond of a SODGER LADDIE.   soldier
        [Chorus:] Sing, lal de lal, &c.

The first of my LOVES was a swaggering blade,
To rattle the thundering drum was his trade;
His leg was so tight and his cheek was so ruddy,
Transported I was with my SODGER LADDIE.

But the godly old Chaplain left him in the lurch,
The sword I forsook for the sake of the church;
He ventur'd the SOUL, and I risked the BODY,
'Twas then I proved false to my SODGER LADDIE.

Full soon I grew sick of my sanctified *Sot*,
The Regiment AT LARGE for a HUSBAND I got;
From the gilded SPONTOON to the FIFE I was ready;[7]
I asked no more but a SODGER LADDIE.

But the PEACE it reduc'd me to beg in despair,[8]
Till I met my old boy in a CUNNINGHAM fair;
His RAGS REGIMENTAL they flutter'd so gaudy,
My heart it rejoic'd at a SODGER LADDIE.

And now I have lived—I know not how long,
And still I can join in a cup and a song;
But whilst with both hands I can hold the glass steady,
Here's to thee, MY HERO, my SODGER LADDIE.

Recitativo — [3]

Then niest outspak a raucle Carlin,   course old woman
Wha ken't fu' weel to cleek the Sterlin;   pilfer
For monie a pursie she had hooked,
An' had in mony a well been douked: ducked
Her LOVE had been a HIGHLAND LADDIE,
But weary fa' the waefu' woodie!   a curse on; noose
Wi' sighs an' sobs she thus began
To wail her braw JOHN HIGHLANDMAN —   fine

---

7   As spontoon is a halberd carried by infantry officers; the fife would have been played by a
     boy.
8   Presumably the Peace of Paris, in 1782, that ended the War of Independence in North
     America and the war with France that accompanied it.

A HIGHLAND lad my love was born,
The lalland laws he held in scorn;   lowland
But he still was faithfu' to his clan,
My gallant, braw JOHN HIGHLANDMAN.

    Chorus—Sing, hey my braw John Highlandman!
        Sing ho my braw John Highlandman!
        There's not a lad in a' the lan'
        Was match for my John Highlandman.

With his Philabeg, an' tartan Plaid,   kilt
An' guid Claymore down by his side,   broadsword
The ladies' hearts he did trepan,   buguile
My gallant, braw JOHN HIGHLANDMAN.
       Sing hey &c.

We ranged a' from Tweed to Spey,
An' liv'd like lords an' ladies gay:
For a lalland face he feared none,
My gallant, braw JOHN HIGHLANDMAN.
       Sing hey &c.

They banish'd him beyond the sea,
But ere the bud was on the tree,
Adown my cheeks the pearls ran,
Embracing my JOHN HIGHLANDMAN.
       Sing hey &c.

But Och! they catch'd him at the last,
And bound him in a dungeon fast,
My curse upon them every one,
They've hang'd my braw JOHN HIGHLANDMAN.
       Sing hey &c.

And now a Widow I must mourn
The Pleasures that will ne'er return;
No comfort but a hearty can,
When I think on JOHN HIGHLANDMAN.
       Sing hey &c.

Recitativo — [4]

A pigmy Scraper wi' his Fiddle,
Wha us'd to trystes an' fairs to driddle,   markets; dawdle
Her strappan limb an' gausy middle,   ample
    (He reach'd nae higher)
Had hol'd his HEARTIE like a riddle,
    An' blawn't on fire.

Wi' hand on hainch, and upward e'e,   hip; eye
He croon'd his gamut, ONE, TWO, THREE,
Then in an ARIOSO key,
    The wee Apollo
Set off wi' ALLEGRETTO glee
    His GIGA⁹ SOLO —

Air [4]. *Tune, Whistle owre the lave o't*

Let me ryke up to dight that tear,
An' go wi' me an' be my DEAR;
An' then your every CARE an' FEAR
    May whistle owre the lave o't.   over the rest of it

    Chorus — I am a Fiddler to my trade,
        An' a' the tunes that e'er I play'd,
        The sweetest still to WIFE or MAID,
        Was whistle owre the lave o't.

At KIRNS an' WEDDINS we'se be there,   harvest-homes; we shall
An' O sae nicely 's we will fare!
We'll bowse about till Dadie CARE   booze
    Sing, Whistle owre the lave o't.
        I am &c.

Sae merrily 's the banes we'll pyke,   bones we'll pick
An' sun oursels about the dyke;
An' at our leisure, when ye like
    We'll whistle owre the lave o't.
        I am &c.

But bless me wi' your heav'n o' charms,
An' while I kittle hair on thairms,   tickle; fiddle-strings
HUNGER, CAULD, an' a' sic harms   such
    May whistle owre the lave o't.
        I am &c.

---

9   A *gigue* is a lively piece in two sections, each repeated. 'Arioso' instrumental playing is in a
sustained, vocal style. 'Allegretto' playing is brisk. Apollo is god of music.

Recitativo — [5]

Her charms had struck a sturdy CAIRD,   tinker
    As weel as poor GUTSCRAPER;
He taks the Fiddler by the beard,
    An' draws a roosty rapier —
He swoor by a' was swearing worth
    To speet him like a Pliver,   spit; plover
Unless he would from that time forth
    Relinquish her for ever:

Wi' ghastly e'e poor TWEEDLEDEE   eye
    Upon his hunkers bended,   squatted
An' pray'd for grace wi' ruefu' face,
    An' so the quarrel ended;
But tho' his little heart did grieve,
    When round the TINKLER prest her,
He feign'd to snirtle in his sleeve   snigger
    When thus the CAIRD address'd her —

Air [5]. *Tune, Clout the Caudron*

My bonie lass I work in brass,
    A TINKLER is my station;
I've travell'd round all Christian ground
    In this my occupation;
I've ta'en the gold, an' been enroll'd
    In many a noble squadron:
But vain they search'd, when off I march'd
    To go an' clout the CAUDRON.   patch
          I've ta'en the gold, &c.

Despise that SHRIMP, that withered IMP,
    With a' his noise an' cap'rin;
An' take a share, with those that bear
    The *budget* and the *apron*!   leather bag
And *by* that STOWP! my faith an' houpe,   tankard
    And by that dear KILBAIGIE,[10]
If e'er ye want, or meet with scant,   poverty
    May I ne'er weet my CRAIGIE!   wet; throat
          And by that Stowp, &c.

---

10 A peculiar sort of Whiskie so called: a great favorite with Poosie Nansie's Clubs. [Burns's note]

The Caird prevail'd — th' unblushing fair
    In his embraces sunk;
Partly wi' LOVE o'ercome sae sair,
    An' partly she was drunk:
Sir VIOLINO with an air,
    That show'd a man o' spunk,   spirit
Wish'd UNISON between the PAIR,
    An' made the bottle clunk
          To their health that night.

But hurchin Cupid shot a shaft,   urchin
    That play'd a DAME a shavie —   trick
The Fiddler RAK'D her FORE AND AFT,
    Behint the chicken cavie: hen-coop
Her lord, a wight of HOMER's craft[11]   fellow
    Tho' limpan wi' the Spavie,   spavin, leg-tumour
He hirpl'd up and lap like daft,   hobbled; leapt
    An' shor'd them DAINTY DAVIE   offered them
          O' *boot* that night.   into the bargain

He was a care-defying blade,
    As ever BACCHUS listed!   enlisted
Tho' Fortune sair upon him laid,
    His heart she ever miss'd it.
He had no WISH but — to be glad,
    Nor WANT but — when he thristed;   thirsted
He hated nought but — to be sad,
    An' thus the Muse suggested
          His sang that night.

Air [6]. *Tune, For a' that an' a' that*

I AM a BARD, of no regard
    Wi' gentle folks an' a' that;
But HOMER LIKE the glowran byke,   gazing crowd
    Frae town to town I draw that.   from

Chorus —   For a' that, an' a' that,
         An' twice as muckle's a' that,   much as
         I've lost but ANE, I've TWA behin',
         I've WIFE ENEUGH for a' that.

I never drank the Muses' STANK,   pond
    Castalia's burn an' a' that,
But there it streams an' richly reams,   foams

---

11 Homer is allowed to be the eldest Ballad singer on record. [Burns's note]

My HELICON I ca' that.[12]   call
        For a' that &c.

Great love I bear to all the FAIR,
        Their humble slave an' a' that;
But lordly WILL, I hold it still
        A mortal sin to thraw that.   frustrate
            For a' that &c.

In raptures sweet this hour we meet
        Wi' mutual love an' a' that;
But for how lang the FLIE MAY STANG,
        Let INCLINATION law that.
            For a' that &c.

Their tricks an' craft hae put me daft,
        They've ta'en me in, an' a' that,
But clear your decks an' here 's the SEX!   [a toast]
        I like the jads for a' that.

            For a' that, an' a' that,
            An' twice as muckle's a' that,
            My DEAREST BLUID to do them guid,
            They're welcome till't for a' that.   to it

                    Recitativo — [7]

So sung the BARD — and Nansie's waw's   walls
Shook with a thunder of applause
        Re-echo'd from each mouth!
They toom'd their pocks, they pawn'd their duds, emptied pockets; clothes
They scarcely left to coor their fuds   cover; tails
        To quench their lowan drouth: glowing thirst
Then owre again, the jovial thrang
        The Poet did request
To lowse his PACK an' wale a sang,   choose
        A BALLAD o' the best.
            He rising, rejoicing,
                Between his TWA DEBORAHS,
            Looks round him an' found them
                Impatient for the Chorus:

---

12 Castalia is a spring on Mount Parnassus, sacred to the Muses; Helicon another mountain,
    with similar springs.

Air [7]. Tune, Jolly Mortals fill your glasses

SEE the smoking bowl before us,
    Mark our jovial, ragged ring!
Round and round take up the Chorus,
    And in raptures let us sing —

    Chorus —   A fig for those by law protected!
                    LIBERTY'S a glorious feast!
                    Courts for cowards were erected,
                    Churches built to please the PRIEST.

What is TITLE, what is TREASURE,
    What is REPUTATION's care?
If we lead a life of pleasure,
    'Tis no matter HOW or WHERE.
               A fig, &c.

With the ready trick and fable
    Round we wander all the day;
And at night, in barn or stable,
    Hug our doxies on the hay.
               A fig, &c.

Does the train-attended CARRIAGE
    Thro' the country lighter rove?
Does the sober bed of MARRIAGE
    Witness brighter scenes of love?
               A fig, &c.

Life is all a VARIORUM,
    We regard not how it goes;
Let them cant about DECORUM,
    Who have character to lose.
               A fig, &c.

Here's to BUDGETS, BAGS and WALLETS!
    Here's to all the wandering train!
Here's our ragged BRATS and CALLETS!   wenches
    One and all, cry out, AMEN!

               A fig for those by LAW protected!
               LIBERTY'S a glorious feast!
               COURTS for cowards were erected,
               CHURCHES built to please the Priest.

ADDRESS OF BEELZEBUB.[1]

To the Rt. Hon.ble JOHN, EARL OF BREADALBANE, President of the Rt. Hon.ble the HIGHLAND SOCIETY, which met, on the 23d of May last, at the Shakespeare, Covent garden, to concert ways and means to frustrate the designs of FIVE HUNDRED HIGHLANDERS, who, as the Society were informed by Mr. McKenzie of Applecross, were so audacious as to attempt an escape from their lawful lords and masters whose property they were, by emigrating from the lands of Mr. Mcdonald of Glengary to the wilds of CANADA, in search of that fantastic thing — LIBERTY —

LONG LIFE, my Lord, an' health be yours,		
Unskaith'd by hunger'd HIGHLAN BOORS!		
Lord grant, nae duddie, desp'rate beggar,		ragged
Wi' durk, claymore, or rusty trigger		
May twin auld SCOTLAND o' a LIFE,	5	deprive
She likes — as BUTCHERS like a KNIFE!		
Faith, you and Applecross were right		
To keep the highlan hounds in sight!		
I doubt na! they wad bid nae better,		ask
Than let them ance out owre the water;	10	once
Then up amang thae lakes an' seas		
They'll mak what rules an' laws they please.		
Some daring Hancocke, or a Frankline,		
May set their HIGHLAN bluid a ranklin;		
Some Washington again may head them,	15	
Or some MONTGOMERY, fearless, lead them;[2]		
Till God knows what may be effected,		
When by such HEADS an' HEARTS directed:		
Poor, dunghill sons of dirt an' mire,		
May to PATRICIAN RIGHTS ASPIRE;	20	
Nae sage North, now, nor sager Sackville,[3]		
To watch an' premier owre the pack vile!		
An' whare will ye get Howes an' Clintons		
To bring them to a right repentance		
To cowe the rebel generation,	25	
An' save the honor o' the NATION?		

1   Written in 1790; first published in the *Scots Magazine*, February 1818.
2   John Hancock (1737-93), President of the Continental Congress at the signing of the Declaration of Independence in 1776; Benjamin Franklin (1706-90), scientist, inventor and writer who helped draft the declaration; George Washington (1732-99), commander in the war with Britain and first President of the new state; Richard Montgomery (1738-75), a retired British soldier who led a rebel unit to capturing Montreal but was killed attacking Quebec.
3   Frederick, Lord North (1713-92), premier 1770-82 and thus responsible for the failure in America; George, 1st Viscount Sackville (1716-85), Secretary of State for American Affairs during the war; William, 5th Viscount Howe (1729-1814), the general in charge of British forces; Sir Henry Clinton (1738-95), general whose inability to relieve the seige of Gen. Cornwallis's army at Yorktown led to its surrender and the final British collapse in 1781.

THEY! an' be d—mn'd! what right hae they
To Meat, or Sleep, or light o' day,
Far less to riches, pow'r, or freedom,
But what your lordships PLEASE TO GIE THEM?

But, hear me, my lord! Glengary, hear!
Your HAND'S OWRE LIGHT ON THEM, I fear;   *too*
Your FACTORS, GRIEVES, TRUSTEES and BAILIES,
I canna say but they do gailies;   *cannot; well enough*
They lay aside a' tender mercies   35
An' tirl the HALLIONS to the BIRSIES;   *strip; rascals; bristles*
Yet, while they're only poin'd and herriet,   *distrained (for debt); harried*
They'll keep their stubborn Highlan spirit.
But smash them! crush them a' to spails!   *splinters*
An' rot the DYVORS i' the JAILS!   40   *bankrupts*
The young dogs, swinge them to the labour,   *flog*
Let WARK an' HUNGER mak them sober!
The HIZZIES, if they're oughtlins fausont,   *trollops; decent*
Let them in DRURY LANE be lesson'd!⁴
An' if the wives, an' dirty brats,   45
Come thiggan at your doors an' yets,   *begging; gates*
Flaffan wi' duds, an' grey wi' beese,   *flapping; rags; vermin*
Frightan awa your deucks an' geese;
Get out a HORSE-WHIP, or a JOWLER,
The langest thong, the fiercest growler,   50
An' gar the tatter'd gipseys pack   *make*
Wi' a' their bastarts on their back!

Go on, my lord! I lang to meet you,
An' in my HOUSE AT HAME to greet you;
Wi' COMMON LORDS ye shanna mingle,   55
The benmost neuk, beside the ingle   *furthest-in corner; fireplace*
At my right hand, assign'd your seat,
'Tween HEROD's hip an' POLYCRATE;
Or, if ye on your station tarrow,   *hesitate*
Between ALMAGRO and PIZARRO,⁵   60
A seat, I'm sure ye're weel deservin 't;
An' till ye come—your humble servant,
                              BEELZEBUB
HELL 1st June Anno Mundi 5790⁶

---

4   London's Drury Lane was a notorious haunt of prostitutes.
5   Herod, king of Judea under Rome at the time of Christ; Polycrates, king of Samos in the Aegean in the mid sixth century B.C.; Diego D'Almargo (1475–1538) and Francisco Pizarro (1478–1541) leaders of the brutal Spanish conquest of Peru.
6   That is, 1790, plus the 4000 years calculated to have elapsed between the creation of the Earth and the birth of Christ: Satan of course does not count years from the latter.

ODE [For General Washington's Birthday].[1]

No Spartan tube, no Attic shell,
  No lyre Eolian I awake;
'Tis Liberty's bold note I swell,
  Thy harp, Columbia, let me take.[2]
See gathering thousands, while I sing,   5
A broken chain, exulting, bring,
  And dash it in a tyrant's face!
And dare him to his very beard,
And tell him, he no more is feared,
No more the Despot of Columbia's race.   10
  A tyrant's proudest insults braved,
They shout, a People freed! They hail an Empire saved.

  Where is Man's godlike form?
  Where is that brow erect and bold,
  That eye that can, unmoved, behold   15
  The wildest rage, the loudest storm,
That e'er created fury dared to raise!
  Avaunt! thou caitiff, servile, base,
  That tremblest at a Despot's nod,
  Yet, crouching under th' iron rod,   20
Canst laud the hand that struck th' insulting blow!
  Art thou of man's imperial line?
  Dost boast that countenance divine?
  Each skulking feature answers, No!
  But come, ye sons of Liberty,   25
  Columbia's offspring, brave as free,
In danger's hour still flaming in the van:
Ye know, and dare maintain, The Royalty of Man.

  Alfred, on thy starry throne,
  Surrounded by the tuneful choir,   30
The Bards that erst have struck the patriot lyre,
And rous'd the freeborn Briton's soul of fire,
  No more thy England own. —[3]
Dare injured nations form the great design,
  To make detested tyrants bleed?[4]   35
Thy England execrates the glorious deed!
  Beneath her hostile banners waving,
  Every pang of honor braving,

---

1 Written in 1794; not published until 1874.
2 'Columbia' here meaning the Americas in general: that continent discovered by Christopher Columbus.
3 Taking Alfred the Great (848–99) as England's great liberator (from the Danes).
4 The French Republic had executed the erstwhile Louis XVI in January 1793.

England in thunder calls — 'The Tyrant's cause is mine!'[5]
   That hour accurst, how did the fiends rejoice,   40
And hell thro' all her confines raise th' exulting voice,
   That hour which saw the generous English name
Linkt with such damned deeds of everlasting shame!

   Thee, Caledonia, thy wild heaths among,   45
   Famed for the martial deed, the heaven-taught song,
      To thee I turn with swimming eyes. —
      Where is that soul of Freedom fled?
      Immingled with the mighty Dead!
   Beneath that hallow'd turf where WALLACE lies!
   Hear it not, Wallace, in thy bed of death!   50
      Ye babbling winds in silence sweep;
      Disturb not ye the hero's sleep,
      Nor give the coward secret breath. —
   Is this the ancient Caledonian form,
   Firm as her rock, resistless as the storm?   55
   Shew me that eye which shot immortal hate,
      Blasting the Despot's proudest bearing:
   Shew me that arm which, nerved with thundering fate,
      Braved Usurpation's boldest daring!
      Dark-quenched as yonder sinking star,   60
      No more that glance lightens afar;
   That palsied arm no more whirls on the waste of war.

---

5   When Britain went to war with the French Republic in February, it was entering a military and political alliance with absolutist monarchies such as Prussia, Austria and Spain. The U.S. government was of course sympathetic to the Republic.

The Fornicator. A New Song—[1]

Tune, Clout the Caldron.

YE jovial boys who love the joys,
    The blissful joys of Lovers;
Yet dare avow with dauntless brow,
    When the bony lass discovers;   *i.e. reveals her pregnancy*
I pray draw near and lend an ear,   5
    And welcome in a Frater,   *brother*
For I've lately been on quarentine,
    A proven Fornicator.

Before the Congregation wide
    I pass'd the muster fairly,   10
My handsome Betsey by my side,
    We gat our ditty rarely;[2]
But my downcast eye by chance did spy
    What made my lips to water,
Those limbs so clean where I, between,   15
    Commence'd a Fornicator.

With rueful face and signs of grace
    I pay'd the buttock-hire,[3]
The night was dark and thro' the park
    I could not but convey her;   20
A parting kiss, what could I less,
    My vows began to scatter,
My Betsey fell — lal de dal lal lal,
    I am a Fornicator.

But for her sake this vow I make,   25
    And solemnly I swear it,
That while I own a single crown,
    She's welcome for to share it;
And my rogueish boy his Mother's joy,
    And darling of his Pater,   30   *father*
For him I boast my pains and cost,
    Although a Fornicator.

Ye wenching blades whose hireling jades
    Have tipt you off blue-boram,[4]
I tell you plain, I do disdain   35

---

1   Written in 1784–5. As well as collecting, arranging and writing traditional folk-songs, Burns also collected and wrote bawdy lyrics. This collection came to be known as *The Merry Muses of Caledonia* and, after many years unofficial circulation, were eventually published in 1965, in the era of the Lady Chatterley trial. This and the following lyric are from this source.
2   'Received our reproof', i.e. from the minister in church, in the 'stool of repentance'.
3   The church fine for fornication.
4   I.e. whose whores have given them pox.

To rank you with the Quorum;
But a bony lass upon the grass
    To teach her esse Mater,   to become a mother
And no reward but for regard,
    O that's a Fornicator.   40

Your warlike Kings and Heros bold,
    Great Captains and Commanders;
Your mighty Cèsars fam'd of old,
    And Conquering Alexanders;
In fields they fought and laurels bought   45
    And bulwarks strong did batter,
But still they grac'd our noble list
    And ranked Fornicator!!!

Why should na poor folk mowe.[1]

Tune, The Campbells are Coming.

WHEN Princes and Prelates and het-headed zealots
  All Europe hae set in a lowe,   blaze
The poor man lies down, nor envies a crown,
  And comforts himsel with a mowe. —   fuck

Chorus
And why shouldna poor folk mowe, mowe, mowe,
  And why shouldna poor folk mowe:
The great folk hae siller, and houses and lands,   silver
  Poor bodies hae naething but mowe. —

2
When Br–nsw–ck's great Prince cam a cruising to Fr–nce
  Republican billies to cowe,[2]
Bauld Br–nsw–c's great Prince wad hae shawn better sense, bold
  At hame with his Princess to mowe. —
    And why should na &c. —

3
Out over the Rhine proud Pr–ss–a wad shine,
  To *spend* his best blood he did vow;
But Frederic had better ne'er forded water,[3]
  But *spent* as he docht in a mowe. —   as he planned [?]
    And why &c. —

4
By sea and by shore! the Emp–r–r swore,[4]
  In Paris he'd kick up a row;
But Paris sae ready just leugh at the laddie   laughed
  And bade him gae tak him a mowe. —
    And why &c. —

5
Auld Kate laid her claws on poor Stanislaus,[5]
  And Poland has bent like a bow:
May the deil in her a— ram a huge pr–ck o' brass!
  And damn her in h–ll with a mowe!
    And why &c. —

---

1   Written in 1792.
2   Charles William Ferdinand, Duke of Brunswick and brother-in-law to George III, invaded France with a mostly Prussian and Austrian army in August 1792, aiming to overthrow the revolution. It was defeated at Valmy.
3   Frederick-William II was King of Prussia.
4   Francis II, Holy Roman Emperor, another member of the coalition against France.
5   Catherine the Great, Empress of Russia; and Stanisław August Poniatowski, last King of the Polish-Lithuanian Commonwealth. Stanisław had sided with his reformist parliament to produce a modernising Constitution for Poland, partly inspired by events in France, in 1791. The following year Russia invaded to reassert its hegemony, and defeated the new state.

6

But truce with commotions and new-fangled notions,
    A bumper I trust you'll allow:
Here's George our gude king and Charlotte his queen,
    And lang may they tak a gude mowe!

A

SERIES OF PLAYS:

IN WHICH
IT IS ATTEMPTED TO DELINIATE

THE STRONGER PASSIONS OF THE MIND.

EACH PASSION BEING THE SUBJECT
OF

A TRAGEDY AND A COMEDY.[1]

LONDON:
PRINTED FOR T. CADELL, JUN. AND W.DAVIES, IN THE STRAND.

1798

[from] INTRODUCTORY DISCOURSE[2]

IT is natural for a writer, who is about to submit his works to the Publick, to feel a strong inclination, by some Preliminary Address, to conciliate the favour of his reader, and dispose him, if possible, to peruse them with a favourable eye. I am well aware, however, that his endeavours are generally fruitless: in his situation our hearts revolt from all appearance of confidence, and we consider his diffidence as hypocrisy. Our own word is frequently taken for what we say of ourselves, but very rarely for what we say of our works. Were these three plays, which this small volume contains, detached pieces only, and unconnected with others that do not yet appear, I should have suppressed this inclination altogether;[3] and have allowed my reader to begin

---

1   By Joanna Baillie (1762–1851). This volume is usually referred to as the 1798 *Plays on the Passions*. Other volumes followed.

2   What follows are extracts only. I have omitted all of Baillie's own footnotes. Where sections of paragraphs have been elided, this is marked thus: […]; where whole paragraphs have been elided, this is marked with asterisks. The complete text can be conveniently read on Google Books, in an 1821 edition of this volume.

3   The three plays are *Count Basil* and *The Tryal*, respectively a tragedy and a comedy delineating the passion of love; and *De Monfort*, representing the passion of hate. *De Monfort's* partner comedy on hate is *The Election*, included in the second volume of *Plays on the Passions*, published in 1802. Baillie's original plan was for a pair of plays to address, as well as love and hate, ambition, fear, hope, remorse, jealousy, pride, envy, revenge, anger, joy, and grief. This plan was subsequently revised, and having got as far as remorse and jealousy in the

what is before him, and to form what opinion of it his taste or his humour might direct, without any previous trespass upon his time or his patience. But they are part of an extensive design: of one which, as far as my information goes, has nothing exactly similar to it in the language: of one which a whole life time will be limited enough to accomplish; and which has, therefore, a considerable chance of being cut short by that hand which nothing can resist.

Before I explain the plan of this work, I must make a demand upon the patience of my reader, whilst I endeavour to communicate to him those ideas regarding human nature, as they in some degree affect almost every species of moral writings, but particularly the Dramatic, that induced me to attempt it; and, as far as my judgment enabled me to apply them, has directed me in the execution of it.

From that strong sympathy which most creatures, but the human above all, feel for others of their kind, nothing has become so much an object of man's curiosity as man himself. We are all conscious of this within ourselves, and so constantly do we meet with it in others, that like every circumstance of continually repeated occurrence, it thereby escapes observation. Every person, who is not deficient in intellect, is more or less occupied in tracing, amongst the individuals he converses with, the varieties of understanding and temper which constitute the characters of men; and receives great pleasure from every stroke of nature that points out to him those varieties. This is, much more than we are aware of, the occupation of children, and of grown people also, whose penetration is but lightly esteemed; and that conversation which degenerates with them into trivial and mischievous tattling, takes its rise not unfrequently from the same source that supplies the rich vein of the satirist and the wit. That eagerness so universally shewn for the conversation of the latter, plainly enough indicates how many people have been occupied in the same way with themselves. Let any one, in a large company, do or say what is strongly expressive of his particular character, or of some passion or humour of the moment, and it will be detected by almost every person present. How often may we see a very stupid countenance animated with a smile, when the learned and the wise have betrayed some native feature of their own minds! And how often will this be the case when they have supposed it to be concealed under a very different disguise! From this constant employment of their minds, most people, I believe, without being conscious of it, have stored up in idea the greater part of those strongly marked varieties of human character, which may be said to divide it into classes;[4] and in one of those classes they involuntarily place every new person they become acquainted with.

* * * * *

In our ordinary intercourse with society, this sympathetick propensity of our minds is exercised upon men, under the common occurrences of life, in which we have often observed them. Here vanity and weakness put themselves forward to view, more conspicuously than the virtues: here men encounter those smaller trials, from which they are not apt to come off victorious; and here, consequently, that which is marked with the whimsical and ludicrous will strike us most forcibly, and make the strongest impression on our memory. To this sympathetick propensity of our minds, so exercised, the genuine and pure comick of every composition, whether drama, fable, story, or satire is addressed.

1836 *Miscellaneous Plays,* Baillie regarded the project as complete.

4   It is perhaps worth pointing out that Baillie does not mean *social* classes: the use of 'class' in the formulations 'working class', 'middle class' etc was just coming into currency around this time.

If man is an object of so much attention to man, engaged in the ordinary occurrences of life, how much more does he excite his curiosity and interest when placed in extraordinary situations of difficulty and distress? It cannot be any pleasure we receive from the sufferings of a fellow-creature which attracts such multitudes of people to a publick execution, though it is the horrour we conceive for such a spectacle that keeps so many away. To see a human being bearing himself up under such circumstances, or struggling with the terrible apprehensions which such a situation impresses, must be the powerful incentive, which makes us press forward to behold what we shrink from, and wait with trembling expectation for what we dread. For though few at such a spectacle can get near enough to distinguish the expression of face, or the minuter parts of a criminal's behaviour, yet from a considerable distance will they eagerly mark whether he steps firmly; whether the motions of his body denote agitation or calmness; and if the wind does but ruffle his garment, they will, even from that change upon the outline of his distant figure, read some expression connected with his dreadful situation. Though there is a greater proportion of people in whom this strong curiosity will be overcome by other dispositions and motives; though there are many more who will stay away from such a sight than will go to it; yet there are very few who will not be eager to converse with a person who has beheld it; and to learn, very minutely, every circumstance connected with it, except the very act itself of inflicting death. To lift up the roof of his dungeon, like the *Diable boiteux*,[5] and look upon a criminal the night before he suffers, in his still hour of privacy, when all that disguise, which respect for the opinion of others, the strong motive by which even the lowest and wickedest of men continue to be moved, would present an object to the mind of every person, not withheld from it by great timidity of character, more powerfully attractive than almost any other.

* * * * *

But it is not in situations of difficulty and distress alone, that man becomes the object of this sympathetick curiosity; he is no less so when the evil he contends with arises in his own breast, and no outward circumstance connected with him either awakens our attention or our pity. What human creature is there, who can behold a being like himself under the violent agitation of those passions which all have, in some degree, experienced, without feeling himself most powerfully excited by the sight? I say, all have experienced, for the bravest man on earth knows what fear is as well as the coward; and will not refuse to be interested for one under the dominion of this passion, provided there be nothing in the circumstances attending it to create contempt. Anger is a passion that attracts less sympathy than any other, yet the unpleasing and distorted features of an angry man will be more eagerly gazed upon, by those who are no wise concerned with his fury or the objects of it, than the most amiable placid countenance in the world. Every eye is directed to him; every voice is hushed to silence in his presence; even children will leave off their gambols as he passes, and gaze after him more eagerly than the gaudiest equipage. The wild tossings of despair; the gnashing of hatred and revenge; the yearnings of affection, and the softened mien of love; all that language of the agitated soul, which every age and nation understands, is never addressed to the dull nor inattentive.

It is not merely under the violent agitations of passion, that man so rouses and interests us; even the smallest indications of an unquiet mind, the restless eye, the muttering lip, the half-checked exclamation, and the hasty start, will set our attention

---

5   *Le Diable boiteux* (1707) is a picaresque novel by French author Alain René Lesage in which a devil reveals to the hero various types of human depravity by lifting the roofs of houses to reveal the private behaviour going on within.

as anxiously upon the watch, as the first distant flashes of a gathering storm. When some great explosion of passion bursts forth, and some consequent catastrophe happens, if we are at all acquainted with the unhappy perpetrator, how minutely will we endeavour to remember every circumstance of his past behaviour! And with what avidity will we seize upon every recollected word or gesture, that is in the smallest degree indicative of the supposed state of his mind, at the time when they took place. If we are not acquainted with him, how eagerly will we listen to similar recollections from another! Let us understand, from observation or report, that any person harbours in his breast, concealed from the world's eye, some powerful rankling passion of what kind soever it be, we will observe every word, every motion, every look, even the distant gait of such a man, with a constancy and attention bestowed upon no other. Nay, should we meet him unexpectedly on our way, a feeling will pass across our minds as though we found ourselves in the neighbourhood of some secret and fearful thing. If invisible, would we not follow him into his lonely haunts, into his closet, into the midnight silence of his chamber? There is, perhaps, no employment which the human mind will with so much avidity pursue, as the discovery of concealed passion, as the tracing the varieties and progress of a perturbed soul.

It is to this sympathetick curiosity of our nature, exercised upon mankind in great and trying occasions, and under the influence of the stronger passions, when the grand, the generous, the terrible attract our attention far more than the base and depraved, that the high and powerfully tragick, of every composition, is addressed.

This propensity is universal. Children begin to shew it very early; it enters into many of their amusements, and that part of them too, for which they shew the keenest relish. It tempts them many times, as well as the mature in years, to be guilty of tricks, vexations, and cruelty; yet God Almighty has implanted it within us, as well as all our other propensities and passions, for wise and good purposes. It is our best and most powerful instructor. From it we are taught the proprieties and decencies of ordinary life, and are prepared for distressing and difficult situations. In examining others we know ourselves. With limbs untorn, with head unsmitten, with senses unimpaired by despair, we know what we ourselves might have been on the rack, on the scaffold, and in the most afflicting circumstances of distress. Unless when accompanied with passions of the dark and malevolent kind, we cannot well exercise this disposition without becoming more just, more merciful, more compassionate; and as the dark and malevolent passions are not the predominant inmates of the human breast, it hath produced more deeds — O many more! of kindness than of cruelty. It holds up for our example a standard of excellence, which, without its assistance, our inward consciousness of what is right and becoming might never have dictated. It teaches us, also, to respect ourselves, and our kind; for it is a poor mind, indeed, that from this employment of its faculties, learns not to dwell upon the noble view of human nature rather than the mean.

Universal, however, as this disposition undoubtedly is, with a generality of mankind it occupies itself in a passing and superficial way. Though a native trait of character or of passion is obvious to them as well as to the sage, yet to their minds it is but the visitor of a moment; they look upon it singly and unconnected: and though this disposition, even so exercised, brings instruction as well as amusement, it is chiefly by storing up in their minds those ideas to which the instructions of others refer, that it can be eminently useful. Those who reflect and reason upon what human nature holds out to their observation, are comparatively but few. No stroke of nature which engages their attention stands insulated and alone. Each presents itself to them with many varied connections; and they comprehend not merely the immediate feeling which gave rise to it, but the relation of that feeling to others which are concealed. We wonder at the changes and caprices of men; they see in them nothing but what is natural and accountable. We stare upon some dark catastrophe of passion, as the Indians did stare upon an eclipse of the moon; they, conceiving the track of ideas through which an impassioned mind has passed, regard it like the philosopher who foretold the phenomenon. Knowing what situation of life he is about to be thrown into, they perceive in the man, who, like Hazael, says, "is thy servant a dog that he should do this thing?" the foul and ferocious murderer.[6] A man of this contemplative character partakes, in some degree, of the entertainment of the Gods, who were supposed to look down upon this world and the inhabitants of it, as we do upon a theatrical exhibition; and if he is of a benevolent disposition, a good man struggling with, and triumphing over adversity, will be to him, also, the most delightful spectacle. But though this eagerness to observe their fellow-creatures in every situation, leads not the generality of mankind to reason and reflect; and those strokes of nature which they are so ready to remark, stand single and unconnected in their minds, yet they may be easily induced to do both: and there is no mode of instruction which they will so eagerly pursue, as that which lays open before them, in a more enlarged and connected view, than their individual observations are capable of supplying, the varieties of the human mind. Above all, to be well exercised in this study will fit a man more particularly for the most important situations of life. He will prove for it the better Judge, the better Magistrate, the better Advocate; and as a ruler or conductor of other men, under every occurring circumstance, he will find himself the better enabled to fulfil his duty, and accomplish his designs. He will perceive the natural effect of every order that he issues upon the minds of his soldiers, his subjects, or his followers; and he will deal to others judgment tempered with mercy; that is to say truly just; for justice appears to us severe only when it is imperfect.

In proportion as moral writers of every class have exercised within themselves this sympathetick propensity of our nature, and have attended to it in others, their works have been interesting and instructive. They have struck the imagination more forcibly, convinced the understanding more clearly, and more lastingly impressed the memory. If unseasoned with any reference to this, the fairy bowers of the poet, with all his gay images of delight, will be admired and forgotten; the important relations of the historian, and even the reasonings of the philosopher will make a less permanent impression.

* * * * *

Our desire to know what men are in the closet as well as in the field, by the blazing hearth, and at the social board, as well as in the council and the throne, is very imperfectly gratified by real history; romance writers, therefore, stepped boldly forth to supply the deficiency; and tale writers, and novel writers, of many descriptions, followed after. If they have not been very skilful in the delineations of nature; if they have represented men and women speaking and acting as men and women never did speak or act; if they have caricatured both our virtues and our vices; if they have given us such pure and unmixed, or such heterogeneous combinations of character as real life never presented, and yet have pleased and interested us, let it not be imputed to the dulness of man in discerning what is genuinely natural in himself. There are many inclinations belonging to us, besides this great master-propensity of which I am treating. Our love of the grand, the beautiful, the novel, and above all of the marvellous, is very strong; and if we are richly fed with what we have a good relish for, we may be weaned to forget our native and favourite aliment. Yet we can never so far

---

6   See 2 Kings 8:13.

forget it, but we will cling to, and acknowledge it again, whenever it is presented before us. In a work abounding with the marvellous and unnatural, if the author has any how stumbled upon an unsophisticated genuine stroke of nature, we will immediately perceive and be delighted with it, though we are foolish enough to admire at the same time, all the nonsense with which it is surrounded. After all the wonderful incidents, dark mysteries, and secrets revealed, which eventful novel[7] so liberally presents to us; after the beautiful fairy ground, and even the grand and sublime scenes of nature with which descriptive novel so often enchants us; those works which most strongly characterize human nature in the middling and lower classes of society, where it is to be discovered by stronger and more unequivocal marks, will ever be the most popular. For though great pains have been taken in our higher sentimental novels to interest us in the delicacies, embarrassments, and artificial distresses of the more refined part of society, they have never been able to cope in the public opinion with these. The one is a dressed and beautiful pleasure-ground, in which we are enchanted for a while, amongst the delicate and unknown plants of cultivation; the other is a rough forest of our native land; the oak, the elm, the hazle, and the bramble are there; and amidst the endless varieties of its paths we can wander for ever. Into whatever scenes the novelist may conduct us, what object soever he may present to our view, still is our attention most sensibly awake to every touch faithful to nature; still are we upon the watch for every thing that speaks to us of ourselves.

The fair field of what is properly called poetry, is enriched with so many beauties, that in it we are often tempted to forget what we really are, and what kind of beings we belong to. Who in the enchanted regions of simile, metaphor, allegory and description, can remember the plain order of things in this every-day world? From heroes whose majestick forms rise like a lofty tower, whose eyes are lightening, whose arms are irresistible, whose course is like the storms of heaven, bold and exalted sentiments we will readily receive; and will not examine them very accurately by that rule of nature which our own breast prescribes to us. A shepherd whose sheep, with fleeces of the purest snow, browse the flowery herbage of the most beautiful vallies; whose flute is ever melodious, and whose shepherdess is ever crowned with roses; whose every care is love, will not be called very strictly to account for the loftiness and refinement of his thoughts. The fair Nymph, who sighs out her sorrows to the conscious and compassionate wilds; whose eyes gleam like the bright drops of heaven; whose loose tresses stream to the breeze, may say what she pleases with impunity. I will venture, however, to say, that amidst all this decoration and ornament, all this loftiness and refinement, let one simple trait of the human heart, one expression of passion genuine and true to nature, be introduced, and it will stand forth alone in the boldness of reality, whilst the false and unnatural around it, fades away upon every side, like the rising exhalations of the morning. With admiration, and often with enthusiasm we proceed on our way through the grand and the beautiful images, raised to our imagination by the lofty Epic muse; but what even here are those things that strike upon the heart; that we feel and remember? Neither the descriptions of war, the sound of the trumpet, the clanging of arms, the combat of heroes, nor the death of the mighty, will interest our minds like the fall of the feeble stranger, who simply expresses the anguish of his soul, at the thoughts of that far-distant home which he must never return to again, and closes his eyes, amongst the ignoble and forgotten; like the timid stripling goaded by the shame of reproach, who urges his trembling steps to the fight, and falls like a

---

7   This odd usage, repeated in the next clause, omitting the article from the expected '*the eventful novel*', is not mentioned in *OED*, but it remains uncorrected in subsequent editions.

tender flower before the first blast of winter. How often will some simple picture of this kind be all that remains upon our minds of the terrifick and magnificent battle, whose description we have read with admiration! How comes it that we relish so much the episodes of an heroic poem?[8] It cannot merely be that we are pleased with a resting place, where we enjoy the variety of contrast; for were the heroic style introduced into it, ninety readers out of an hundred would pass over it altogether. It is not that we meet such a story, so situated, with a kind of sympathetic good will, as in passing through a country of castles and of palaces, we should pop unawares upon some humble cottage, resembling the dwellings of our native land, and gaze upon it with affection. The highest pleasures which we receive from poetry, as well as from the real objects which surround us in the world, are derived from the sympathetick interest we all take in beings like ourselves; and I will even venture to say, that were the grandest scenes which can enter into the imagination of man, presented to our view, and all reference to man completely shut out from our thoughts, the objects that composed it would convey to our minds little better than dry ideas of magnitude, colour, and form; and the remembrance of them would rest upon our minds like the measurement and distances of the planets.

If the study of human nature then, is so useful to the poet, the novelist, the historian, and the philosopher, of how much greater importance must it be to the dramatick writer? To them it is a powerful auxiliary, to him it is the centre and strength of the battle. If characteristick views of human nature enliven not their pages, there are many excellencies with which they can, in some degree, make up for the deficiency, it is what we receive from them with pleasure rather than demand. But in his works no richness of invention, harmony of language, nor grandeur of sentiment will supply the place of faithfully delineated nature. The poet and the novelist may represent to you their great characters from the cradle to the tomb. They may represent them in any mood or temper, and under the influence of any passion which they see proper, without being obliged to put words into their mouths, those great betrayers of the feigned and adopted. They may relate every circumstance however trifling and minute, that serves to develop their tempers and dispositions. They tell us what kind of people they intend their men and women to be, and as such we receive them. If they are to move us in any scene of distress, every circumstance regarding the parties concerned in it, how they looked, how they moved, how they sighed, how the tears gushed from their eyes, how the very light and shadow fell upon them, is carefully described, and the few things that are given them to say along with all this assistance, must be very unnatural indeed if we refuse to sympathize with them. But the characters of the drama must speak directly for themselves. Under the influence of every passion, humour, and impression; in the artificial veilings of hypocrisy and ceremony, in the openness of freedom and confidence, and in the lonely hour of meditation they speak. He who made us hath placed within our breast a judge that judges instantaneously of every thing they say. We expect to find them creatures like ourselves; and if they are untrue to nature, we feel that we are imposed upon; as though the poet had introduced to us for brethren, creatures of a different race, beings of another world.

* * * * *

[…] But in presenting to us those views of great characters, and of the human mind in difficult and trying situations which particularly belong to Tragedy, the far greater proportion, even of those who may be considered as respectable dramatick poets, have very much failed. From the beauty of those original dramas to which they have ever

---

8   Baillie is using 'episode' its older sense of 'digression' or 'interpolated narrative'.

looked back with admiration, they have been tempted to prefer the embellishments of poetry to faithfully delineated nature. They have been more occupied in considering the works of the great Dramatists who have gone before them, and the effects produced by their writings, than the varieties of human character which first furnished materials for those works, or those principles in the mind of man by means of which such effects were produced. Neglecting the boundless variety of nature, certain strong outlines of character, certain bold features of passion, certain grand vicissitudes and striking dramatick situations have been repeated from one generation to another; whilst a pompous and solemn gravity, which they have supposed to be necessary for the dignity of tragedy, has excluded almost entirely from their works those smaller touches of nature, which so well develop the mind; and by showing men in their hours of state and exertion only, they have consequently shewn them imperfectly. Thus, great and magnanimous heroes, who bear with majestick equanimity every vicissitude of fortune; who in every temptation and trial stand forth in unshaken virtue, like a rock buffeted by the waves; who encompast with the most terrible evils, in calm possession of their souls, reason upon the difficulties of state; and, even upon the brink of destruction, pronounce long eulogiums on virtue, in the most eloquent and beautiful language, have been held forth to our view as objects of imitation and interest; as though they had entirely forgotten that it is only from creatures like ourselves that we feel, and therefore, only from creatures like ourselves that we receive the instruction of example. [...]

* * * * *

They have, indeed, from this regard to the works of preceding authors, and great attention to the beauties of composition, and to dignity of design, enriched their plays with much striking, and sometimes sublime imagery, lofty thoughts, and virtuous sentiments; but in striving so eagerly to excel in those things that belong to tragedy in common with many other compositions, they have very much neglected those that are peculiarly her own. [...] Every species of moral writing has its own way of conveying instruction, which it can never, but with disadvantage, exchange for any other. The Drama improves us by the knowledge we acquire of our own minds, from the natural desire we have to look into the thoughts, and observe the behaviour of others. Tragedy brings to our view men placed in those elevated situations, exposed to those great trials, and engaged in those extraordinary transactions, in which few of us are called upon to act. As examples applicable to ourselves, therefore, they can but feebly affect us; it is only from the enlargement of our ideas in regard to human nature, from that admiration of virtue, and abhorrence of vice which they excite, that we can expect to be improved by them. But if they are not represented to us as real and natural characters, the lessons we are taught from their conduct and sentiments will be no more to us than those which we receive from the pages of the poet or the moralist.

But the last part of the task which I have mentioned as peculiarly belonging to tragedy, unveiling the human mind under the dominion of those strong and fixed passions, which seemingly unprovoked by outward circumstances, will from small beginnings brood within the breast, till all the better dispositions, all the fair gifts of nature are borne down before them, her poets in general have entirely neglected, and even her first and greatest have but imperfectly attempted. They have made use of the passions to mark their several characters, and animate the scenes, rather than to open to our view the nature and portraitures of those great disturbers of the human breast, with whom we are all, more or less, called upon to contend. [...] The impassioned character is generally brought into view under those irresistible attacks of their power, which it is impossible to repell; whilst those gradual steps that led him to this state, in some of which a stand might have been made against the foe, are left entirely in the shade. [...]

It is characteristick of the more powerful passions that they will encrease and nourish themselves on very slender aliment; it is from within that they are chiefly supplied with what they feed on; and it is in contending with opposite passions and affections of the mind that we best[9] discover their strength, not with events. But in tragedy it is events more frequently than opposite affections which are opposed to them; and those of such force and magnitude that the passions themselves are almost obscured by the spendour and importance of the transactions to which they are attached. [...]

From this general view, which I have endeavoured to communicate to my reader, of tragedy, and those principles in the human mind upon which the success of her efforts depends, I have been led to believe, that an attempt to write a series of tragedies, of simpler construction, less embellished with poetical decorations, less constrained by that lofty seriousness which has so generally been considered as necessary for the support of tragick dignity, and in which the chief object should be to delineate the progress of the higher passions in the human breast, each play exhibiting a particular passion, might not be unacceptable to the publick. And I have been the more readily induced to act upon this idea, because I am confident, that tragedy, written upon this plan, is fitter to produce stronger moral effect than upon any other. [...] We cannot, it is true, amidst its wild uproar [of the 'tempest' of passion], listen to the voice of reason, and save ourselves from destruction; but we can foresee its coming, we can mark its rising signs, we can know the situations that will most expose us to its rage, and we can shelter our heads from the coming blast. [...] Above all, looking back to the first rise, and tracing the progress of passion, points out to us those stages in the approach of the enemy, when he might have been combated most successfully; and where the suffering him to pass may be considered as occasioning all the misery that ensues.

* * * * *

It was the saying of a sagacious Scotchman, 'let who will make the laws of a nation, if I may have the writing of its ballads.'[10] Something similar may be said in regard to the Drama. Its lessons reach not, indeed, to the lowest classes of the labouring people, who are the broad foundation of society, which can generally never be moved without endangering every thing that is constructed upon it, and who are our potent and formidable ballad readers; but they reach to the classes next in order to them, and who will always have over them no inconsiderable influence. The impressions made by it are communicated, at the same instant of time, to a greater number of individuals, than those of any other species of writing; and they are strengthened in every spectator, by observing their effects upon those who surround him. From this observation, the mind of the reader will suggest of itself, what it would be unnecessary, and, perhaps, improper in me here to enlarge upon. The theatre is a school in which much good or evil may be learned. At the beginning of its career the Drama was employed to mislead and excite; and were I not unwilling to refer to transactions of the present times, I might abundantly confirm what I have said by recent examples. The authour, therefore, who aims in any degree to improve the mode of its instruction, and point to more useful lessons than it is generally employed to dispense, is certainly praiseworthy, though want of abilities may unhappily prevent him from being successful in his efforts.

* * * * *

---

9   The first edition reads 'least' here, which makes no sense; later editions correct this and I follow them at this point.

10 This is a paraphrase from *An Account of a Conversation Concerning a Right Regulation of Governments* (1704) by Andrew Fletcher of Saltoun, political theorist and member of the last Scottish parliament before the Union.

It may, perhaps, be supposed from my publishing these plays, that I have written them for the closet rather than the stage. If upon perusing them with attention, the reader is disposed to think they are better calculated for the first than the last, let him impute it to want of skill in the authour, and not to any previous design. A play, but of small poetical merit, that is suited to strike and interest the spectator, to catch the attention of him who will not, and of him who cannot read, is a more valuable and useful production than one whose elegant and harmonious pages are admired in the libraries of the tasteful and refined. To have received approbation from an audience of my countrymen, would have been more pleasing to me than any other praise. A few tears from the simple and young would have been, in my eyes, pearls of great price; and the spontaneous, untutored plaudits of the rude and uncultivated would have come to my heart as offerings of no mean value. I should, therefore, have been better pleased to have introduced them to the world from the stage than from the press. I possess, however, no likely channel to the former mode of publick introduction; and upon further reflection it appeared to me that by publishing them in this way, I have an opportunity afforded me of explaining the design of my work, and enabling the publick to judge, not only of each play by itself, but as making a part likewise of the whole; an advantage which, perhaps, does more than over-balance the splendour and effect of theatrical representation.

It may be thought that with this extensive plan before me, I should not have been in a hurry to publish, but have waited to give a larger portion of it to the publick, which would have enabled them to make a truer estimate of its merit. To bring forth only three plays of the whole, and the last without its companion, may seem like the haste of those vain people, who as soon as they have written a few pages of a discourse, or a few couplets of a poem, cannot be easy till every body has seen them. I do protest, in honest simplicity! It is distrust and not confidence, that has led me at this early stage of an undertaking, to bring it before the publick. […] I have not proceeded so far, indeed, merely upon the strength of my own judgment; but the friends to whom I have shewn my manuscripts are partial to me, and their approbation which in the case of any indifferent person would be in my mind absolutely decisive, goes but a little way in relieving me from these apprehensions. To step beyond the circle of my own immediate friends in quest of opinion, from the particular temper of my mind I feel an uncommon repugnance: I can with less pain to myself bring them before the publick at once, and submit to its decision. It is to my countrymen at large that I call for assistance. If this work is fortunate enough to attract their attention, let their strictures as well as their praise come to my aid: the one will encourage me in a long and arduous undertaking, the other will teach me to improve it as I advance. For there are many errours that may be detected, and improvements that may be suggested in the prosecution of this work, which from the observations of a great variety of readers are more likely to be pointed out to me, than from those of a small number of persons, even of the best judgment. I am not possessed of that confidence in mine own powers, which enables the concealed genius, under the pressure of present discouragement, to pursue his labours in security, looking firmly forward to other more enlightened times for his reward. If my own countrymen with whom I live and converse, who look upon the same race of men, the same state of society, the same passing events with myself, receive not my offering, I presume not to look to posterity.

Before I close this discourse, let me crave the forbearance of my reader, if he has discovered in the course of it any unacknowledged use of the thoughts of other authours, which he thinks ought to have been noticed; and let me beg the same favour, if in reading the following plays, any similar neglect seems to occur. There are few writers who have sufficient originality of thought to strike out for themselves new ideas upon every occasion. When a thought presents itself to me, as suited to the purpose I am aiming at, I would neither be thought proud enough to reject it, on finding that another has used it before me, nor mean enough to make use of it without acknowledging the obligation, when I can at all guess to whom such acknowledgments are due. But I am situated where there is no library to consult; my reading through the whole of my life has been of a loose, scattered, unmethodical kind, with no determined direction, and I have not been blessed by nature with the advantages of a retentive or accurate memory. Do not, however, imagine from this, I at all wish to insinuate that I ought to be acquitted of every obligation to preceding authours; and that when a palpable similarity of thought and expression is observable between us, it is a similarity produced by accident alone, and with perfect unconsciousness on my part. I am frequently sensible, from the manner in which an idea arises to my imagination, and the readiness with which words, also, present themselves to clothe it in, that I am only making use of some dormant part of that hoard of ideas which the most indifferent memories lay up, and not the native suggestions of my own mind. […] If this volume should appear, to any candid and liberal critick, to merit that he should take the trouble of pointing out to me in what parts of it I seem to have made use of other authours' writings, which according to the fair laws of literature ought to have been acknowledged, I shall think myself obliged to him. I shall examine the sources he points out as having supplied my own lack of ideas; and if this book should have the good fortune to go through a second edition, I shall not fail to own my obligations to him, and the authours from whom I may have borrowed.

How little credit soever, upon perusing these plays, the reader may think me entitled to in regard to the execution of the work, he will not, I flatter myself, deny me some credit in regard to the plan. I know of no series of plays, in any language, expressly descriptive of the different passions; and I believe there are few plays existing in which the display of one strong passion is the chief business of the drama, so written that they could properly make part of such a series. […]

I have now only to thank my reader, whoever he may be, who has followed me through the pages of this discourse, for having had the patience to do so. May he, in going through what follows (a wish the sincerity of which he cannot doubt) find more to reward his trouble than I dare venture to promise him; and for the pains he has already taken, and that, which he intends to take for me, I request that he will accept of my grateful acknowledgments.

DE MONFORT:

A TRAGEDY

PERSONS OF THE DRAMA.

MEN.

DE MONFORT.
REZENVELT.
COUNT FREBERG, *Friend to* De Monfort *and* Rezenvelt.
MANUEL, *Servant to* De Monfort.
JEROME, De Monfort's *old Landlord.*
GRIMBALD, *an artful knave.*
BERNARD, *a Monk.*
Monks, Gentlemen, Officers, Page, &c. &c.

WOMEN.

JANE DE MONFORT, *sister to* De Monfort.
COUNTESS FREBERG, *Wife to* Freberg.
THERESA, *Servant to the* Countess.
Abbess, Nuns, *and a* Lay Sister, Ladies, &c.

Scene, a Town in Germany.

ACT I. — SCENE I.

JEROME's *House. A large old-fashioned Chamber.*

Jer. (*speaking without.*) This way, good masters.

Enter JEROME, *bearing a light, and followed by* Manuel, *and* Servants *carrying luggage.*

	Rest your burdens here.
	This spacious room will please the Marquis best.
	He takes me unawares; but ill prepar'd:
	If he had sent, e'en tho' a hasty notice,
	I had been glad.
Man.	Be not disturb'd, good Jerome;
	Thy house is in most admirable order;
	And they who travel o'cold winter nights
	Think homeliest quarters good.
Jer.	He is not far behind?
Man.	A little way.
	(*To the servants.*) Go you and wait below till he arrive.

Jer.	(*Shaking* Manuel *by the hand.*)
	Indeed, my friend, I'm glad to see you here,
	Yet marvel wherefore.
Man.	I marvel wherefore too, my honest Jerome:
	But here we are, pri'thee be kind to us.
Jer.	Most heartily I will. I love your master:
	He is a quiet and a lib'ral man:
	A better inmate never cross'd my door.
Man.	Ah! but he is not now the man he was.
	Lib'ral he'll be, God grant he may be quiet.
Jer.	What has befallen him?
Man.	I cannot tell thee;
	But faith, there is no living with him now.
Jer.	And yet, methinks, if I remember well,
	You were about to quit his service, Manuel,
	When last he left this house. You grumbled then.
Man.	I've been upon the eve of leaving him
	These ten long years; for many times is he
	So difficult, capricious, and distrustful,
	He galls my nature—yet, I know not how,
	A secret kindness binds me to him still.
Jer.	Some, who offend from a suspicious nature,
	Will afterwards such fair confession make
	As turns e'en the offence into a favour.
Man.	Yes, some indeed do so: so will not he;
	He'd rather die than such confession make.
Jer.	Ay, thou art right, for now I call to mind
	That once he wrong'd me with unjust suspicion,
	When first he came to lodge beneath my roof;
	And when it so fell out that I was proved
	Most guiltless of the fault, I truly thought
	He would have made profession of regret;
	But silent, haughty, and ungraciously
	He bore himself as one offended still.
	Yet shortly after, when unwittingly
	I did him some slight service, o' the sudden
	He overpower'd me with his grateful thanks;
	And would not be restrain'd from pressing on me
	A noble recompense. I understood
	His o'erstrain'd gratitude and bounty well,
	And took it as he meant.
Man.	'Tis often thus.
	I would have left him many years ago,
	But that with all his faults there sometimes come
	Such bursts of natural goodness from his heart,
	As might engage a harder churl than I
	To serve him still.—And then his sister too,
	A noble dame, who should have been a queen:

	The meanest of her hinds, at her command,[1]

The meanest of her hinds, at her command,[1]
Had fought like lions for her, and the poor,
E'en o'er their bread of poverty had bless'd her —
She would have griev'd if I had left my Lord.

Jer. Comes she along with him?

Man. No, he departed all unknown to her,
Meaning to keep conceal'd his secret route;
But well I knew it would afflict her much,
And therefore left a little nameless billet,
Which after our departure, as I guess,
Would fall into her hands, and tell her all.
What could I do! O 'tis a noble lady!

Jer. All this is strange — something disturbs his mind —
Belike he is in love.

Man.   No, Jerome, no.
Once on a time I serv'd a noble master,
Whose youth was blasted with untoward love,
And he with hope and fear and jealousy
For ever toss'd, led an unquiet life:
Yet, when unruffled by the passing fit,
His pale wan face such gentle sadness wore
As mov'd a kindly heart to pity him;
But Monfort, even in his clamest hour,
Still bears that gloomy sternness in his eye
Which sullenly repells all sympathy.
O no! good Jerome, no, it is not love.

Jer. Hear I not horses trampling at the gate?
(*Listening.*)
He is arriv'd — stay thou — I had forgot —
A plague upon't! my head is so confus'd —
I will return i'the instant to receive him.

(EXIT *hastily.*)

(*A great bustle without.* EXIT Manuel *with lights, and returns again, lighting in* De Monfort, *as if just alighted from his journey.*)

Man. Your ancient host, my lord, receives you gladly,
And your apartment will be soon prepar'd.

De Mon. 'Tis well.

Man. Where shall I place the chest you gave in charge?
So please you, say my lord.

De Mon. (*Throwing himself into a chair.*) Where-e'er thou wilt.

Man. I would not move that luggage till you came.
(*Pointing to certain things.*)

De Mon. Move what thou wilt, and trouble me no more.
(Manuel, *with the assistance of other Servants, sets about putting the things in order, and* De Monfort *remains sitting in a thoughtful posture.*)

Enter JEROME, *bearing wine, &c. on a salver. As he approaches* DE MONFORT, MANUEL *pulls him by the sleeve.*

---

1   Hinds: farm labourers.

Man.	(*Aside to* Jerome.) No, do not now; he will not be disturb'd.
Jer.	What! not to bid him welcome to my house,
	And offer some refreshment?
Man.	No, good Jerome.
	Softly, a little while: I pri'thee do.

(Jerome *walks softly on tip-toes, till he gets near* De Monfort, *behind backs, then peeping on one side to see his face.*)

Jer.	(*Aside to* Manuel) Ah, Manuel, what an alter'd man is here!
	His eyes are hollow, and his cheeks are pale —
	He left this house a comely gentleman.
De Mon.	Who whispers there?
Man.	'Tis your old landlord, sir.
Jer.	I joy to see you here — I crave your pardon —
	I fear I do intrude —
De Mon.	No, my kind host, I am oblig'd to thee.
Jer.	How fares it with your honour?
De Mon.	Well enough.
Jer.	Here is a little of the fav'rite wine
	That you were wont to praise. Pray honour me.
	(*Fills a glass.*)
De Mon.	(*After drinking*) I thank you, Jerome, 'tis delicious.
Jer.	Ay, my dear wife did ever make it so.
De Mon.	And how does she?
Jer.	Alas, my lord! she's dead.
De Mon.	Well, then she is at rest.
Jer.	How well, my lord?
De Mon.	Is she not with the dead, the quiet dead,
	Where all is peace. Not e'en the impious wretch,
	Who tears the coffin from its earthy vault,
	And strews the mould'ring ashes to the wind
	Can break their rest.
Jer.	Woe's me! I thought you would have griev'd for her.
	She was a kindly soul! Before she died,
	When pining sickness bent her cheerless head,
	She set my house in order —
	And but the morning ere she breath'd her last,
	Bade me preserve some flaskets of this wine,
	That should the Lord de Monfort come again
	His cup might sparkle still.
	(De Monfort *walks across the stage, and wipes his eyes.*)
	Indeed I fear I have distress'd you, sir;
	I surely thought you would be griev'd for her.
De Mon.	(*Taking* Jerome's *hand.*) I am, my friend. How long has she been dead?
Jer.	Two sad long years.
De Mon.	Would she were living still!
	I was too troublesome, too heedless of her.
Jer.	O no! she lov'd to serve you.
	(*Loud knocking without.*)

De Mon.	What fool comes here, at such untimely hours,
	To make this cursed noise. (*To* Manuel.) Go to the gate.

[EXIT Manuel.

	All sober citizens are gone to bed;
	It is some drunkards on their nightly rounds,
	Who mean it but in sport.
Jer.	I hear unusual voices — here they come.

Re-enter MANUEL, *shewing in Count* FREBERG *and his* LADY.

Freb.	(*Running to embrace* De Monfort.)
	My dearest Monfort! most unlook'd for pleasure!
	Do I indeed embrace thee here again?
	I saw thy servant standing by the gate,
	His face recall'd, and learnt the joyful tidings.
	Welcome, thrice welcome here!
De Mon.	I thank thee, Freberg, for this friendly visit,
	And this fair Lady too. (*Bowing to the* LADY.)
Lady.	I fear, my Lord,
	We do intrude at an untimely hour:
	But now, returning from a midnight mask,
	My husband did insist that we should enter.
Freb.	No, say not so; no hour untimely call,
	Which doth together bring long absent friends.
	Dear Monfort, why hast thou play'd so sly,
	To come upon us thus so suddenly?
De Mon.	O! many varied thoughts do cross our brain,
	Which touch the will, but leave the memory trackless;
	And yet a strange compounded motive make,
	Wherefore a man should bend his evening walk
	To th' east or west, the forest or the field.
	Is it not often so?
Freb .	I ask no more, happy to see you here
	From any motive. There is one behind,
	Whose presence would have been a double bliss:
	Ah! how is she? The noble Jane De Monfort.
De Mon.	(*Confused.*) She is — I have — I left my sister well.
Lady.	(*to* Freberg.) My Freberg, you are heedless of respect.
	You surely mean to say the Lady Jane.
Freb.	Respect! No, madam; Princess, Empress, Queen,
	Could not denote a creature so exalted
	As this plain appellation doth,
	The noble Jane De Monfort.
Lady.	(*Turning from him displeased to* Monfort.)
	You are fatigued, my Lord; you want repose;
	Say, should we not retire?
Freb.	Ha! is it so?
	My friend, your face is pale; have you been ill?
De Mon.	No, Freberg, no; I think I have been well.

Freb.	(*Shaking his head.*) I fear thou hast not, Monfort—Let it pass.
	We'll re-establish thee: we'll banish pain.
	I will collect some rare, some cheerful friends,
	And we shall spend together glorious hours,
	That gods might envy. Little time so spent
	Doth far outvalue all our life beside.
	This is indeed our life, our waking life,
	The rest dull breathing sleep.
De Mon.	Thus, it is true, from the sad years of life
	We sometimes do short hours, yea minutes strike,
	Keen, blissful, bright, never to be forgotten;
	Which, through the dreary gloom of time o'erpast
	Shine like fair sunny spots on a wild waste.
	But few they are, as few the heaven-fir'd souls
	Whose magick power creates them. Bless'd art thou,
	If in the ample circle of thy friends
	Thou canst but boast a few.
Freb.	Judge for thyself: in truth I do not boast.
	There is amongst my friends, my later friends,
	A most accomplish'd stranger. New to Amberg,
	But just arriv'd; and will ere long depart.
	I met him in Franconia two years since.[2]
	He is so full of pleasant anecdote,
	So rich, so gay, so poignant is his wit,
	Time vanishes before him as he speaks,
	And ruddy morning thro' the lattice peeps
	Ere night seems well begun.
De Mon.	How is he call'd?
Freb .	I will surprise thee with a welcome face:
	I will not tell thee now.
Lady.	(*to* Mon.) I have, my lord, a small request to make,
	And must not be denied. I too may boast
	Of some good friends, and beauteous countrywomen:
	To-morrow night I open wide my doors
	To all the fair and gay: beneath my roof
	Musick, and dance, and revelry shall reign.
	I pray you come and grace it with your presence.
De Mon.	You honour me too much to be denied.
Lady.	I thank you, sir; and in return for this,
	We shall withdraw, and leave you to repose.
Freb.	Must it be so? Good night—sweet sleep to thee.
	(*To* De Monfort.)
De Mon.	(*to* Freb.) Good night. (*To Lady.*) Good night, fair Lady.
Lady.	Farewel!
	[EXEUNT Freberg *and* Lady.]
De Mon.	(*to* Jer.) I thought Count Freberg had been now in France.
Jer.	He meant to go, as I have been inform'd.

---

2 Franconia (Franken) is an ancient Duchy in south-east Germany, now mostly part of Bavaria, centred on the cities of Bamberg and Nuremberg. Amberg is an old town immediately to the East.

De Mon.   Well, well, prepare my bed; I will to rest.

[E<small>XIT</small> Jerome.

De Mon.   (*alone*) I know not how it is, my heart stands back,
          And meets not this man's love. — Friends! rarest friends!
          Rather than share his undiscerning praise
          With every table-wit, and book-form'd sage,
          And paltry poet puling to the moon,
          I'd court from him proscription, yea abuse,
          And think it proud distinction.

[E<small>XIT</small>.

SCENE II.

A Small Apartment in J<small>EROME</small>'s *House: a table and breakfast set out. Enter* D<small>E</small> M<small>ONFORT</small>, *followed by* M<small>ANUEL</small>, *and sits down by the table, with a cheerful face*

De Mon.   Manuel, this morning's sun shines pleasantly:
          These old apartments too are light and cheerful.
          Our landlord's kindness has reviv'd me much;
          He serves as though he lov'd me. This pure air
          Braces the listless nerves, and warms the blood:
          I feel in freedom here.
          (*Filling a cup of coffee, and drinking.*)
Man.   Ah! sure, my Lord,
          No air is purer than the air at home.
De Mon.   Here can I wander with assured steps,
          Nor dread, at every winding of the path,
          Lest an abhorred serpent cross my way,
          To move — (*Stopping short.*)
Man.   What says your honour?
          There are no serpents in our pleasant fields.
De Mon.   Thinkst thou there are no serpents in the world,
          But those who slide along the grassy sod,
          And sting the luckless foot that presses them?
          There are who in the path of social life
          Do bask their spotted skins in Fortune's sun,
          And sting the soul — Ay, till its healthful frame
          Is chang'd to secret, fest'ring, sore disease,
          So deadly is the wound.
Man.   Heav'n guard your honour from such horrid skathe:
          They are but rare, I hope?
De Mon.   (*Shaking his head.*) We mark the hollow eye, the wasted frame,
          The gait disturb'd of wealthy honour'd men,
          But do not know the cause.
Man.   'Tis very true. God keep you well, my lord!
De Mon.   I thank thee, Manuel, I am very well.
          I shall be gay too, by the setting sun.
          I go to revel it with sprightly dames,

	And drive the night away.
	(*Filling another cup and drinking.*)
Man.	I should be glad to see your honour gay.
De Mon.	And thou too shalt be gay. There, honest Manuel,
	Put these broad pieces in thy leathern purse,
	And take at night a cheerful jovial glass.
	Here is one too, for Bremer; he loves wine;
	And one for Jacques: be joyful altogether.

Enter SERVANT.

Ser.	My Lord, I met e'en now, a short way off,
	Your countryman the Marquis Rezenvelt.
De Mon.	(*Starting from his seat, and letting the cup fall from his hand.*)
	Who, sayst thou?
Ser.	Marquis Rezenvelt, an' please you.
De Mon.	Thou ly'st—it is not so—it is impossible.
Ser.	I saw him with these eyes, plain as yourself.
De Mon.	Fool! 'tis some passing stranger thou hast seen,
	And with a hideous likeness been deceiv'd.
Ser.	No other stranger could deceive my sight.
De Mon.	(*Dashing his clenched hand violently upon the table, and overturning every thing.*)
	Heaven blast thy sight! it lights on nothing good.
Ser.	I surely thought no harm to look upon him.
De Mon.	What, dost thou still insist? He must it be?
	Does it so please thee well? (Servant *endeavours to speak.*)
	Hold thy damn'd tongue.
	By heaven I'll kill thee. (*Going furiously up to him.*)
Man.	(*In a soothing voice.*)
	Nay, harm him not, my lord; he speaks the truth;
	I've met his groom, who told me certainly
	His Lord is here. I should have told you so,
	But thought, perhaps, it might displease your honour.
De Mon.	(*Becoming all at once calm, and turning sternly to* Manuel.)
	And how dar'st thou to think it would displease me?
	What is't to me who leaves or enters Amberg?
	But it displeases me, yea e'en to frenzy,
	That every idle fool must hither come,
	To break my leisure with the paltry tidings
	Of all the cursed things he stares upon.
	(Servant *attempts to speak*—De Monfort *stamps with his foot.*)
	Take thine ill-favour'd visage from my sight,
	And speak of it no more.

[EXIT Servant.

	And go thou too; I choose to be alone.

[EXIT Manuel.

(De Monfort *goes to the door by which they went out; opens it, and looks.*)
But is he gone indeed? Yes, he is gone.

(*Goes to the opposite door, opens it, and looks: then gives loose to all the fury of gesture, and walks up and down in great agitation*)
It is too much: by heaven it is too much!
He haunts me — stings me — like a devil haunts —
He'll make a raving maniac of me — Villain!
The air wherein thou draw'st thy fulsome breath
Is poison to me — Oceans shall divide us! (*Pauses.*)
But no; thou thinkst I fear thee, cursed reptile!
And hast a pleasure in the damned thought.
Though my heart's blood should curdle at thy sight,
I'll stay and face thee still.
(*Knocking at the chamber door.*)
                    Ha! Who knocks there?

Freb.	(*Without.*) It is thy friend, De Monfort.
De Mon.	(Opening the door). Enter, then.

Enter FREBERG.

Freb.	(*Taking his hand kindly.*)
	How art thou now? How hast thou pass'd the night?
	Has kindly sleep refresh'd thee?
De Mon.	Yes, I have lost an hour or two in sleep,
	And so should be refresh'd.
Freb.	And art thou not?
	Thy looks speak not of rest. Thou art disturb'd.
De Mon.	No, somewhat ruffled from a foolish cause,
	Which soon will pass away.
Freb.	(*Shaking his head.*) Ah no, De Monfort! something in thy face
	Tells me another tale. Then wrong me not:
	If any secret grief distract thy soul,
	Here am I all devoted to thy love;
	Open thy heart to me. What troubles thee?
De Mon.	I have no grief: distress me not, my friend.
Freb.	Nay, do not call me so. Wert thou my friend,
	Wouldst thou not open all thine inmost soul,
	And bid me share its every consciousness?
De Mon.	Freberg, thou knowst not man; not nature's man,
	But only him who, in smooth studied works
	Of polish'd sages, shines deceitfully
	In all the splendid foppery of virtue.
	That man was never born whose secret soul
	With all its motley treasure of dark thoughts,
	Foul fantasies, vain musings, and wild dreams,
	Was ever open'd to another's scan.
	Away, away! it is delusion all.
Freb.	Well, be reserved then: perhaps I'm wrong.
De Mon.	How goes the hour?
Freb.'	Tis early: a long day is still before us,
	Let us enjoy it. Come along with me;

	I'll introduce you to my pleasant friend.
De Mon.	Your pleasant friend?
Freb.	Yes, he of whom I spake.

(*Taking his hand.*)
There is no good I would not share with thee,
And this man's company, to minds like thine,
Is the best banquet feast I could bestow.
But I will speak in mystery no more,
It is thy townsman, noble Rezenvelt.
(De Mon. *pulls his hand hastily from Freberg, and shrinks back.*)
Ha! what is this? Art thou pain-stricken, Monfort?
Nay, on my life, thou rather seem'st offended:
Does it displease thee that I call him friend?

De Mon. No, all men are thy friends.

Freb. No, say not all men. But thou art offended.
I see it well. I thought to do thee pleasure.
But if his presence is not welcome here,
He shall not join our company to-day.

De Mon. What dost thou mean to say? What is't to me
Whether I meet with such a thing as Rezenvelt
To-day, to-morrow, every day, or never.

Freb . In truth, I thought you had been well with him.
He prais'd you much.

De Mon. I thank him for his praise—Come, let us move:
This chamber is confin'd and airless grown.
(*Starting.*)
I hear a stranger's voice!

Freb. 'Tis Rezenvelt.
Let him be told that we are gone abroad.

De Mon. (*Proudly.*) No! let him enter. Who waits there? Ho! Manuel!

Enter MANUEL.

What stranger speaks below?

Man. The Marquis Rezenvelt.
I have not told him that you are within.

De Mon. (*Angrily.*) And wherefore did'st thou not? Let him ascend.
(*A long pause. De Montfort walking up and down with a quick pace.*)

Enter REZENVELT, *and runs freely up to* De Monfort.

Rez. (*to* De Mon.) My noble Marquis, welcome.

De Mon. Sir, I thank you.

Rez. (*to* Freb.) My gentle friend, well met. Abroad so early?

Freb. It is indeed an early hour for me.
How sits thy last night's revel on thy spirits?

Rez. O, light as ever. On my way to you
E'en now I learnt De Montfort was arriv'd,
And turn'd my steps aside; so here I am.

	(*Bowing gaily to* De Monfort.)
De Mon.	(*Proudly.*) I thank you, Sir; you do me too much honour.
Rez.	Nay, say not so; not too much honour, Marquis,
	Unless, indeed, 'tis more than pleases you.
De Mon.	(*Confused.*) Having no previous notice of your coming,
	I look'd not for it.
Rez.	Ay, true indeed; when I approach you next,
	I'll send a herald to proclaim my coming,
	And bow to you by sound of trumpet, marquis.

De Mon. (*to* Freb.) (*Turning haughtily from Rezenvelt with affected indifference.*)
How does your cheerful friend, that good old man?
Freb.   My cheerful friend? I know not whom you mean.
De Mon. Count Waterlan.
Freb.   I know not one so nam'd.
De Mon. (*Very confused.*) O pardon me — it was at Bâle I knew him.[3]
Freb.   You have not yet inquir'd for honest Reisdale.
I met him as I came, and mention'd you.
He seem'd amaz'd; and fain he would have learnt
What cause procur'd us so much happiness.
He question'd hard, and hardly would believe;
I could not satisfy his strong desire.
Rez.   And know you not what brings De Montfort here?
Freb.   Truly, I do not.
Rez.   O! 'tis love of me.
I have but two short days in Amberg been,
And here with postman's speed he follows me,
Finding his home so dull and tiresome grown.
Freb.   (*to* De Mon.) Is Rezenvelt so sadly miss'd with you?
Your town so chang'd?
De Mon.   Not altogether so:
Some witlings and jest-mongers still remain
For fools to laugh at.
Rez.   But he laughs not, and therefore he is wise.
He ever frowns on them with sullen brow
Contemptuous; therefore he is very wise;
Nay, daily frets his most refined soul
With their poor folly to its inmost core;
Therefore he is most eminently wise.
Freb.   Fy, Rezenvelt! You are too early gay;
Such spirits rise but with the ev'ning glass.
They suit not placid morn.
(To De Monfort, *who after walking impatiently up and down, comes close
to his ear, and lays hold of his arm.*)
                          What would you, Monfort?
De Mon. Nothing — Yet, what is't o'clock?
No, no — I had forgot — 'tis early still.
(*Turns away again.*)
Freb. (*to* Rez.) Waltser informs me that you have agreed

---

3   The French name for the Swiss city more often called Basel..

	To read his verses o'er, and tell the truth.
	It is a dangerous task.
Rez.	Yet I'll be honest:
	I can but lose his favour and a feast.

(*Whilst they speak,* De Monfort *walks up and down impatiently and irresolute; at last pulls the bell violently.*)

Enter SERVANT.

De Mon.	(*to* Ser.) What dost thou want? —
Ser.	I thought your honour rung.
De Mon.	I have forgot—Stay; are my horses saddled?
Ser.	I thought, my Lord, you would not ride to-day,
	After so long a journey.
De Mon.	(*Impatiently.*) Well—'tis good.
	Begone!—I want thee not.

[EXIT Servant.

Rez.	(*Smiling significantly.*) I humbly crave your pardon, gentle Marquis.
	It grieves me that I cannot stay with you,
	And make my visit of a friendly length.
	I trust your goodness will excuse me now;
	Another time I shall be less unkind.
	(*To* Freberg.) Will you not go with me?
Freb.	Excuse me, Monfort, I'll return again.

[EXEUNT Rezenvelt *and* Freberg.

De Mon.	(*Alone, tossing his arms distractedly.*)
	Hell hath no greater torment for th' accurs'd
	Than this man's presence gives—
	Abhorred fiend! he hath a pleasure too,
	A damned pleasure in the pain he gives!
	Oh! the side glance of that detested eye!
	That conscious smile! that full insulting lip!
	It touches every nerve: it makes me mad.
	What, does it please thee? Dost thou woo my hate?
	Hate shalt thou have! determin'd, deadly hate,
	Which shall awake no smile. Malignant villain!
	The venom of thy mind is rank and devilish,
	And thin the film that hides it.
	Thy hateful visage ever spoke thy worth:
	I loath'd thee when a boy.
	That men should be besotted with him thus![4]
	And Freberg likewise so bewitched is,
	That like a hireling flatt'rer, at his heels
	He meanly paces, off'ring brutish praise.
	O! I could curse him too.

[EXIT.

---

4   The first two editions have 'That — — should be besotted with him thus!' The blank is filled
    with 'men' in the third edition (1800).

A very splendid apartment in Count FREBERG'*s house, fancifully decorated. A wide folding door opened, shews another magnificent room lighted up to receive company. Enter through the folding doors the* Count *and* Countess, *richly dressed.*

Freb.	(*Looking round.*) In truth, I like those decorations well:
	They suit those lofty walls. And here, my love,
	The gay profusion of a woman's fancy
	Is well display'd. Noble simplicity
	Becomes us less, on such a night as this
	Than gaudy show.
Lady.	Is it not noble then? (*He shakes his head.*) I thought it so;
	And as I know you love simplicity,
	I did intend it should be simple too.
Freb.	Be satisfied, I pray; we want to-night
	A cheerful banquet-house, and not a temple.
	How runs the hour?
Lady.	It is not late, but soon we shall be rous'd
	With the loud entry of our frolick guests.

Enter a PAGE, *richly dressed.*

Page.	Madam, there is a Lady in your hall,
	Who begs to be admitted to your presence.
Lady.	Is it not one of our invited friends?
Page.	No, far unlike to them; it is a stranger.
Lady.	How looks her countenance?
Page.	So queenly, so commanding, and so noble,
	I shrunk at first in awe; but when she smil'd,
	For so she did to see me thus abash'd,
	Methought I could have compass'd sea and land
	To do her bidding.
Lady.	Is she young or old?
Page.	Neither, if right I guess; but she is fair;
	For time hath laid his hand so gently on her,
	As he too had been aw'd.
Lady.	The foolish stripling!
	She has bewitch'd thee. Is she large in stature?
Page.	So stately and so graceful is her form,
	I thought at first her stature was gigantick,
	But on a near approach I found, in truth,
	She scarcely does surpass the middle size.
Lady.	What is her garb?
Page.	I cannot well describe the fashion of it.
	She is not deck'd in any gallant trim,
	But seems to me clad in the usual weeds
	Of high habitual state; for as she moves
	Wide flows her robe in many a waving fold,

	As I have seen unfurled banners play
	With a soft breeze.
Lady.	Thine eyes deceive thee, boy,
	It is an apparition thou hast seen.
Freb.	(*Starting from his seat, where he has been sitting during the conversation between* the Lady *and the* Page.)
	It is an apparition he has seen.
	Or it is Jane De Monfort.

[EXIT, *hastily.*

Lady.	(*Displeased.*) No; such description surely suits not her.
	Did she enquire for me?
Page.	She ask'd to see the lady of Count Freberg.
Lady.	Perhaps it is not she — I fear it is —
	Ha! here they come. He has but guess'd too well.

Enter FREBERG, *leading in* JANE DE MONFORT.

Freb.	(*Presenting her to* Lady.) Here, madam, welcome a most worthy guest.
Lady.	Madam, a thousand welcomes. Pardon me;
	I could not guess who honour'd me so far;
	I should not else have waited coldly here.
Jane.	I thank you for this welcome, gentle Countess.
	But take those kind excuses back again;
	I am a bold intruder on this hour,
	And am entitled to no ceremony.
	I came in quest of a dear truant friend,
	But Freberg has inform'd me —
	(*To* Freberg.) And he is well, you say?
Freb.	Yes, well, but joyless.
Jane .	It is the usual temper of his mind:
	It opens not, but with the thrilling touch
	Of some strong heart-string o' the sudden press'd.
Freb.	It may be so, I've known him otherwise:
	He is suspicious grown.
Jane.	Not so, Count Freberg, Monfort is too noble.
	Say rather, that he is a man in grief,
	Wearing at times a strange and scowling eye;
	And thou, less generous than beseems a friend,
	Hast thought too hardly of him.
Freb.	(*Bowing with great respect.*) So will I say;
	I'll own nor word nor will, that can offend you.
Lady.	De Monfort is engag'd to grace our feast,
	Ere long you'll see him here.
Jane .	I thank you truly, but this homely dress
	Suits not the splendour of such scenes as these.
Freb .	(*Pointing to her dress.*) Such artless and majestick elegance,
	So exquisitely just, so nobly simple,
	Will make the gorgeous blush.
Jane.	(*Smiling.*) Nay, nay, be more consistent, courteous knight,

	And do not praise a plain and simple guise
	With such profusion of unsimple words.
	I cannot join your company to-night.
Lady.	Not stay to see your brother?
Jane.	Therefore it is I would not, gentle hostess.
	Here will he find all that can woo the heart
	To joy and sweet forgetfulness of pain;
	The sight of me would wake his feeling mind
	To other thoughts. I am no doting mistress,
	No fond distracted wife, who must forthwith
	Rush to his arms and weep. I am his sister:
	The eldest daughter of his father's house:
	Calm and unwearied is my love for him;
	And having found him, patiently I'll wait,
	Nor greet him in the hour of social joy,
	To dash his mirth with tears. —
	The night wears on; permit me to withdraw.
Freb.	Nay, do not, do not injure us so far!
	Disguise thyself, and join our friendly train.
Jane.	You wear not masks to-night?
Lady.	We wear not masks, but you may be conceal'd
	Behind the double foldings of a veil.
Jane.	(*After pausing to consider.*) In truth, I feel a little so inclin'd.
	Methinks unknown, I e'en might speak to him,
	And gently prove the temper of his mind:
	But for the means I must become your debtor.
	(*To* Lady.)
Lady.	Who waits? (*Enter her* Woman.) Attend this lady to my wardrobe,
	And do what she commands you.
	[EXEUNT Jane *and* Waiting-woman.
Freb.	(*Looking after* Jane, *as she goes out, with admiration.*)
	Oh! what a soul she bears! see how she steps!
	Nought but the native dignity of worth
	E'er taught the moving form such noble grace.
Lady.	Such lofty mien, and high assumed gait
	I've seen ere now, and men have call'd it pride.
Freb.	No, 'faith! thou never didst, but oft indeed
	The paltry imitation thou hast seen.
	(*Looking at her.*) How hang those trappings on thy motly gown?
	They seem like garlands on a May-day queen,
	Which hinds have dress'd in sport.
Lady.	I'll doff it, then, since it displeases you.
Freb.	No, no, thou art lovely still in every garb.
	But see the guests assemble.

Enter groups of well dressed people, who pay their compliments to Freberg *and his* Lady; *and followed by her pass into the inner apartment, where more company appear assembling, as if by another entry.*

Freb.	(*Who remains on the front of the stage, with a friend or two.*)
	How loud the hum of this gay-meeting crowd!
	'Tis like a bee-swarm in the noonday sun.
	Musick will quell the sound. Who waits without?
	Musick strike up.
	(*A grand piece of musick is playing, and when it ceases, enter from the inner apartment* REZENVELT, *with several gentlemen, all richly dressed.*)
Freb.	(*to those just entered.*)
	What lively gallants quit the field so soon?
	Are there no beauties in that moving crowd
	To fix your fancy?
Rez.	Ay, marry, are there! men of ev'ry mind
	May in that moving crowd some fair one find,
	To suit their taste, though whimsical and strange,
	As ever fancy own'd.
	Beauty of every cast and shade is there,
	From the perfection of a faultless form,
	Down to the common, brown, unnoted maid,
	Who looks but pretty in her Sunday gown.
1st Gent.	There is, indeed, a gay variety.
Rez.	And if the liberality of nature
	Suffices not, there's store of grafted charms,
	Blending in one the sweets of many plants
	So obstinately, strangely opposite,
	As would have well defied all other art
	But female cultivation. Aged youth,
	With borrow'd locks in rosy chaplets bound,
	Cloathes her dim eye, parch'd lip, and skinny cheek
	In most unlovely softness.
	And youthful age, with fat round trackless face,
	The down-cast look of contemplation deep,
	Most pensively assumes.
	Is it not even so? The native prude,
	With forced laugh, and merriment uncouth,
	Plays off the wild coquet's successful charms
	With most unskilful pains; and the coquet,
	In temporary crust of cold reserve,
	Fixes her studied looks upon the ground
	Forbiddingly demure.
Freb.	Fy! thou art too severe.
Rez.	Say, rather, gentle.
	I' faith! the very dwarfs attempt to charm
	With lofty airs of puny majesty,
	While potent damsels, of a portly make,
	Totter like nurselings, and demand the aid
	Of gentle sympathy.
	From all those diverse modes of dire assault,
	He owns a heart of hardest adamant,
	Who shall escape to-night.

Freb.	(*to* De Monfort, *who has entered during* Rezenvelt's *speech, and heard the greatest part of it.*) Ha, ha, ha, ha!
	How pleasantly he gives his wit the rein,
	Yet guides its wild career!
	(De Monfort *is silent.*)
Rez.	(*Smiling archly.*) What, think you, Freberg, the same powerful spell
	Of transformation reigns o'er all to-night?
	Or that De Monfort is a woman turn'd,
	So widely from his native self to swerve,
	As grace my gai'ty with a smile of his?
De Mon.	Nay, think not, Rezenvelt, there is no smile
	I can bestow on thee. There is a smile,
	A smile of nature too, which I can spare,
	And yet, perhaps, thou wilt not thank me for it.
	(*Smiles contemptuously.*)
Rez.	Not thank thee! It were surely most ungrateful
	No thanks to pay for nobly giving me
	What, well we see, has cost thee so much pain.
	For nature hath her smiles, of birth more painful
	Than bitt'rest execrations.
Freb.	These idle words will lead us to disquiet:
	Forbear, forbear, my friends. Go, Rezenvelt,
	Accept the challenge of those lovely dames,
	Who through the portal come with bolder steps
	To claim your notice.
	(*Enter a group of Ladies from the other apartment.* Rezenvelt *shrugs up his shoulders, as if unwilling to go.*)
1st Gent.	(*to* Rez.) Behold in sable veil a lady comes,
	Whose noble air doth challenge fancy's skill
	To suit it with a countenance as goodly.
	(*Pointing to* Jane De Monfort, *who now enters in a thick black veil.*)
Rez.	Yes, this way lies attraction. (*To* Freberg.) With permission,
	(*Going up to* Jane.)
	Fair lady, though within that envious shroud
	Your beauty deigns not to enlighten us,
	We bid you welcome, and our beauties here
	Will welcome you the more for such concealment.
	With the permission of our noble host—
	(*Taking her hand, and leading her to the front of the stage.*)
Jane .	(*to* Freb.) Pardon me this presumption, courteous sir:
	I thus appear, (*pointing to her veil*), not careless of respect
	Unto the generous lady of the feast.
	Beneath this veil no beauty shrouded is,
	That, now, or pain, or pleasure can bestow.
	Within the friendly cover of its shade
	I only wish, unknown, again to see
	One who, alas! is heedless of my pain.
De Mon.	Yes, it is ever thus. Undo that veil,
	And give thy count'nance to the cheerful light.

	Men now all soft, and female beauty scorn,

Men now all soft, and female beauty scorn,
And mock the gentle cares which aim to please.
It is most damnable! undo thy veil,
And think of him no more.

Jane. I know it well, e'en to a proverb grown,
Is lovers' faith, and I had borne such slight:
But he who has, alas! forsaken me,
Was the companion of my early days,
My cradle's mate, mine infant play-fellow.
Within our op'ning minds with riper years,
The love of praise and gen'rous virtue sprung:
Thro' varied life our pride, our joys, were one;
At the same tale we wept: he is my brother.

De Mon. And he forsook thee? — No, I dare not curse him:
My heart upbraids me with a crime like his.

Jane. Ah! do not thus distress a feeling heart.
All sisters are not to the soul entwin'd
With equal bands; thine has not watch'd for thee,
Weep'd for thee, cheer'd thee, shar'd thy weal and woe,
As I have done for him.

De Mon. (*Eagerly.*) Ha! has she not?
By heaven! the sum of all thy kindly deeds
Were but as chaff pois'd against massy gold,
Compar'd to that which I do owe her love.
Oh, pardon me! I mean not to offend —
I am too warm — but she of whom I speak
Is the dear sister of my earliest love;
In noble, virtuous worth to none a second:
And though behind those sable folds were hid
As fair a face as ever woman own'd,
Still would I say she is as fair as thee.
How oft amidst the beauty-blazing throng,
I've proudly to th' inquiring stranger told
Her name and lineage! yet within her house,
The virgin mother of an orphan race
Her dying parents left, this noble woman
Did, like a Roman matron, proudly sit,
Despising all the blandishments of love;
While many a youth his hopeless love conceal'd,
Or, humbly distant, woo'd her like a queen.
Forgive, I pray you! O forgive this boasting!
In faith! I mean you no discourtesy.

Jane. (*Off her guard, in a soft natural tone of voice.*) Oh no! nor do me any.

De Mon. What voice speaks now? Withdraw, withdraw this shade!
For if thy face bear semblance to thy voice,
I'll fall and worship thee. Pray! pray undo!
(*Puts forth his hand eagerly to snatch away the veil, whilst she shrinks back, and Rezenvelt steps between to prevent him.*)

Rez. Stand off: no hand shall lift this sacred veil.

De Mon.	What, dost thou think De Monfort fall'n so low,
	That there may live a man beneath heav'n's roof,
	Who dares to say he shall not?
Rez.	He lives who dares to say —
Jane.	(*Throwing back her veil, much alarmed, and rushing between them.*)
	Forbear, forbear!

(Rezenvelt, *very much struck, steps back respectfully, and makes her a very low bow. De Monfort* stands for a while motionless, gazing upon her, till she, looking expressively to him, extends her arms, and he, rushing into them, bursts into tears. Freberg *seems very much pleased. The company then advancing from the inner apartment, gather about them, and the Scene closes.*)

SCENE II.

De Monfort's *apartments. Enter* DE MONFORT, *with a disordered air, and his hand pressed upon his forehead, followed by* JANE.

De Mon.	No more, my sister, urge me not again:
	My secret troubles cannot be reveal'd.
	From all participation of its thoughts
	My heart recoils: I pray thee be contented.
Jane.	What, must I, like a distant humble friend,
	Observe thy restless eye, and gait disturb'd,
	In timid silence, whilst with yearning heart
	I turn aside to weep? O no! De Monfort!
	A nobler task thy noble mind will give;
	Thy true entrusted friend I still shall be.
De Mon.	Ah, Jane, forbear! I cannot e'en to thee.
Jane .	Then, fy upon it! fy upon it, Monfort!
	There was a time when e'en with murder stain'd,
	Had it been possible that such dire deed
	Could e'er have been the crime of one so piteous,
	Thou wouldst have told it me.
De Mon.	So would I now — but ask of this no more.
	All other trouble but the one I feel
	I had disclos'd to thee. I pray thee spare me.
	It is the secret weakness of my nature.
Jane.	Then secret let it be; I urge no farther.
	The eldest of our valiant father's hopes,
	So sadly orphan'd, side by side we stood,
	Like two young trees, whose boughs, in early strength
	Screen the weak saplings of the rising grove,
	And brave the storm together —
	I have so long, as if by nature's right,
	Thy bosom's inmate and adviser been,
	I thought through life I should have so remain'd,
	Nor ever known a change. Forgive me, Monfort,
	A humbler station will I take by thee:

	The close attendant of thy wand'ring steps;

The close attendant of thy wand'ring steps;
The cheerer of this home, with strangers sought;
The soother of those griefs I must not know,
This is mine office now: I ask no more.

De Mon. Oh, Jane! thou dost constrain me with thy love!
Would I could tell it thee!

Jane. Thou shalt not tell me. Nay I'll stop mine ears,
Nor from the yearnings of affection wring
What shrinks from utt'rance. Let it pass, my brother.
I'll stay by thee; I'll cheer thee, comfort thee:
Pursue with thee the study of some art,
Or nobler science, that compels the mind
To steady thought progressive, driving forth
All floating, wild, unhappy fantasies;
Till thou, with brow unclouded, smil'st again,
Like one who from dark visions of the night,
When th' active soul within its lifeless cell
Holds it own world, with dreadful fancy press'd
Of some dire, terrible, or murd'rous deed,
Wakes to the dawning morn, and blesses heaven.

De Mon. It will not pass away; 'twill haunt me still.

Jane. Ah! say not so, for I will haunt thee too;
And be to it so close an adversary,
That, though I wrestle darkling with the fiend,
I shall o'ercome it.

De Mon. Thou most gen'rous woman!
Why do I treat thee thus? It should not be—
And yet I cannot—O that cursed villain!
He will not let me be the man I would.

Jane. What sayst thou, Monfort? Oh! what words are these?
They have awak'd my soul to dreadful thoughts.
I do beseech thee, speak!
(*He shakes his head, and turns from her; she following him.*)
By the affection thou didst ever bear me;
By the dear mem'ry of our infant days;
By kindred living ties, ay, and by those
Who sleep i' the tomb, and cannot call to thee,
I do conjure thee speak.
(*He waves her off with his hand and covers his face with the other, still turning from her.*)
Ha! wilt thou not?
(*Assuming dignity.*)
Then, if affection, most unwearied love,
Tried early, long, and never wanting found,
O'er gen'rous man hath more authority,
More rightful power than crown or sceptre give,
I do command thee.
(*He throws himself into a chair, greatly agitated.*)
De Monfort, do not thus resist my love.

Here I entreat thee on my bended knees.
(*Kneeling.*)
Alas! my brother!
(De Monfort *starts up, and catching her in his arms, raises her up, then placing her in the chair, kneels at her feet.*)

De Mon.   Thus let him kneel who should the abased be,
And at thine honour'd feet confession make!
I'll tell thee all—but, oh! thou wilt despise me.
For in my breast a raging passion burns,
To which thy soul no sympathy will own.
A passion which hath made my nightly couch
A place of torment; and the light of day,
With the gay intercourse of social man
Feel like th' oppressive airless pestilence.
O Jane! thou wilt despise me.

Jane.   Say not so:
I never can despise thee, gentle brother.
A lover's jealousy and hopeless pangs
No kindly heart contemns.

De Mon.   A lover, sayst thou?
No, it is hate! black, lasting, deadly hate;
Which thus hath driven me forth from kindred peace,
From social pleasure, from my native home,
To be a sullen wand'rer on the earth,
Avoiding all men, cursing and accurs'd.

Jane.   De Monfort, this is fiend-like, frightful, terrible!
What being, by th'Almighty Father form'd,
Of flesh and blood, created even as thou,
Could in thy breast such horrid tempest wake,
Who art thyself his fellow?
Unknit thy brows, and spread those wrath-clench'd hands.
Some sprite accurst within thy bosom mates
To work thy ruin. Strive with it, my brother!
Strive bravely with it; drive it from thy breast:
'Tis the degrader of a noble heart;
Curse it, and bid it part.

De Mon.   It will not part. (*His hand on his breast.*)
                         I've lodged it here too long;
With my first cares I felt its rankling touch,
I loath'd him when a boy.

Jane.   Who did'st thou say?

De Mon.   Oh! that detested Rezenvelt!
E'en in our early sports, like two young whelps
Of hostile breed, instinctively reverse,
Each 'gainst the other pitch'd his ready pledge,
And frown'd defiance. As we onward pass'd
From youth to man's estate, his narrow art
And envious gibing malice, poorly veil'd
In the affected carelessness of mirth,

Still more detestable and odious grew.
There is no living being on this earth
Who can conceive the malice of his soul,
With all his gay and damned merriment,
To those, by fortune or by merit plac'd
Above his paltry self. When, low in fortune,
He look'd upon the state of prosp'rous men,
As nightly birds, rous'd from their murky holes,
Do scowl and chatter at the light of day,
I could endure it; even as we bear
Th' impotent bite of some half-trodden worm,
I could endure it. But when honours came,
And wealth and new-got titles fed his pride;
Whilst flatt'ring knaves did trumpet forth his praise,
And grov'ling idiots grinn'd applauses on him;
Oh! then I could no longer suffer it!
It drove me frantic. — What! what would I give!
What would I give to crush the bloated toad,
So rankly do I loathe him!

Jane. And would thy hatred crush the very man
Who gave to thee that life he might have ta'en?
That life which thou so rashly didst expose
To aim at his! Oh! this is horrible!

De Mon. Ha! thou hast heard it, then? From all the world,
But most of all from thee, I thought it hid.

Jane. I heard a secret whisper, and resolv'd
Upon the instant to return to thee.
Did'st thou receive my letter?

De Mon. I did! I did! 'twas that which drove me hither.
I could not bear to meet thine eye again.

Jane. Alas! that, tempted by a sister's tears,
I ever left thy house! these few past months,
These absent months, have brought us all this woe.
Had I remain'd with thee it had not been.
And yet, methinks, it should not move you thus.
You dar'd him to the field; both bravely fought;
He more adroit disarm'd you; courteously
Return'd the forfeit sword, which, so return'd,
You did refuse to use against him more;
And then, as says report, you parted friends.

De Mon. When he disarm'd this curs'd, this worthless hand
Of its most worthless weapon, he but spar'd
From dev'lish pride, which now derives a bliss
In seeing me thus fetter'd, sham'd, subjected
With the vile favour of his poor forbearance;
While he securely sits with gibing brow,
And basely bates me, like a muzzled cur
Who cannot turn again. —
Until that day, till that accursed day,

I knew not half the torment of this hell,
Which burns within my breast. Heaven's lightnings blast him!

Jane. O this is horrible! Forbear, forbear!
Lest heaven's vengeance light upon thy head,
For this most impious wish.

De Mon. Then let it light.
Torments more fell than I have felt already
It cannot send. To be annihilated;
What all men shrink from; to be dust, be nothing,
Were bliss to me, compar'd to what I am.

Jane. Oh! wouldst thou kill me with these dreadful words?

De Mon. (*Raising his hands to heaven.*) Let me but once upon his ruin look,
Then close mine eyes for ever!
(Jane, *in great distress, staggers back, and supports herself upon the side scene.* De Monfort, *alarm'd, runs up to her with a softened voice.*)
Ha! how is this? thou'rt ill; thou'rt very pale.
What have I done to thee? Alas, alas!
I meant not to distress thee.—O my sister!

Jane. (*Shaking her head.*) I cannot speak to thee.

De Mon. I have kill'd thee.
Turn, turn thee not away! look on me still!
Oh! droop not thus, my life, my pride, my sister!
Look on me yet again.

Jane. Thou too, De Monfort,
In better days, wert wont to be my pride.

De Mon. I am a wretch, most wretched in myself,
And still more wretched in the pain I give.
O curse that villain! that detested villain!
He has spread mis'ry o'er my fated life:
He will undo us all.

Jane. I've held my warfare through a troubled world,
And borne with steady mind my share of ill;
For then the helpmate of my toil wert thou.
But now the wane of life comes darkly on,
And hideous passion tears me from thy heart,
Blasting thy worth.—I cannot strive with this.

De Mon. (*Affectionately.*) What shall I do?

Jane. Call up thy noble spirit;
Rouse all the gen'rous energy of virtue;
And with the strength of heaven-endued man,
Repel the hideous foe. Be great; be valiant.
O, if thou couldst! e'en shrouded as thou art
In all the sad infirmities of nature,
What a most noble creature wouldst thou be!

De Mon. Ay, if I could: alas! alas! I cannot.

Jane. Thou canst, thou mayst, thou wilt.
We shall not part till I have turn'd thy soul.

Enter MANUEL.

De Mon.	Ha! some one enters. Wherefore com'st thou here?
Man.	Count Freberg waits your leisure.
De Mon.	(*Angrily.*) Be gone, be gone. — I cannot see him now.

[EXIT Manuel.

Jane.	Come to my closet; free from all intrusion,
	I'll school thee there; and thou again shalt be
	My willing pupil, and my gen'rous friend;
	The noble Monfort I have lov'd so long,
	And must not, will not lose.
De Mon.	Do as thou wilt; I will not grieve thee more.

[EXEUNT.

SCENE III.

Count FREBERG's *House. Enter the* COUNTESS, *followed by the* PAGE, *and speaking as she enters.*

Lady.	Take this and this. (*Giving two packets.*)
	And tell my gentle friend,
	I hope to see her ere the day be done.
Page.	Is there no message for the Lady Jane?
Lady.	No, foolish boy, that would too far extend
	Your morning's route, and keep you absent long.
Page.	O no, dear Madam! I'll the swifter run.
	The summer's light'ning moves not as I'll move,
	If you will send me to the Lady Jane.
Lady.	No, not so slow, I ween. The summer's light'ning!
	Thou art a lad of taste and letters grown:
	Would'st poetry admire, and ape they master.
	Go, go; my little spaniels are unkempt;
	My cards unwritten, and my china broke:
	Thou art too learned for a lady's page.
	Did I not bid thee call Theresa here?
Page.	Madam she comes.

Enter THERESA, *carrying a robe over her arm.*

Lady.	(*to* Ther.) What has employ'd you all this dreary while?
	I've waited long.
Ther.	Madam, the robe is finish'd.
Lady.	Well, let me see it.
	(Theresa *spreads out the robe.*)
	(*Impatiently to the* Page.) Boy, hast thou ne'er a hand to lift that fold?
	See where it hangs.
	(Page *takes the other side of the robe, and spreads it out to its full extent before her, whilst she sits down and looks at it with much dissatisfaction.*)
Ther.	Does not my lady like this easy form?

Lady.	That sleeve is all awry.
Ther.	Your pardon, madam;
	'Tis but the empty fold that shapes it thus.
	I took the pattern from a graceful shape;
	The Lady Jane De Monfort wears it so.
Lady.	Yes, yes, I see 'tis thus with all of you.
	Whate'er she wears is elegance and grace,
	Whilst ev'ry ornament of mine, forsooth,
	Must hang likfe trappings on a May-day queen.
	(*Angrily to the* Page, *who is smiling to himself.*)
	Youngster be gone. Why do you loiter here?

[EXIT Page.

Ther .	What would you, madam, chuse to wear to-night?
	One of your newest robes?
Lady.	I hate them all.
Ther .	Surely, that purple scarf became you well,
	With all those wreaths of richly hanging flowers.
	Did I not overhear them say, last night,
	As from the crouded ball-room ladies past,
	How gay and handsome, in her costly dress,
	The Countess Freberg look'd.
Lady.	Did'st thou o'erhear it?
Ther.	I did, and more than this.
Lady.	Well, all are not so greatly prejudic'd;
	All do not think me like a May-day queen,
	Which peasants deck in sport.
Ther.	And who said this?
Lady.	(*Putting her handkerchief to her eyes.*) E'en my good lord, Theresa.
Ther.	He said it but in jest. He loves you well.
Lady.	I know as well as thee he loves me well;
	But what of that? he takes no pride in me.
	Elsewhere his praise and admiration go,
	And Jane De Monfort is not mortal woman.
Ther.	The wond'rous character this lady bears
	For worth and excellence; from early youth
	The friend and mother of her younger sisters
	Now greatly married, as I have been told,
	From her most prudent care, may well excuse
	The admiration of so good a man
	As my good master is. And then, dear madam,
	I must confess, when I myself did hear
	How she was come thro' the rough winter's storm,
	To seek and comfort an unhappy brother,
	My heart beat kindly to her.
Lady.	Ay, ay, there is a charm in this I find:
	But wherefore may she not have come as well
	Through wintery storms to seek a lover too?
Ther .	No, madam, no, I could not think of this.
Lady.	That would reduce her in your eyes, mayhap,

To woman's level. — Now I see my vengeance!
I'll tell it round that she is hither come,
Under pretence of finding out De Monfort,
To meet with Rezenvelt. When Freberg hears it
'Twill help, I ween, to break this magick charm.

Ther. Ah no! there is —

Lady.   Well, hold thy foolish tongue.
Carry that robe into my chamber, do:
I'll try it there myself.

                                        [EXEUNT.

DE MONFORT *discovered sitting by a table reading. After a little time he lays down his book, and continues in a thoughtful posture. Enter to him* JANE DE MONFORT.

Jane.	Thanks, gentle brother.—
	(*Pointing to the book.*)
	Thy willing mind has rightly been employ'd:
	Did not thy heart warm at the fair display
	Of peace and concord and forgiving love?
De Mon.	I know resentment may to love be turn'd;
	Tho' keen and lasting, into love as strong:
	And fiercest rivals in th'ensanguin'd field
	Have cast their brandish'd weapons to the ground,
	Joining their mailed breasts in close embrace,
	With gen'rous impulse fir'd. I know right well
	The darkest, fellest wrongs have been forgiven
	Seventy times o'er from blessed heavenly love:
	I've heard of things like these; I've heard and wept.
	But what is this to me?
Jane.	All, all, my brother!
	It bids thee too that noble precept learn,
	To love thine enemy.
De Mon.	Th' uplifted stroke that would a wretch destroy
	Gorg'd with my richest spoil, stain'd with my blood,
	I would arrest, and cry, hold! hold! have mercy:
	But when the man most adverse to my nature,
	Who e'en from childhood hath, with rude malevolence,
	Withheld the fair respect all paid beside,
	Turning my very praise into derision;
	Who galls and presses me where'er I go,
	Would claim the gen'rous feelings of my heart,
	Nature herself doth lift her voice aloud,
	And cries, it is impossible.
Jane. (	*Shaking her head.*)—Ah, Monfort, Monfort!
De Mon.	I can forgive th' envenom'd reptile's sting,
	But hate his loathsome self.
Jane.	And canst thou do no more for love of heaven?
De Mon.	Alas! I cannot now so school my mind
	As holy men have taught, nor search it truly:
	But this, my Jane, I'll do for love of thee;
	And more it is than crowns could win me to,
	Or any power but thine. I'll see the man.
	Th' indignant risings of abhorrent nature;
	The stern contraction of my scowling brows,
	That, like the plant, whose closing leaves do shrink
	At hostile touch, still knit at his approach;
	The crooked curving lip, by instinct taught,
	In imitation of disgustful things

	To pout and swell, I strictly will repress;
	And meet him with a tamed countenance,
	E'en as a townsman, who would live at peace,
	And pay him the respect his station claims.
	I'll crave his pardon too for all offence
	My dark and wayward temper may have done;
	Nay more, I will confess myself his debtor
	For the forbearance I have curs'd so oft.
	Life spar'd by him, more horrid than the grave
	With all its dark corruption! This I'll do.
	Will it suffice thee? More than this I cannot.
Jane.	No more than this do I require of thee
	In outward act, tho' in thy heart, my friend,
	I hop'd a better change, and yet will hope.
	I told thee Freberg had propos'd a meeting.
De Mon.	I know it well.
Jane.	And Rezenvelt consents.
	He meets you here; so far he shews respect.
De Mon.	Well, let it be; the sooner past the better.
Jane .	I'm glad to hear you say so, for, in truth,
	He has propos'd for it an early hour.
	'Tis almost near his time; I came to tell you.
De Mon.	What, comes he here so soon? shame on his speed!
	It is not decent thus to rush upon me.
	He loves the secret pleasure he will feel
	To see me thus subdued.
Jane.	O say not so! he comes with heart sincere.
De Mon.	Could we not meet elsewhere? from home—i' the fields,
	Where other men—must I alone receive him?
	Where is your agent, Freberg, and his friends,
	That I must meet him here?
	(*Walks up and down, very much disturbed.*)
	Now didst thou say?—how goes the hour?—e'en now!
	I would some other friend were first arriv'd.
Jane.	See, to thy wish comes Freberg and his dame.
De Mon.	His lady too! why comes he not alone?
	Must all the world stare upon our meeting?

Enter COUNT FREBERG *and his* COUNTESS.

Freb.	A happy morrow to my noble marquis
	And his most noble sister.
Jane.	Gen'rous Freberg,
	Your face, methinks, forebodes a happy morn
	Open and cheerful. What of Rezenvelt?
Freb.	I left him at his home, prepar'd to follow:
	He'll soon appear. (*To De Monfort.*) And now, my worthy friend,
	Give me your hand; this happy change delights me.
	(*De Monfort gives him his hand coldly, and they walk to the bottom of the*
	stage together, in earnest discourse, whilst Jane *and the* Countess *remain*

	in the front.)
Lady.	My dearest madam, will you pardon me?
	I know Count Freberg's bus'ness with De Monfort,
	And had a strong desire to visit you,
	So much I wish the honour of your friendship.
	For he retains no secret from mine ear.
Jane.	(*archly.*) Knowing your prudence. — You are welcome, madam,

Jane. (*archly.*) Knowing your prudence. — You are welcome, madam,
So shall Count Freberg's lady ever be.
(De Monfort *and* Freberg *returning towards the front of the stage, still engaged in discourse.*)

Freb. He is indeed a man, within whose breast,
Firm rectitude and honour hold their seat,
Tho' unadorned with that dignity
Which were their fittest garb. Now, on my life!
I know no truer heart than Rezenvelt.

De Mon. Well, Freberg, well, — there needs not all this pains
To garnish out his worth; let it suffice;
I am resolv'd I will respect the man,
As his fair station and repute demand.
Methinks I see not at your jolly feasts
The youthful knight, who sang so pleasantly.

Freb. A pleasant circumstance detains him hence;
Pleasant to those who love high gen'rous deeds
Above the middle pitch of common minds;
And, tho' I have been sworn to secrecy,
Yet must I tell it thee.
This knight is near akin to Rezenvelt
To whom an old relation, short while dead,
Bequeath'd a good estate, some leagues distant.
But Rezenvelt, now rich in fortune's store,
Disdain'd the sordid love of further gain,
And gen'rously the rich bequest resign'd
To this young man, blood of the same degree
To the deceas'd, and low in fortune's gifts,
Who is from hence to take possession of it:
Was it not nobly done?

De Mon.   'Twas right and honourable.
This morning is oppressive, warm, and heavy:
There hangs a foggy closeness in the air;
Dost thou not feel it?

Freb. O no! to think upon a gen'rous deed
Expands my soul, and makes me lightly breath.

De Mon. Who gives the feast to night? His name escapes me.
You say I am invited.

Freb.   Old Count Waterlan.
In honour of your townsman's gen'rous gift
He spreads the board.

De Mon. He is too old to revel with the gay.

Freb. But not too old is he to honour virtue.

	I shall partake of it with open soul;
	For, on my honest faith, of living men
	I know not one, for talents, honour, worth,
	That I should rank superior to Rezenvelt.
De Mon.	How virtuous he hath been in three short days!
Freb.	Nay, longer, Marquis, but my friendship rests
	Upon the good report of other men;
	And that has told me much.

(De Monfort *aside, going some steps hastily from* Freberg, *and rending his cloak with agitation as he goes.*)
Would he were come! by heaven I would he were!
This fool besets me so.
(*Suddenly correcting himself, and joining the* Ladies, *who have retired to the bottom of the stage, he speaks to* Countess Freberg *with affected cheerfulness.*)
The sprightly dames of Amberg rise by times,
Untarnish'd with the vigils of the night.

Lady.	Praise us not rashly, 'tis not always so.
De Mon.	He does not rashly praise who praises you;
	For he were dull indeed —

(*Stopping short, as if he heard something.*)

| Lady. | How dull indeed? |
| De Mon. | I should have said — It has escap'd me now — |

(*Listening again, as if he heard something.*)

Jane.	(*to* De Mon.) What, hear you aught?
De Mon.	(*hastily.*) 'Tis nothing.
Lady.	(*to* De Mon.) Nay, do not let me lose it so, my lord.
	Some fair one has bewitch'd your memory,
	And robs me of the half-form'd compliment.
Jane.	Half-utter'd praise is to the curious mind,
	As to the eye half-veiled beauty is,
	More precious than the whole. Pray pardon him.
	Some one approaches. (*Listening.*)
Freb.	No, no, it is a servant who ascends;
	He will not come so soon.
De Mon.	(*Off his guard.*) 'Tis Rezenvelt: I heard his well-known foot!
	From the first stair-case, mounting step by step.
Freb.	How quick an ear thou hast for distant sound!
	I heard him not.

(De Monfort *looks embarrassed, and is silent.*)

Enter REZENVELT.

(De Monfort, *recovering himself, goes up to receive* Rezenvelt, *who meets him with a cheerful countenance.*)

De Mon.	(*to* Rez.) I am, my lord, beholden to you greatly.
	This ready visit makes me much your debtor.
Rez.	Then may such debts between us, noble marquis,
	Be oft incurr'd, and often paid again.
	(*To* Jane.) Madam, I am devoted to your service,

116

	And ev'ry wish of yours commands my will.
	(*To* Countess.) Lady, good morning. (*To* Freb.) Well, my gentle friend,
	You see I have not linger'd long behind.
Freb.	No, thou art sooner than I look'd for thee.
Rez.	A willing heart adds feather to the heel,
	And makes the clown a winged mercury.
De Mon.	Then let me say, that with a grateful mind
	I do receive these tokens of good will;
	And must regret that, in my wayward moods,
	I have too oft forgot the due regard
	Your rank and talents claim.
Rez.	No, no, De Monfort,
	You have but rightly curb'd a wanton spirit,
	Which makes me too neglectful of respect.
	Let us be friends, and think of this no more.
Freb.	Ay, let it rest with the departed shades
	Of things which are no more; whilst lovely concord,
	Follow'd by friendship sweet, and firm esteem,
	Your future days enrich. O heavenly friendship!
	Thou dost exalt the sluggish souls of men,
	By thee conjoin'd, to great and glorious deeds;
	As two dark clouds, when mix'd in middle air,
	With vivid lightnings flash, and roar sublime.
	Talk not of what is past, but future love.
De Mon.	(*With dignity.*) No, Freberg, no, it must not. (*To* Rezenvelt.) No, my lord,
	I will not offer you an hand of concord,
	And poorly hide the motives which constrain me.
	I would that, not alone these present friends,
	But ev'ry soul in Amberg were assembled,
	That I, before them all, might here declare
	I owe my spared life to your forbearance.
	(*Holding out his hand.*) Take this from one who boasts no feeling warmth,
	But never will deceive.
	(Jane *smiles upon* De Monfort *with great approbation, and* Rezenvelt *runs up to him with open arms.*)
Rez.	Away with hands! I'll have thee to my breast.
	Thou art, upon my faith, a noble spirit!
De Mon.	(*Shrinking back from him.*)
	Nay, if you please, I am not so prepar'd —
	My nature is of temp'rature too cold —
	I pray you pardon me. (Jane's *countenance changes.*)
	But take this hand, the token of respect;
	The token of a will inclin'd to concord;
	The token of a mind that bears within
	A sense impressive of the debt it owes you:
	And cursed be its power, unnerv'd its strength,
	If e'er again it shall be lifted up
	To do you any harm.
Rez.	Well, be it so, De Monfort, I'm contented;

	I'll take thy hand, since I can have no more.
	(*Carelessly.*) I take of worthy men whate'er they give.
	Their heart I gladly take; if not, their hand:
	If that too is withheld, a courteous word,
	Or the civility of placid looks;
	And, if e'en these are too great favours deem'd,
	'Faith, I can set me down contentedly
	With plain and homely greeting, or, God save ye!
De Mon.	(*Aside, starting away from him some paces.*)
	By the good light, he makes a jest of it!
	(Jane *seems greatly distressed, and* Freberg *endeavours to cheer her.*)
Freb.	(*to* Jane.) Cheer up, my noble friend; all will go well;
	For friendship is no plant of hasty growth.
	Though rooted in esteem's deep-fixed soil,
	The gradual culture of kind intercourse
	Must bring it to perfection.
	(*To the* Countess.) My love, the morning, now, is far advanced;
	Our friends elsewhere expect us; take your leave.
Lady.	(*to* Jane.) Farewell! dear madam, till the ev'ning hour.
Freb.	(*to* De Mon.) Good day, De Monfort. (*To* Jane.) Most devoutly yours.
Rez.	(*to* Freb.) Go not too fast, for I will follow you.

[EXEUNT Freberg *and his* Lady.

	(*To* Jane.) The Lady Jane is yet a stranger here:
	She might, perhaps, in the purlieus of Amberg
	Find somewhat worth her notice.
Jane.	I thank you, Marquis, I am much engag'd;
	I go not out to-day.
Rez.	Then fare ye well! I see I cannot now
	Be the proud man who shall escort you forth,
	And show to all the world my proudest boast,
	The notice and respect of Jane De Monfort.
De Mon.	(*Aside, impatiently.*) He says farewell, and goes not!
Jane.	(*to* Rez.) You do me honour.
Rez.	Madam, adieu! (*To* Jane.) Good morning, noble marquis.

[EXIT

(Jane *and* De Monfort *look expressively to one another, without speaking, and then* EXEUNT, *severally.*)

SCENE II.

A splendid Banquetting Room. DE MONFORT, REZENVELT, FREBERG, MASTER OF THE HOUSE, *and* GUESTS, *are discovered sitting at table, with wine, &c. before them.*

SONG. — A GLEE.[1]

Pleasant is the mantling bowl,
And the song of merry soul;

---

1   A glee is an unaccompanied song for three or more voices.

And the red lamps cheery light,
And the goblet glancing bright;
Whilst many a cheerful face, around,
Listens to the jovial sound.
Social spirits, join with me;
Bless the God of jollity.

Freb.   (to De Mon.) (*Who rises to go away.*)
          Thou wilt not leave us, Monfort? wherefore so?
De Mon.   (*Aside to* Freberg.) I pray thee take no notice of me now.
          Mine ears are stunned with these noisy fools;
          Let me escape.
                                           [EXIT, *hastily.*

Master of the House. What, is De Monfort gone?
Freb.   Time presses him.
Rez.   It seem'd to sit right heavily upon him,
          We must confess.
Mast.   (to Freb.) How is your friend? he wears a noble mien,
          But most averse, methinks, from social pleasure.
          Is this his nature?
Freb.   No, I've seen him cheerful,
          And at the board, with soul-enliven'd face,
          Push the gay goblet round. — But it wears late.
          We shall seem topers more than social friends,
          If the returning sun surprise us here.
          (*To* Mast.) Good rest, my gen'rous host; we will retire.
          You wrestle with your age most manfully,
          But brave it not too far. Retire to sleep.
Mast.   I will, my friend, but do you still remain,
          With noble Rezenvelt, and all my guests.
          Ye have not fourscore years upon your head;
          Do not depart so soon. God save you all!
                       [EXIT Master, *leaning upon a* Servant.
Freb.   (to the Guests.) Shall we resume?
Guests.   The night is too far spent.
Freb.   Well then, good rest to you.
Rez.   (to Guests.) Good rest, my friends.
                    [EXEUNT *all but* Freberg *and* Rezenvelt.
Freb.   Alas, my Rezenvelt!
          I vainly hop'd the hand of gentle peace,
          From this day's reconciliation sprung,
          These rude unseemly jarrings had subdu'd;
          But I have mark'd, e'en at the social board,
          Such looks, such words, such tones, such untold things,
          Too plainly told, 'twixt you and Monfort pass,
          That I must now despair.
          Yet who could think, two minds so much refin'd,
          So near in excellence, should be remov'd,
          So far remov'd, in gen'rous sympathy?

Rez.	Ay, far remov'd indeed.
Freb.	And yet, methought, he made a noble effort,
	And with a manly plainness bravely told
	The galling debt he owes to your forbearance.
Rez.	'Faith! so he did, and so did I receive it;
	When, with spread arms, and heart e'en mov'd to tears,
	I frankly proffer'd him a friend's embrace:
	And, I declare, had he as such receiv'd it,
	I from that very moment had forborne
	All opposition, pride-provoking jest,
	Contemning carelessness, and all offence;
	And had caress'd him as a worthy heart,
	From native weakness such indulgence claiming:
	But since he proudly thinks that cold respect,
	The formal tokens of his lordly favour,
	So precious are, that I would sue for them
	As fair distinction in the world's eye,
	Forgetting former wrongs, I spurn it all;
	And but that I do bear the noble woman,
	His worthy, his incomparable sister,
	Such fix'd, profound regard, I would expose him;
	And, as a mighty bull, in senseless rage,
	Rous'd at the baiter's will, with wretched rags
	Of ire-provoking scarlet, chaffs and bellows,
	I'd make him at small cost of paltry wit,
	With all his deep and manly faculties,
	The scorn and laugh of fools.
Freb.	For heaven's sake, my friend! restrain your wrath!
	For what has Monfort done of wrong to you,
	Or you to him, bating one foolish quarrel,
	Which you confess from slight occasion rose,
	That in your breasts such dark resentment dwells,
	So fix'd, so hopeless?
Rez.	O! from our youth he has distinguish'd me
	With ev'ry mark of hatred and disgust.
	For e'en in boyish sports I still oppos'd
	His proud pretensions to pre-eminence;
	Nor would I to his ripen'd greatness give
	That fulsome adulation of applause
	A senseless crowd bestow'd. Tho' poor in fortune,
	I still would smile at vain-assuming wealth:
	But when unlook'd-for fate on me bestow'd
	Riches and splendour equal to his own,
	Tho' I, in truth, despise such poor distinction,
	Feeling inclin'd to be at peace with him,
	And with all men beside, I curb'd my spirit,
	And sought to soothe him. Then, with spiteful rage,
	From small offence he rear'd a quarrel with me,
	And dar'd me to the field. The rest you know.

	In short, I still have been th' opposing rock,
	O'er which the stream of his o'erflowing pride
	Hath foam'd and bellow'd. Seest thou how it is?
Freb.	Too well I see, and warn thee to beware.
	Such streams have oft, by swelling floods surcharg'd,
	Borne down with sudden and impetuous force,
	The yet unshaken stone of opposition,
	Which had for ages stopp'd their flowing course.
	I pray thee, friend, beware.
Rez.	Thou canst not mean — he will not murder me?
Freb.	What a proud heart, with such dark passion toss'd,
	May, in the anguish of its thoughts, conceive,
	I will not dare to say.
Rez.	Ha, ha! thou knowst him not.
	Full often have I mark'd it in his youth,
	And could have almost lov'd him for the weakness;
	He's form'd with such antipathy, by nature,
	To all infliction of corporeal pain,
	To wounding life, e'en to the sight of blood,
	He cannot if he would.
Freb.	Then fy upon thee!
	It is not gen'rous to provoke him thus.
	But let us part: we'll talk of this again.
	Something approaches. — We are here too long.
Rez.	Well, then, to-morrow I'll attend your call.
	Here lies my way. Good night.

[Exit.

Enter GRIMBALD.

Grim.	Forgive, I pray, my lord, a stranger's boldness.
	I have presum'd to wait your leisure here,
	Though at so late an hour.
Freb.	But who art thou?
Grim.	My name is Grimbald, sir,
	A humble suitor to your honour's goodness,
	Who is the more embolden'd to presume,
	In that the noble Marquis of De Monfort
	Is so much fam'd for good and gen'rous deeds.
Freb.	You are mistaken, I am not the man.
Grim.	Then, pardon me; I thought I could not err.
	That mien so dignified, that piercing eye
	Assur'd me it was he.
Freb.	My name is not De Monfort, courteous stranger;
	But, if you have a favour to request,
	I may, with him, perhaps, befriend your suit.
Grim.	I thank your honour, but I have a friend
	Who will commend me to De Monfort's favour:
	The Marquis Rezenvelt has known me long,
	Who, says report, will soon become his brother.

121

Freb.	If thou wouldst seek thy ruin from De Monfort,
	The name of Rezenvelt employ, and prosper;
	But, if aught good, use any name but his.
Grim.	How may this be?
Freb.	I cannot now explain.
	Early to-morrow call upon Count Freberg;
	So am I call'd, each burgher knows my house,
	And there instruct me how to do you service.
	Good-night.

[EXIT.

Grim.	(*Alone.*) Well, this mistake may be of service to me:
	And yet my bus'ness I will not unfold
	To this mild, ready, promise-making courtier;
	I've been by such too oft deceiv'd already:
	But if such violent enmity exist
	Between De Monfort and this Rezenvelt,
	He'll prove my advocate by opposition.
	For, if De Monfort would reject my suit,
	Being the man whom Rezenvelt esteems,
	Being the man he hates, a cord as strong,
	Will he not favour me? I'll think of this.

[EXIT.

SCENE III.

A lower Apartment in JEROME's *house, with a wide folding glass door, looking into a garden, where the trees and shrubs are brown and leafless. Enter* DE MONFORT *with his arms crossed, with a thoughtful frowning aspect, and paces slowly across the stage,* Jerome *following behind him, with a timid step. De Monfort hearing him, turns suddenly about.*

De Mon.	(*Angrily.*) Who follows me to this sequester'd room?
Jer .	I have presum'd, my lord. 'Tis somewhat late:
	I am inform'd you eat at home to-night;
	Here is a list of all the dainty fare
	My busy search has found; please to peruse it.
De Mon.	Leave me: begone! Put hemlock in thy soup,
	Or deadly night-shade, or rank hellebore,[2]
	And I will mess upon it.
Jer.	Heaven forbid!
	Your honour's life is all too precious, sure—
De Mon.	(*Sternly.*) Did I not say begone?
Jer.	Pardon, my lord, I'm old, and oft forget.

[EXIT.

De Mon.	(*Looking after him, as if his heart smote him.*)
	Why will they thus mistime their foolish zeal,
	That I must be so stern?

---

2   All of these are of course highly poisonous plants, also used in tiny quantities for medicinal purposes.

O, that I were upon some desert coast!
Where howling tempests and the lashing tide
Would stun me into deep and senseless quiet;
As the storm-beaten trav'ller droops his head,
In heavy, dull, lethargic weariness,
And, 'midst the roar of jarring elements,
Sleeps to awake no more.
What am I grown? all things are hateful to me.

Enter MANUEL.

	(*Stamping with his foot.*) Who bids thee break upon my privacy?
Man.	Nay, good my lord! I heard you speak aloud,
	And dreamt not surely that you were alone.
De Mon.	What, dost thou watch, and pin thine ears to holes,
	To catch those exclamations of the soul,
	Which heaven alone should hear? Who hir'd thee, pray?
	Who basely hir'd thee for a task like this?
Man.	My lord, I cannot hold. For fifteen years,
	Long-troubled years, I have your servant been,
	Nor hath the proudest lord in all the realm,
	With firmer, with more honourable faith
	His sov'reign serv'd, than I have served you;
	But if my honesty be doubted now,
	Let him who is more faithful take my place,
	And serve you better.
De Mon.	Well, be it as thou wilt. Away with thee.
	Thy loud-mouth'd boasting is no rule for me
	To judge thy merit by.

Enter JEROME *hastily, and pulls* MANUEL *away.*

Jer.	Come, Manuel, come away; thou art not wise.
	The stranger must depart and come again,
	For now his honour will not be disturb'd.
	[EXIT Manuel *sulkily.*
De Mon.	A stranger, said'st thou.
	(*Drops his handkerchief.*)
Jer.	I did, good sir, but he shall go away;
	You shall not be disturb'd.
	(*Stooping to lift the handkerchief.*)
	You have dropp'd somewhat.
De Mon.	(*Preventing him.*) Nay, do not stoop, my friend! I pray thee not!
	Thou art too old to stoop. —
	I'm much indebted to thee. — Take this ring —
	I love thee better than I seem to do.
	I pray thee do it — thank me not. — What stranger?
Jer.	A man who does most earnestly entreat
	To see your honour; but I know him not.

De Mon.	Then let him enter.

[EXIT Jerome.

A pause. Enter GRIMBALD.

De Mon.	You are the stranger who would speak with me?
Grim.	I am so far unfortunate, my lord.
	That, though my fortune on your favour hangs,
	I am to you a stranger.
De Mon.	How may this be? What can I do for you?,
Grim.	Since thus your lordship does so frankly ask,
	The tiresome preface of apology
	I will forbear, and tell my tale at once. —
	In plodding drudgery I've spent my youth,
	A careful penman in another's office;
	And now, my master and employer dead,
	They seek to set a stripling o'er my head,
	And leave me on to drudge, e'en to old age,
	Because I have no friend to take my part.
	It is an office in your native town,
	For I am come from thence, and I am told
	You can procure it for me. Thus, my lord,
	From the repute of goodness which you bear,
	I have presum'd to beg.
De Mon.	They have befool'd thee with a false report.
Grim.	Alas! I see it is in vain to plead.
	Your mind is pre-possess'd against a wretch,
	Who has, unfortunately for his weal,
	Offended the revengeful Rezenvelt.
De Mon.	What dost thou say?
Grim.	What I, perhaps, had better leave unsaid.
	Who will believe my wrongs if I complain?
	I am a stranger, Rezenvelt my foe,
	Who will believe my wrongs?
De Mon.	(*Eagerly catching him by the coat.*)
	I will believe them!
	Though they were base as basest, vilest deeds,
	In ancient record told, I would believe them.
	Let not the smallest atom of unworthiness
	That he has put upon thee be conceal'd.
	Speak boldly, tell it all; for, by the light!
	I'll be thy friend, I'll be thy warmest friend,
	If he has done thee wrong.
Grim.	Nay, pardon me, it were not well advis'd,
	If I should speak so freely of the man,
	Who will so soon your nearest kinsman be.
De Mon.	What canst thou mean by this?
Grim.	That Marquis Rezenvelt
	Has pledg'd his faith unto your noble sister,
	And soon will be the husband of her choice.

124

	So I am told, and so the world believes.
De Mon.	'Tis false! 'tis basely false!
	What wretch could drop from his envenom'd tongue
	A tale so damn'd? — It chokes my breath —
	(*Stamping with his foot.*) What wretch did tell it thee?
Grim.	Nay, every one with whom I have convers'd
	Has held the same discourse. I judge it not.
	But you, my lord, who with the lady dwell.
	You best can tell what her deportment speaks;
	Whether her conduct and unguarded words
	Belie such rumour.
	(De Monfort *pauses, staggers backwards, and sinks into a chair; then*
	starting up hastily.)
De Mon.	Where am I now? 'midst all the cursed thoughts
	That on my soul like stinging scorpions prey'd,
	This never came before — Oh, if it be!
	The thought will drive me mad. — Was it for this
	She urg'd her warm request on bended knee?
	Alas! I wept, and thought of sister's love,
	No damned love like this.
	Fell devil! 'tis hell itself has lent thee aid
	To work such sorcery! (*Pauses.*) I'll not believe it.
	I must have proof clear as the noon-day sun
	For such foul charge as this! Who waits without!
	(*Paces up and down, furiously agitated.*)
Grim.	(*Aside.*) What have I done? I've carried this too far.
	I've rous'd a fierce ungovernable madman.

Enter JEROME.

De Mon.	(*In a loud angry voice.*) Where did she go, at such an early hour,
	And with such slight attendance?
Jer.	Of whom inquires your honour?
De Mon.	Why, of your lady. Said I not my sister?
Jer.	The Lady Jane, your sister?
De Mon.	(*In a faltering voice.*) Yes, I did call her so.
Jer .	In truth, I cannot tell you where she went.
	E'en now, from the short-beechen walk hard-by,
	I saw her through the garden-gate return.
	The Marquis Rezenvelt, and Freberg's Countess,
	Are in her company. This way they come,
	As being nearer to the back apartments;
	But I shall stop them, if it be your will,
	And bid them enter here.
De Mon.	No, stop them not. I will remain unseen,
	And mark them as they pass. Draw back a little.
	(Grimbald *seems alarm'd, and steals off unnoticed. De Monfort grasps*
	Jerome *tightly by the hand, and drawing back with him two or three steps,*
	not to be seen from the garden, waits in silence with his eyes fixed on the

glass-door.)

De Mon.	I hear their footsteps on the grating sand.
	How like the croaking of a carrion bird,
	That hateful voice sounds to the distant ear!
	And now she speaks—her voice sounds cheerly too—
	O curse their mirth!—
	Now, now, they come; keep closer still! keep steady!
	(*Taking hold of* Jerome *with both hands*.)
Jer.	My lord, you tremble much.
De Mon.	What, do I shake?
Jer.	You do, in truth, and your teeth chatter too.
De Mon.	See! see they come! he strutting by her side.
	(Jane, Rezenvelt, *and* Countess Freberg *appear through the glass-door, pursuing their way up a short walk leading to the other wing of the house*.)
	See how he turns his odious face to her's!
	Utt'ring with confidence some nauseous jest.
	And she endures it too—Oh! this looks vilely!
	Ha! mark that courteous motion of his arm—
	What does he mean?—He dares not take her hand!
	(*Pauses and looks eagerly*.) By heaven and hell he does!
	(*Letting go his hold of* Jerome, *he throws out his hands vehemently, and thereby pushes him against the scene*.)
Jer.	Oh! I am stunn'd! my head is crack'd in twain:
	Your honour does forget how old I am.
De Mon.	Well, well, the wall is harder than I wist.
	Begone, and whine within.
	[EXIT Jerome, *with a sad rueful countenance*.
	(De Monfort *comes forward to the front of the stage, and makes a long pause, expressive of great agony of mind*.)
	It must be so: each passing circumstance;
	Her hasty journey here; her keen distress
	Whene'er my soul's abhorrence I express'd;
	Ay, and that damned reconciliation,
	With tears extorted from me: Oh, too well!
	All, all too well bespeak the shameful tale.
	I should have thought of heav'n and hell conjoin'd,
	The morning star mix'd with infernal fire,
	Ere I had thought of this—
	Hell's blackest magick, in the midnight hour,
	With horrid spells and incantation dire,
	Such combination opposite, unseemly,
	Of fair and loathsome, excellent and base,
	Did ne'er produce.—But every thing is possible,
	So as it may my misery enhance!
	Oh! I did love her with such pride of soul!
	When other men, in gay pursuit of love,
	Each beauty follow'd, by her side I stay'd;
	Far prouder of a brother's station there,
	Than all the favours favour'd lovers boast.

126

We quarrell'd once, and when I could no more
The alter'd coldness of her eye endure,
I slipp'd o'tip-toe to her chamber-door;
And when she ask'd who gently knock'd—Oh! oh!
Who could have thought of this?
(*Throws himself into a chair, covers his face with his hand, and bursts into
    tears. After some time, he starts up from his seat furiously.*)
Hell's direst torment seize th' infernal villain!
Detested of my soul! I will have vengeance!
I'll crush thy swelling pride—I'll still thy vaunting—
I'll do a deed of blood—Why shrink I thus?
If by some spell or magick sympathy,
Piercing the lifeless figure on that wall
Could pierce his bosom too, would I not cast it?
(*Throwing a dagger against the wall.*)
Shall groans and blood affright me? No, I'll do it.
Tho' gasping life beneath my pressure heav'd,
And my soul shudder'd at the horrid brink,
I would not flinch.—Fie, this recoiling nature!
O that his sever'd limbs were strew'd in air,
So as I saw it not!

(*Enter* Rezenvelt *behind, from the glass door. De Monfort turns round, and on seeing him,
starts back, then drawing his sword, rushes furiously upon him.*)

Detested robber; now all forms are over:
Now open villainy, now open hate!
Defend thy life.

Rez.   De Monfort, thou art mad.

De Mon.   Speak not, but draw. Now for thy hated life!
(*They fight:* Rezenvelt *parries his thrusts with great skill, and at last
    disarms him.*)
Then take my life, black fiend, for hell assists thee.

Rez.   No, Monfort, but I'll take away your sword,
Not as a mark of disrespect to you,
But for your safety. By to-morrow's eve
I'll call on you myself and give it back;
And then, if I am charg'd with any wrong,
I'll justify myself. Farewell, strange man!

[EXIT.

(De Monfort *stands for some time quite motionless, like one stupified. Enter to him a*
SERVANT: *he starts.*)

De Mon.   Ha! who art thou?

Ser.   'Tis I, an' please your honour.

De Mon.   (*Staring wildly at him.*) Who art thou?

Ser.   Your servant Jacques.

De Mon.   Indeed I knew thee not.
Leave me, and when Rezenvelt is gone,
Return and let me know.

Ser.   He's gone already, sir.

De Mon.   How, gone so soon?

Ser.	Yes, as his servant told me,
	He was in haste to go; as night comes on,
	And at the evening hour he must take horse,
	To visit some old friend whose lonely mansion
	Stands a short mile beyond the farther wood;
	And, as he loves to wander thro' those wilds
	Whilst yet the early moon may light his way,
	He sends his horses round the usual road,
	And crosses it alone.
	I would not walk thro' those wild dens alone
	For all his wealth. For there, as I have heard,
	Foul murders have been done, and ravens scream;
	And things unearthly, stalking through the night,
	Have scar'd the lonely trav'ller from his wits.
	(De Monfort *stands fixed in thought*.)
	I've ta'en your steed, an' please you, from her field,
	And wait your farther orders.
	(De Monfort *heeds him not*.)
	His hoofs are sound, and where the saddle gall'd,
	Begins to mend. What further must be done?
	(De Monfort *still heeds him not*.)
	His honour heeds me not. Why should I stay?
De Mon.	(*Eagerly, as he is going*.) He goes alone, saidst thou?
Ser.	His servant told me so.
De Mon.	And at what hour?
Ser.	He 'parts from Amberg by the fall of eve.
	Save you, my lord? how chang'd your count'nance is!
	Are you not well?
De Mon.	Yes, I am well: begone!
	And wait my orders by the city wall:
	I'll that way bend, and speak to thee again.

[EXIT Servant.

(De Monfort *walks rapidly two or three times across the stage; then seizes his dagger from the wall, looks steadfastly at its point, and* EXIT, *hastily*.)

ACT IV.—SCENE I.

Moon-light. A wild path in a wood, shaded with trees. Enter DE MONFORT, *with a strong expression of disquiet, mixed with fear, upon his face, looking behind him, and bending his ear to the ground, as if he listened to something.*

De Mon.   How hollow groans the earth beneath my tread!
    Is there an echo here? Methinks it sounds
    As tho' some heavy footstep follow'd me.
    I will advance no farther.
    Deep settled shadows rest across the path,
    And thickly-tangled boughs o'er-hang this spot.
    O that a tenfold gloom did cover it!
    That 'midst the murky darkness I might strike;
    As in the wild confusion of a dream,
    Things horrid, bloody, terrible do pass,
    As tho' they pass'd not; nor impress the mind
    With the fix'd clearness of reality.
    (*An owl is heard screaming near him.*)
    (*Starting.*) What sound is that?
    (*Listens, and the owl cries again.*)
                       It is the screech-owl's cry.
    Foul bird of night! what spirit guides thee here?
    Art thou instinctive drawn to scenes of horrour?
    I've heard of this. (*Pauses and listens.*)
    How those fall'n leaves so rustle on the path,
    With whisp'ring noise, as though the earth around me
    Did utter secret things!
    The distant river, too, bears to mine ear
    A dismal wailing. O mysterious night!
    Thou art not silent; many tongues hast thou.
    A distant gath'ring blast sounds through the wood,
    And dark clouds fleetly hasten o'er the sky:
    O! that a storm would rise, a raging storm;
    Amidst the roar of warring elements;
    I'd lift my hand and strike: but this pale light,
    The calm distinctness of each stilly thing,
    Is terrible. (*Starting.*) Footsteps, are near—
    He comes, he comes! I'll watch him farther on—
    I cannot do it here.

                                          [EXIT.

Enter REZENVELT, *and continues his way slowly across the stage: but just as he is going off the owl screams, he stops and listens, and the owl screams again.*

Rez.   Ha! does the night-bird greet me on my way?
    How much his hooting is in harmony
    With such a scene as this! I like it well.
    Oft when a boy, at the still twilight hour,

I've leant my back against some knotted oak,
And loudly mimick'd him, till to my call
He answer would return, and, thro' the gloom,
We friendly converse held.
Between me and the star-bespangl'd sky,
Those aged oaks their crossing branches wave,
And through them looks the pale and placid moon.
How like a crocodile, or winged snake,
Yon sailing cloud bears on its dusky length!
And now transformed by the passing wind,
Methinks it seems a flying Pegasus.
Ay, but a shapeless band of blacker hue
Comes swiftly after. —
A hollow murm'ring wind sounds through the trees;
I hear it from afar; this bodes a storm.
I must not linger here —
(*A bell heard at some distance.*) What bell is this?
It sends a solemn sound upon the breeze.
Now, to a fearful superstitious mind,
In such a scene, 'twould like a death-knell come:
For me it tells but of a shelter near,
And so I bid it welcome.

[EXIT.

SCENE II.

The inside of a Convent Chapel, of old Gothick architecture, almost dark; two torches only are seen at a distance, burning over a new-made grave. The noise of loud wind, beating upon the windows and roof, is heard. Enter two MONKS.

1*st Monk.*	The storm increases: hark how dismally
	It howls along the cloisters. How goes time?
2*d Monk*	It is the hour: I hear them near at hand;
	And when the solemn requiem has been sung
	For the departed sister, we'll retire.
	Yet, should this tempest still more violent grow,
	We'll beg a friendly shelter till the morn.
1*st Monk.*	See, the procession enters: let us join.

(*The organ strikes up a solemn prelude. Enter a procession of* Nuns, *with the* Abbess, *bearing torches. After compassing the grave twice, and remaining there some time, the organ plays a grand dirge, they advance to the front of the stage.*)

SONG, BY THE NUNS.

Departed soul, whose poor remains
This hallow'd lowly grave contains;
Whose passing storm of life is o'er,

130

Whose pains and sorrows are no more!
Bless'd be thou with the bless'd above!
Where all is joy, and purity, and love.

Let him, in might and mercy dread,
Lord of the living and the dead;
In whom the stars of heav'n rejoice,
To whom the ocean lifts his voice,
Thy spirit purified to glory raise,
To sing with holy saints his everlasting praise.

Departed soul, who in this earthly scene
Hast our lowly sister been.
Swift be thy way to where the blessed dwell!
Until we meet thee there, farewell! farewell!

Enter a LAY SISTER, *with a wild terrified look, her hair and dress all scattered, and rushes forward amongst them.*

Abb.	Why com'st thou here, with such disorder'd looks,
	To break upon our sad solemnity?
Sist.	Oh! I did hear thro' the receding blast,
	Such horrid cries! they made my blood run chill.
Abb.	'Tis but the varied voices of the storm,
	Which many times will sound like distant screams:
	It has deceiv'd thee.
Sist.	O no, for twice it call'd, so loudly call'd,
	With horrid strength, beyond the pitch of nature;
	And murder! murder! was the dreadful cry.
	A third time it return'd with feeble strength,
	But o' the sudden ceas'd, as though the words
	Were rudely smother'd in the grasped throat;
	And all was still again, save the wild blast
	Which at a distance growl'd —
	Oh! it will never from my mind depart!
	That dreadful cry, all I' the instant still'd,
	For then, so near, some horrid deed was done,
	And none to rescue.
Abb.	Where didst thou hear it?
Sist.	In the higher cells,
	As now a window, open'd by the storm,
	I did attempt to close.
1st Monk.	I wish our brother Bernard were arriv'd;
	He is upon his way.
Abb.	Be not alarm'd; it still may be deception.
	'Tis meet we finish our solemnity,
	Nor show neglect unto the honour'd dead.
	(*Gives a sign, and the organ plays again: just as it ceases a loud knocking is heard without.*)

Abb.	Ha! who may this be? hush!
	(*Knocking heard again.*)
2d Monk.	It is the knock of one in furious haste,
	Hush! hush! What footsteps come? Ha! brother Bernard.

Enter BERNARD *bearing a lantern.*

1st Monk.	See, what a look he wears of stiffen'd fear!
	Where hast thou been, good brother?
Bern.	I've seen a horrid sight!
	(*All gathering round him and speaking at once.*)
	What hast thou seen?
Bern.	As on I hasten'd, bearing thus my light,
	Across the path, not fifty paces off,
	I saw a murther'd corse stretch'd on his back,
	Smear'd with new blood, as though but freshly slain.
Abb.	A man or woman?
Bern.	A man, a man!
Abb.	Didst thou examine if within its breast
	There yet is lodg'd some small remains of life?
	Was it quite dead?
Bern.	Nought in the grave is deader.
	I look'd but once, yet life did never lodge
	In any form so laid.
	A chilly horror seiz'd me, and I fled.
1st Monk.	And does the face seem all unknown to thee?
Bern.	The face! I would not on the face have look'd
	For e'en a kingdom's wealth, for all the world.
	O no! the bloody neck, the bloody neck!
	(*Shaking his head, and shuddering with horrour. Loud knocking heard without.*)
Sist.	Good mercy! who comes next?
Bern.	Not far behind
	I left our brother Thomas on the road;
	But then he did repent him as he went,
	And threatened to return.
2d Monk.	See, here he comes.
	Enter brother THOMAS, *with a wild terrified look.*
1st Monk.	How wild he looks!
Bern.	(*Going up to him eagerly.*) What, hast thou seen it too?
Thom.	Yes, yes! it glar'd upon me as it pass'd.
Bern.	What glar'd upon thee?
	(*All gathering round* Thomas *and speaking at once.*)
	O! what hast thou seen?
Thom.	As, striving with the blast, I onward came,
	Turning my feeble lantern from the wind,
	Its light upon a dreadful visage gleam'd,
	Which paus'd, and look'd upon me as it pass'd.
	But such a look, such wildness of despair,

	Such horror-strain'd features never yet
	Did earthly visage show. I shrank and shudder'd.
	If damned spirits may to earth return
	I've seen it.
Bern.	Was there any blood upon it?
Thom.	Nay, as it pass'd, I did not see its form;
	Nought but the horrid face.
Bern.	It is the murderer.
1st Monk.	What way went it?
Thom.	I durst not look till I had pass'd it far,
	Then turning round, upon the rising bank,
	I saw, between me and the paly sky,
	A dusky form, tossing and agitated.
	I stopp'd to mark it, but, in truth, I found
	'Twas but a sapling bending to the wind,
	And so I onward hied, and look'd no more.
1st Monk.	But we must look to't; we must follow it:
	Our duty so commands. (*To* 2*d* Monk.) Will you go, brother?
	(*To* Bernard.) And you, good Bernard?
Bern.	If I needs must go.
1st Monk.	Come, we must all go.
Abb.	Heaven be with you, then!

[EXEUNT *Monks.*

Sist.	Amen! amen! Good heav'n, be with us all!
	O what a dreadful night!
Abb.	Daughters retire; peace to the peaceful dead!
	Our solemn ceremony now is finish'd.

[EXEUNT.

SCENE III.

A large room in the Convent, very dark. Enter the ABBESS, Lay Sister *bearing a light, and several* Nuns; Sister *sets down the light on a table at the bottom of the stage, so that the room is still very gloomy.*

Abb.	They have been longer absent than I thought:
	I fear he has escap'd them.
1st Nun.	Heaven forbid!
Sist.	No, no, found out foul murder ever is,
	And the foul murd'rer too.
2d Nun.	The good Saint Francis will direct their search;
	The blood so near this holy convent shed
	For threefold vengeance calls.
Abb.	I hear a noise within the inner court,
	They are return'd; (*listening;*) and Bernard's voice I hear:
	They are return'd.
Sist.	Why do I tremble so?
	It is not I who ought to tremble thus.

2d Nun.	I hear them at the door.
Bern.	(*Without.*) Open the door, I pray thee, brother Thomas; I cannot now unhand the prisoner. (*All speak together, shrinking back from the door, and staring upon one* *another.*) He is with them!

(*A folding door at the bottom of the stage is opened, and enter* **Bernard**, **Thomas**, *and the other*
two **Monks**, *carrying lanterns in their hands, and bringing in* **De Monfort**. *They are likewise*
followed by other **Monks**. *As they lead forward* **De Monfort** *the light is turned away, so that*
he is seen obscurely; but when they come to the front of the stage they all turn the light side of
their lanterns on him at once, and his face is seen in all the strengthened horrour of despair, with
his hands and cloathes bloody.)

	(**Abbess** *and* **Nuns** *speak at once, and starting back.*) Holy saints be with us!
Bern.	(*to* Abb.) Behold the man of blood!
Abb.	Of misery too; I cannot look upon him.
Bern.	(*to* Nuns.) Nay, holy sisters, turn not thus away. Speak to him, if, perchance, he will regard you: For from his mouth we have no utt'rance heard, Save one deep and smother'd exclamation, When first we seiz'd him.
Abb.	(*to* De Mon.) Most miserable man, how art thou thus? (*Pauses.*) Thy tongue is silent, but those bloody hands Do witness horrid things. What is thy name?
De Mon.	(*Roused; looks steadfastly at the* **Abbess** *for some time; then speaking in a* *short hurried voice.*) I have no name.
Abb.	(*to* Bern.) Do it thyself; I'll speak to him no more.
Sist.	O holy saints! that this should be the man, Who did against his fellow lift the stroke, Whilst he so loudly call'd. — Still in mine ear it sounds: O murder! murder!
De Mon.	(*Starting.*) He calls again!
Sist.	No, he did call, but now his voice is still'd. 'Tis past.
De Mon.	(*In great anguish.*) 'Tis past.
Sist.	Yes, it is past, art thou not he who did it? (De Monfort *utters a deep groan, and is supported from falling by the* Monks. *A noise is heard without.*)
Abb.	What noise is this of heavy lumb'ring steps, Like men who with a weighty burthen come?
Bern.	It is the body: I have orders given That here it should be laid.

(*Enter men bearing the body of* **Rezenvelt**, *covered with a white cloth, and set it down in*
the middle of the room: they then uncover it. **De Monfort** *stands fixed and motionless with*
horrour, only that a sudden shivering seems to pass over him when they uncover the corps.
The **Abbess** *and* **Nuns** *shrink back and retire to some distance; all the rest fixing their eyes*
steadfastly upon **De Monfort**. *A long pause.*)

Bern.	(*to* De Mon.) Seest thou the lifeless corps, those bloody wounds, See how he lies, who but so shortly since

	A living creature was, with all the powers
	Of sense, and motion, and humanity!
	Oh! what a heart had he who did this deed!
1st Monk.	(*Looking at the body.*) How hard those teeth against the lips are press'd,
	As though he struggled still!
2d Monk	The hands too, clench'd: the last efforts of nature.
	(*De Monfort still stands motionless. Brother* Thomas *then goes to the body, and raising up the head a little, turns it towards* De Monfort.)
Thom.	Knowst thou this ghastly face?
De Mon.	(*Putting his hands before his face in violent perturbation.*)
	Oh, do not! do not! Veil it from my sight!
	Put me to any agony but this!
Thom.	Ha! dost thou then confess the dreadful deed?
	Hast thou against the laws of awful heav'n
	Such horrid murder done? What fiend could tempt thee?
	(*Pauses, and looks steadfastly at De Monfort.*)
De Mon.	I hear thy words, but do not hear their sense —
	Hast thou not cover'd it?
Bern.	(*to* Thom.) Forbear, my brother, for thou seest right well
	He is not in a state to answer thee.
	Let us retire and leave him for a while.
	These windows are with iron grated o'er;
	He cannot 'scape, and other duty calls.
Thom.	Then let it be.
Bern.	(*to Monks, &c.*) Come, let us all depart.
	(EXEUNT Abbess *and* Nuns, *followed by the* Monks. *One* Monk *lingering a little behind.*)
De Mon.	All gone! (*Perceiving the Monk.*)
	O stay thou here!
Monk	It must not be.
De Mon.	I'll give thee gold; I'll make thee rich in gold,
	If thou wilt stay e'en but a little while.
Monk.	I must not, must not stay.
De Mon.	I do conjure thee!
Monk.	I dare not stay with thee. (*Going.*)
De Mon.	And wilt thou go?
	(*Catching hold of him eagerly.*)
	O! throw thy cloak upon this grizly form!
	The unclos'd eyes do stare upon me still.
	O do not leave me thus!
	[Monk *covers the body, and* EXIT.
De Mon.	(*Alone, looking at the covered body, but at a distance.*)
	Alone with thee! but thou art nothing now,
	'Tis done, 'tis number'd with the things o'erpast,
	Would! would it were to come!
	What fated end, what darkly gathering cloud
	Will close on all this horrour?
	O that dire madness would unloose my thoughts,
	And fill my mind with wildest fantasies,

Dark, restless, terrible! ought, ought but this!
(*Pauses and shudders.*)
How with convulsive life he heav'd beneath me,
E'en with the death's wound gor'd. O horrid, horrid!
Methinks I feel him still. — What sound is that?
I heard a smother'd groan. — It is impossible!
(*Looking steadfastly at the body.*)
It moves! it moves! the cloth doth heave and swell.
It moves again. — I cannot suffer this —
Whate'er it be I will uncover it.
(*Runs to the corps, and tears off the cloth in despair.*)
All still beneath.
Nought is there here but fix'd and grizly death.
How sternly fixed! Oh! those glazed eyes!
They look upon me still.
(*Shrinks back with horrour.*)
Come, madness! come unto me senseless death!
I cannot suffer this! Here, rocky wall,
Seatter these brains, or dull them.
(*Runs furiously, and, dashing his head against the wall, falls upon the floor.*)

Enter two MONKS, *hastily.*

1*st Monk.*   See; wretched man, he hath destroy'd himself.
2*d Monk.*   He does but faint. Let us remove him hence.
1*st Monk.*   We did not well to leave him here alone.
2*d Monk.*   Come, let us bear him to the open air.

[EXEUNT, *bearing out* De Monfort.

Before the gates of the Convent. Enter JANE DE MONFORT, FREBERG, *and* MANUEL. *As they are proceeding towards the gate,* JANE *stops short and shrinks back.*

Freb.	Ha! wherefore? has a sudden illness seiz'd thee?
Jane.	No, no, my friend. — And yet I am very faint —
	I dread to enter here!
Man.	Ay, so I thought:
	For, when between the trees, that abbey tower
	First shew'd its top, I saw your count'nance change.
	But breathe a little here; I'll go before,
	And make enquiry at the nearest gate.
Freb.	Do so, good Manuel.
	(Manuel *goes and knocks at the gate.*)
	Courage, dear madam: all may yet be well.
	Rezenvelt's servant, frighten'd with the storm,
	And seeing that his master join'd him not,
	As by appointment, at the forest's edge,
	Might be alarm'd, and give too ready ear
	To an unfounded rumour.
	He saw it not; he came not here himself.
Jane.	(*Looking eagerly to the gate, where* Manuel *talks with the* Porter.)
	Ha! see, he talks with some one earnestly.
	And sees't thou not that motion of his hands?
	He stands like one who hears a horrid tale.
	Almighty God!
	(Manuel *goes into the convent.*)
	He comes not back; he enters.
Freb.	Bear up, my noble friend.
Jane.	I will, I will! But this suspense is dreadful.
	(*A long pause.* Manuel *re-enters from the convent, and comes forward slowly, with a sad countenance.*)
	Is this the pace of one who bears good tidings?
	O God! his face doth tell the horrid fact;
	There is nought doubtful here.
Freb.	How is it, Manuel?
Man.	I've seen him through a crevice in his door:
	It is indeed my master.
	(*Bursting into tears.*)
	(Jane *faints, and is supported by* Freberg. — *Enter* ABBESS *and several* NUNS *from the convent who gather about her, and apply remedies. She recovers.*)
1st Nun.	The life returns again.
2d Nun.	Yes, she revives.
Abb. (*to* FREB.)	Let me entreat this noble lady's leave
	To lead her in. She seems in great distress:
	We would with holy kindness soothe her woe,
	And do by her the deeds of christian love.
Freb.	Madam, your goodness has my grateful thanks.
	[EXEUNT, *supporting* Jane *into the convent.*

SCENE II.

De Monfort is discovered sitting in a thoughtful posture. He remains so for some time. His face afterwards begins to appear agitated, like one whose mind is harrowed with the severest thoughts; then, starting from his seat, he clasps his hands together, and holds them up to heaven.

<table>
<tr><td>De Mon.</td><td>O that I ne'er had known the light of day!
That filmy darkness on mine eyes had hung,
And clos'd me out from the fair face of nature!
O that my mind in mental darkness pent,
Had no perception, no distinction known,
Of fair or foul, perfection nor defect;
Nor thought conceiv'd of proud pre-eminence!
O that it had! O that I had been form'd
An idiot from the birth! a senseless changeling,
Who eats his glutton's meal with greedy haste,
Nor knows the hand which feeds him. —
(<i>Pauses; then in a calmer sorrowful voice.</i>)
What am I now? how ends the day of life?
For end it must; and terrible this gloom,
This storm of horrours that surrounds its close.
This little term of nature's agony
Will soon be o'er, and what is past is past:
But shall I then, on the dark lap of earth
Lay me to rest, in still unconsciousness,
Like senseless clod that doth no pressure feel
From wearing foot of daily passenger;
Like a steeped rock o'er which the breaking waves
Bellow and foam unheard? O would I could!</td></tr>
</table>

Enter MANUEL, *who springs forward to his master, but is checked upon perceiving* De Monfort *draw back and look sternly at him.*

<table>
<tr><td>Man.</td><td>My lord, my master! O my dearest master!
(De Monfort <i>still looks at him without speaking.</i>)
Nay, do not thus regard me; good my lord!
Speak to me: am I not your faithful Manuel?</td></tr>
<tr><td>De Mon.</td><td>(In a hasty broken voice.) Art thou alone?</td></tr>
<tr><td>Man.</td><td>No, Sir, the lady Jane is on her way;
She is not far behind.</td></tr>
<tr><td>De Mon.</td><td>(Tossing his arm over his head in an agony.)
This is too much! All I can bear but this!
It must not be. — Run and prevent her coming.
Say, he who is detain'd a prisoner here
Is one to her unknown. I now am nothing.
I am a man of holy claims bereft;
Out from the pale of social kindred cast;
Nameless and horrible. —
Tell her De Monfort far from hence is gone
Into a desolate and distant land,</td></tr>
</table>

Ne'er to return again. Fly, tell her this;
For we must meet no more.

Enter JANE DE MONFORT, *bursting into the chamber and followed by* FREBERG, ABBESS, *and*
several NUNS.

Jane.   We must! we must! My brother, O my brother!
            (De Monfort *turns away his head and hides his face with his arm.* Jane *stops*
                short, and, making a great effort, turns to Freberg, *and the others who followed*
                her, and with an air of dignity stretches out her hand, beckoning them to retire.
                All retire but Freberg, who seems to hesitate.)
            And thou too, Freberg: call it not unkind.
                                [EXIT Freberg: Jane *and* De Monfort *only remain.*
Jane.   My hapless Monfort!
            (De Monfort *turns round and looks sorrowfully upon her; she opens her arms*
                to him, and he, rushing into them, hides his face upon her breast, and weeps.)
Jane.   Ay, give thy sorrow vent: here mayst thou weep.
De Mon.   (*In broken accents.*) Oh! this, my sister, makes me feel again
            The kindness of affection.
            My mind has in a dreadful storm been tost;
            Horrid and dark. — I thought to weep no more. —
            I've done a deed — But I am human still.
Jane.   I know thy suff'rings: leave thy sorrow free:
            Thou art with one who never did upbraid;
            Who mourns, who loves thee still.
De Mon.   Ah! sayst thou so? no, no; it should not be.
            (*Shrinking from her.*) I am a foul and bloody murderer,
            For such embrace unmeet: O leave me! leave me!
            Disgrace and publick shame abide me now;
            And all, alas! who do my kindred own,
            The direful portion share. — Away, away!
            Shall a disgrac'd and publick criminal
            Degrade thy name, and claim affinity
            To noble worth like thine? — I have no name —
            I'm nothing now, not e'en to thee; depart.
            (*She takes his hand, and grasping it firmly, speaks with a determined voice.*)
Jane.   De Monfort, hand in hand we have enjoy'd
            The playful term of infancy together;
            And in the rougher path of ripen'd years
            We've been each other's stay. Dark lowers our fate,
            And terrible the storm that gathers over us;
            But nothing, till that latest agony
            Which severs thee from nature, shall unloose
            This fix'd and sacred hold. In thy dark prison-house;
            In the terrifick face of armed law;
            Yea, on the scaffold, if it needs must be,
            I never will forsake thee.
De Mon.   (*Looking at her with admiration.*)
            Heav'n bless thy gen'rous soul, my noble Jane!
            I thought to sink beneath this load of ill,

	Depress'd with infamy and open shame;
	I thought to sink in abject wretchedness:
	But for thy sake I'll rouse my manhood up,
	And meet it bravely; no unseemly weakness,
	I feel my rising strength, shall blot my end,
	To clothe thy cheek with shame.
Jane.	Yes, thou art noble still.
De Mon.	With thee I am; who were not so with thee?
	But, ah, my sister! short will be the term:
	Death's stroke will come, and in that state beyond,
	Where things unutterable wait the soul,
	New from its earthly tenement discharg'd,
	We shall be sever'd far.
	Far as the spotless purity of virtue
	Is from the murd'rer's guilt, far shall we be.
	This is the gulf of dread uncertainty
	From which the soul recoils.
Jane.	The God who made thee is a God of mercy;
	Think upon this.
De Mon.	(*Shaking his head.*) No, no! this blood! this blood!
Jane.	Yea, e'en the sin of blood may be forgiv'n,
	When humble penitence hath once aton'd.
De Mon.	(*Eagerly.*)What, after terms of lengthen'd misery,
	Imprison'd anguish of tormented spirits,
	Shall I again, a renovated soul,
	Into the blessed family of the good
	Admittance have? Thinkst thou that this may be?
	Speak, if thou canst: O speak me comfort here!
	For dreadful fancies, like an armed host,
	Have push'd me to despair. It is most horrible—
	O speak of hope! if any hope there be.
	(Jane *is silent, and looks sorrowfully upon him; then clasping her hands, and turning her eyes to heaven, seems to mutter a prayer.*)
De Mon.	Ha! dost thou pray for me? heav'n hear thy prayer!
	I fain would kneel.—Alas! I dare not do it.
Jane.	Not so; all by th' Almighty Father form'd
	May in their deepest mis'ry call on him.
	Come kneel with me, my brother.
	(*She kneels and prays to herself; he kneels by her, and clasps his hands fervently, but speaks not. A noise of chains clanking is heard without, and they both rise.*)
De Mon.	Hear'st thou that noise? They come to interrupt us.
Jane.	(*Moving towards a side door.*) Then let us enter here.
De Mon.	(*Catching hold of her with a look of horror.*)
	Not there—not there—the corps—the bloody corps!
Jane.	What, lies he there?—Unhappy Rezenvelt!
De Mon.	A sudden thought has come across my mind;
	How came it not before? Unhappy Rezenvelt!
	Sayst thou but this?
Jane.	What should I say? he was an honest man;
	I still have thought him such, as such lament him.

140

(De Monfort *utters a deep groan.*)
What means this heavy groan?

De Mon.   It hath a meaning.

Enter ABBESS *and* MONKS, *with two* OFFICERS *of justice carrying fetters in their hands to put upon* DE MONFORT.

Jane.   (*Starting.*) What men are these?
1st Off.   Lady, we are the servants of the law,
               And bear with us a power, which doth constrain
               To bind with fetters this our prisoner.
               (*Pointing to* De Monfort.)
Jane.   A stranger uncondemn'd? this cannot be.
1st Off.   As yet, indeed, he is by law unjudg'd,
               But is so far condemn'd by circumstance,
               That law, or custom sacred held as law,
               Doth fully warrant us, and it must be.
Jane.   Nay, say not so; he has no power to escape:
               Distress hath bound him with a heavy chain;
               There is no need of yours.
1st Off.   We must perform our office.
Jane.   O! do not offer this indignity!
1st Off.   Is it indignity in sacred law
               To bind a murderer? (*To* 2d *Officer.*) Come, do thy work.
Jane.   Harsh are thy words, and stern thy harden'd brow;
               Dark is thine eye; but all some pity have
               Unto the last extreme of misery.
               I do beseech thee! if thou art a man—
               (*Kneeling to him.*)
               (De Monfort, *roused at this, runs up to* Jane, *and raises her hastily from the ground; then stretches himself up proudly.*)
De Mon.   (*to* Jane.) Stand thou erect in native dignity;
               And bend to none on earth the suppliant knee,
               Though cloth'd in power imperial. To my heart
               It gives a feller gripe than many irons.
               (*Holding out his hands.*)
               Here, officers of law, bind on those shackles,
               And, if they are too light bring heavier chains.
               Add iron to iron, load, crush me to the ground;
               Nay, heap ten thousand weight upon my breast,
               For that were best of all.
               (*A long pause, whilst they put irons upon him. After they are on,* Jane *looks a thim sorrowfully, and lets her head sink on her breast.* De Monfort *stretches out his hand, looks at them, and then at* Jane; *crosses them over his breast, and endeavours to suppress his feelings.*)
1st Off.   I have it, too, in charge to move you hence,
               (*To* De Monfort.)
               Into another chamber, more secure.
De Mon.   Well, I am ready, sir.
               (*Approaching* Jane, *whom the* Abbess *is endeavouring to comfort, but to no purpose.*)
               Ah! wherefore thus, most honour'd and most dear?

Shrink not at the accoutrements of ill,
Daring the thing itself.
(*Endeavouring to look cheerful.*)
Wilt thou permit me with a gyved hand?
(*She gives him her hand, which he raises to his lips.*)
This was my proudest office.

[EXEUNT, De Monfort *leading out* Jane.

SCENE III.

An long narrow gallery in the convent, with the doors of the cells on each side. The stage darkened. A Nun *is discovered at a distance listening. Enter another* Nun *at the front of the stage, and starts back.*

1*st Nun.*   Ha! who is this not yet retir'd to rest?
               My sister, is it you?
               (*To the other who advances.*)

2*d Nun.*   Returning from the sister Nina's cell,
               Passing yon door where the poor pris'ner lies,
               The sound of one who struggl'd with despair
               Struck on me as I went: I stopp'd and listen'd;
               Oh God! such piteous groans!

1*st Nun.*   Yes, since the ev'ning sun it hath been so.
               The voice of mis'ry oft hath reach'd mine ear,
               E'en in the cell above.

2*d Nun.*   How is it thus?
               Methought he brav'd it with a manly spirit,
                And led, with shakl'd hands, his sister forth,
               Like one resolv'd to bear misfortune boldly.

1*st Nun.*   Yes, with heroic courage, for a while
               He seem'd inspir'd; but, soon depress'd again,
               Remorse and dark despair o'erwhelm'd his soul,
               And so he hath remain'd.

Enter Father BERNARD, *advancing from the further end of the gallery, bearing a crucifix.*

1*st Nun.*   How goes it, father, with your penitent?
               We've heard his heavy groans.

Bern.   Retire, my daughters; many a bed of death,
               With all its pangs and horror I have seen,
               But never ought like this.

2*d Nun.*   He's dying, then?

Bern.   Yes, death is dealing with him.
               From violent agitation of his mind,
               Some stream of life within his breast has burst;
               For many a time, within a little space,
               The ruddy-tide has rush'd into his mouth.
               God grant his pains be short!

1*st Nun.*   Amen, amen!

2*d Nun.*   How does the lady?

Bern.	She sits and bears his head upon her lap;
	And like a heaven-inspir'd angel, speaks
	The word of comfort to his troubled soul:
	Then does she wipe the cold drops from his brow,
	With such a look of tender wretchedness,
	It wrings the heart to see her.
1st Nun.	Ha! hear ye nothing?
2d Nun.	(*Alarmed.*) Yes, I heard a noise.
1st Nun.	And see'st thou nothing?
	(*Creeping close to her sister.*)
Bern.	'Tis a nun in white.

Enter LAY SISTER *in her night cloathes, advancing from the dark end of the gallery.*

	(*To* Sister.) Wherefore, my daughter, hast thou left thy cell?
	It is not meet at this untimely hour.
Sist.	I cannot rest. I hear such dismal sounds,
	Such wailings in the air, such shrilly shrieks,
	As though the cry of murder rose again
	From the deep gloom of night. I cannot rest:
	I pray you let me stay with you, good sisters!
	(*Bell tolls.*)
Nuns.	(*Starting.*) What bell is that?
Bern.	It is the bell of death.
	A holy sister was upon the watch
	To give this notice. (*Bell tolls again.*) Hark! Another knell!
	The wretched struggler hath his warfare clos'd;
	May heaven have mercy on him.
	(*Bell tolls again.*)
	Retire, my daughters; let us all retire,
	For scenes like this to meditation call.

                              [EXEUNT, *bell tolling again.*

SCENE IV.

A hall or large room in the convent. The bodies of DE MONFORT *and* REZENVELT *are discovered laid out upon a low table or platform, covered with black.* FREBERG, BERNARD, ABBESS, MONKS, *and* NUNS *attending.*

Abb.	(*to* Freb.) Here must they lie, my lord, until we know
	Respecting this the order of the law.
Freb.	And you have wisely done, my rev'rend mother.
	(*Goes to the table, and looks at the bodies, but without uncovering them.*)
	Unhappy men! ye, both in nature rich,
	With talents and with virtues were endu'd.
	Ye should have lov'd, yet deadly rancour came,
	And in the prime and manhood of your days
	Ye sleep in horrid death. O direful hate!
	What shame and wretchedness his portion is,
	Who, for a secret inmate, harbours thee!

	And who shall call him blameless who excites,
	Ungen'rously excites, with careless scorn,
	Such baleful passion in a brother's breast,
	Whom heav'n commands to love. Low are ye laid:
	Still all contention now. —Low are ye laid:
	I lov'd you both, and mourn your hapless fall.
Abb.	They were your friends, my lord?
Freb.	I lov'd them both. How does the Lady Jane?
Abb.	She bears misfortune with intrepid soul.
	I never saw in woman bow'd with grief
	Such moving dignity.
Freb.	Ay, still the same.

I've known her long; of worth most excellent;
But in the day of woe she ever rose
Upon the mind with added majesty,
As the dark mountain more sublimely tow'rs
Mantled in clouds and storm.

Enter MANUEL *and* JEROME.

Man.	(*Pointing.*) Here, my good Jerome, there's a piteous sight.
Jer.	A piteous sight! yet I will look upon him:
	I'll see his face in death. Alas, alas!
	I've seen him move a noble gentleman;
	And when with vexing passion undisturb'd,
	He look'd most graciously.

(*Lifts up in mistake the cloth from the body of* Rezenvelt, *and starts back with horrour.*)
Oh! this was the bloody work! Oh, oh! oh, oh!
That human hands could do it!
(*Drops the cloth again.*)

Man.	That is the murder'd corps; here lies De Monfort.

(*Going to uncover the other body.*)

Jer.	(*Turning away his head.*) No, no! I cannot look upon him now.
Man.	Didst thou not come to see him?
Jer.	Fy! cover him—inter him in the dark—
	Let no one look upon him.
Bern.	(*to* Jer.) Well dost thou show the abhorrence nature feels
	For deeds of blood, and I commend thee well.
	In the most ruthless heart compassion wakes
	For one who, from the hand of fellow man,
	Hath felt such cruelty.

(*Uncovering the body of* Rezenvelt.)
This is the murder'd corse:
(*Uncovering the body of* De Monfort.)
But see, I pray!
Here lies the murderer. What think'st thou here?
Look on those features, thou hast seen them oft,
With the last dreadful conflict of despair,
So fix'd in horrid strength.

	See those knit brows; those hollow sun'ken eyes;
	The sharpen'd nose, with nostrils all distent;
	That writhed mouth, where yet the teeth appear,
	In agony, to gnash the nether lip.
	Thinkst thou, less painful than the murd'rer's knife
	Was such a death as this?
	Ay, and how changed too those matted locks!
Jer.	Merciful heaven! his hair is grisly grown,
	Chang'd to white age, that was, but two days since,
	Black as the raven's plume. How may this be?
Bern.	Such change, from violent conflict of the mind,
	Will sometimes come.
Jer.	Alas, alas! most wretched!
	Thou wert too good to do a cruel deed,
	And so it kill'd thee. Thou hast suffer'd for it.
	God rest thy soul! I needs must touch thy hand,
	And bid thee long farewell.
	(*Laying his hand on* De Monfort.)
Bern.	Draw back, draw back! see where the lady comes.

Enter JANE DE MONFORT. FREBERG, *who has been for sometime retired by himself at the bottom of the stage, now steps forward to lead her in, but checks himself on seeing the fixed sorrow of her countenance, and draws back respectfully.* JANE *advances to the table, and looks attentively at the covered bodies.* MANUEL *points out the body of* DE MONFORT, *and she gives a gentle inclination of the head, to signify that she understands him. She then bends tenderly over it, without speaking.*

Man.	(*to* Jane, *as she raises her head.*) Oh, madam! my good lord.
Jane.	Well says thy love, my good and faithful Manuel;
	But we must mourn in silence.
Man.	Alas! the times that I have followed him!
Jane.	Forbear, my faithful Manuel. For this love
	Thou hast my grateful thanks; and here's my hand:
	Thou hast lov'd him, and I'll remember thee:
	Where'er I am, in whate'er spot of earth
	I linger out the remnant of my days,
	I will remember thee.
Man.	Nay, by the living God! where'er you are,
	There will I be. I'll prove a trusty servant:
	I'll follow you, even to the world's end.
	My master's gone; and I, indeed, am mean,
	Yet will I show the strength of nobler men,
	Should any dare upon your honour'd worth
	To put the slightest wrong. Leave you, dear lady!
	Kill me, but say not this!
	(*Throwing himself at her feet.*)
Jane.	(*Raising him.*) Well, then! be thou my servant, and my friend.
	Art thou, good Jerome, too, in kindness come?
	I see thou art. How goes it with thine age?
Jer.	Ah, madam! woe and weakness dwell with age:

	Would I could serve you with a young man's strength!
	I'd spend my life for you.
Jane.	Thanks, worthy Jerome.
	O! who hath said, the wretched have no friends?
Freb.	In every sensible and gen'rous breast
	Affliction finds a friend; but unto thee,
	Thou most exalted and most honourable,
	The heart in warmest adoration bows,
	And even a worship pays.
Jane.	Nay, Freberg! Freberg! grieve me not, my friend.

Jane. Nay, Freberg! Freberg! grieve me not, my friend.
He, to whose ear my praise most welcome was,
Hears it no more; and, oh, our piteous lot!
What tongue will talk of him? Alas, alas!
This more than all will bow me to the earth;
I feel my misery here.
The voice of praise was wont to name us both:
I had no greater pride.
(*Covers her face with her hands, and bursts into tears. Here they all hang about her:* Freberg *supporting her tenderly,* Manuel *embracing her knees, and old* Jerome *catching hold of her robe affectionately.* Bernard, Abbess, Monks, *and* Nuns *likewise gather round her, with looks of sympathy.*)

Enter Two OFFICERS *of law.*

1st Off. Where is the prisoner?
Into our hands he straight must be consign'd.

Bern. He is not subject now to human laws;
The prison that awaits him is the grave.

1st Off. Ha! sayst thou so? there is foul play in this.

Man. (*to* Off.) Hold thy unrighteous tongue, or hie thee hence,
Nor in the presence of this honour'd dame,
Utter the slightest meaning of reproach.

1st Off. I am an officer on duty call'd,
And have authority to say, how died?
(*Here Jane shakes off the weakness of grief, and repressing* Manuel, *who is about to reply to the* Officer, *steps forward with dignity.*)

Jane. Tell them by whose authority you come,
He died that death which best becomes a man,
Who is with keenest sense of conscious ill
And deep remorse assail'd, a wounded spirit.
A death that kills the noble and the brave,
And only them. He had no other wound.

1st Off. And shall I trust to this.

Jane. Do as thou wilt:
To one who can suspect my simple word
I have no more reply. Fulfil thine office.

1st Off. No, lady. I believe your honour'd word,
And will no further search.

Jane. I thank your courtesy: thanks, thanks to all!
My rev'rend mother, and ye honour'd maids;
Ye holy men, and you, my faithful friends;

146

The blessing of the afflicted rest with you:
And he, who to the wretched is most piteous,
Will recompense you. — Freberg, thou art good;
Remove the body of the friend you lov'd,
'Tis Rezenvelt I mean. Take thou this charge:
'Tis meet, that with his noble ancestors,
He lie entomb'd in honourable state.
And now, I have a sad request to make,
Nor will these holy sisters scorn my boon;
That I, within these sacred cloister walls,
May raise a humble, nameless tomb to him,
Who, but for one dark passion, one dire deed,
Had claim'd a record of as noble worth,
As e'er enrich'd the sculptur'd pedestal.

[EXEUNT.

FINIS.

Thomas Carlyle, 'Signs of the Times.' *Edinburgh Review* 49 (June 1829): 439–459.[1]

IT is no very good symptom either of nations or individuals, that they deal much in vaticination. Happy men are full of the present, for its bounty suffices them; and wise men also, for its duties engage them. Our grand business undoubtedly is, not to *see* what lies dimly at a distance, but to *do* what lies clearly at hand.

> Know'st thou *Yesterday*, its aim and reason?
> Work'st thou well *To-day*, for worthy things?
> Calmly wait the *Morrow's* hidden season,
> And fear not thou, what hap soe'er it brings![2]

But man's 'large discourse of reason' *will* look 'before and after;' and, impatient of the 'ignorant present time,' will indulge in anticipation far more than profits him.[3] Seldom can the unhappy be persuaded that the evil of the day is sufficient for it;[4] and the ambitious will not be content with present splendour — but paints yet more glorious triumphs, on the cloud-curtain of the future.

The case, however, is still worse with nations. For here the prophets are not one, but many; and each incites and confirms the other — so that the fatidical fury spreads wider and wider, till at last even a Saul must join in it.[5] For there is still a real magic in the action and reaction of minds on one another. The casual deliration of a few becomes, by this mysterious reverberation, the frenzy of many; men lose the use, not only of their understandings, but of their bodily senses; while the most obdurate, unbelieving hearts melt, like the rest, in the furnace where all are cast, as victims and as fuel. It is grievous to think, that this noble omnipotence of Sympathy has been so rarely the Aaron's-rod of Truth and Virtue,[6] and so often the Enchanter's-rod of Wickedness and Folly! No solitary miscreant, scarcely any solitary maniac, would venture on such actions and imaginations, as large communities of sane men have, in such circumstances, entertained as sound wisdom. Witness long scenes of the French Revolution! a whole people drunk with blood and arrogance — and then with terror and cruelty — and with desperation, and blood again! Levity is no protection against such visitations, nor the utmost earnestness of character.

---

1   This essay first appeared as article VII in this issue of the *Edinburgh Review*. Like all *Edinburgh Review* articles, it was ostensibly an anonymous review of other publications; like many *Edinburgh Review* articles, it makes no mention of these whatsoever. In its original form it had no title other than the details of the reviewed books, but 'Signs of the Times' appears as a running head at the top of each page. The title comes from Jesus's words in Matthew 16.3: 'O ye hypocrites, ye can discern the face of the sky; but can ye not discern the signs of the times?'.

2   This translates lines by Johann Wolfgang von Goethe, the German poet of the period, which appear on an engraving sent by Goethe to Carlyle in 1825.

3   This sentence combines a series of fragments from Shakespeare: *Hamlet* IV.iv.36–7 ('large discourse,/Looking before and after') and I.ii.150 ('discourse of reason'); and towards the end of *Macbeth* I.v ('This ignorant present').

4   Jesus again, in the Sermon on the Mount: 'Take therefore no thought for the morrow: for the morrow shall take thought for the thing of itself. Sufficient unto the day is the evil thereof' (Matthew 6.34).

5   Fatidical: prophetic. Before he is made King of Israel, Saul is given the gift of prophesy, and the people ask, 'Is Saul also among the prophets?' (I Samuel 10.11–12).

6   After the flight from Egypt, Aaron is chosen by God to be High Priest when his rod 'bloomed blossoms, and yielded almonds' (Numbers 17.8), and the rods of the other candidates did not.

The New England Puritan burns witches, wrestles for months with the horrors of Satan's invisible world, and all ghastly phantasms, the daily and hourly precursors of the Last Day; then suddenly bethinks him that he is frantic, weeps bitterly, prays contritely — and the history of that gloomy season lies behind him like a frightful dream.

And Old England too has had her share of such frenzies and panics; though happily, like other old maladies, they have grown milder of late: and since the days of Titus Oates, have mostly passed without loss of men's lives,[7] or indeed without much other loss than that of reason, for the time, in the sufferers. In this mitigated form, however, the distemper is of pretty regular recurrence — and may be reckoned on at intervals, like other natural visitations; so that reasonable men deal with it, as the Londoners do with their fogs — go cautiously out into the groping crowd, and patiently carry lanterns at noon; knowing, by a well-grounded faith, that the sun is still in existence, and will one day reappear. How often have we heard, for the last fifty years, that the country was wrecked, and fast sinking; whereas, up to this date, the country is entire and afloat! The 'State in Danger' is a condition of things, which we have witnessed a hundred times; and as for the church, it has seldom been out of 'danger' since we can remember it.

All men are aware, that the present is a crisis of this sort; and why it has become so. The repeal of the Test Acts, and then of the Catholic disabilities,[8] has struck many of their admirers with an indescribable astonishment. Those things seemed fixed and immovable — deep as the foundations of the world; and, lo! in a moment they have vanished, and their place knows them no more! Our worthy friends mistook the slumbering Leviathan for an island[9] — often as they had been assured, that Intolerance was, and could be, nothing but a Monster; and so, mooring under the lee, they had anchored comfortably in his scaly rind, thinking to take good cheer — as for some space they did. But now their Leviathan has suddenly dived under; and they can no longer be fastened in the stream of time; but must drift forward on it, even like the rest of the world — no very appalling fate, we think, could they but understand it; which, however, they will not yet, for a season. Their little island is gone; sunk deep amid confused eddies; and what is left worth caring for in the universe? What is it to them, that the great continents of the earth are still standing; and the polestar and all our loadstars, in the heavens, still shining and eternal? Their cherished little haven is gone, and they will not be comforted! And therefore, day after day, in all manner of periodical or perennial publications, the most lugubrious predictions are sent forth. The king has virtually abdicated; the church is a widow, without jointure;[10] public principle is gone; private honesty is going; society, in short, is fast falling in pieces; and a time of unmixed evil is come on us. At such a period, it was to be expected that the rage of prophecy should be more than usually excited. Accordingly, the Millennarians have come forth on the right hand, and the Millites on the left. The Fifth-monarchy men prophesy from the Bible, and the Utilitarians from Bentham. The one announce that the last of the seals

---

7   Titus Oates was the fabricator of a Catholic conspiracy to assassinate Charles II: between 1678 and 1681 at least 15 men were executed for involvement in this imaginary "Popish Plot" before it was exposed as a fraud.

8   The Test Acts, passed in the 1670s, barred non-conformist (i.e. non Church of England) protestants from various positions in public life in England, Wales and Ireland; draconian restrictions were placed on Catholics from 1698. The Test Act was repealed in 1828, and the last restrictions on Catholics were lifted in 1829.

9   Alluding to an episode in the voyages of St Brendan, in which the monks land on a whale, mistaking it for an island: the whale moves off when they light a cooking-fire.

10 Jointure was the property or income settled on an upper-class woman at her marriage to support her in the event of her husband's death.

is to be opened, positively, in the year 1860; and the other assures us, that 'the greatest happiness principle' is to make a heaven of earth, in a still shorter time.[11] We know these symptoms too well, to think it necessary or safe to interfere with them. Time and the hours will bring relief to all parties. The grand encourager of Delphic or other noises is — the Echo.[12] Left to themselves, they will soon dissipate, and die away in space.

Meanwhile, we too admit that the present is an important time — as all present time necessarily is. The poorest day that passes over us is the conflux of two Eternities! and is made up of currents that issue from the remotest Past, and flow onwards into the remotest Future. We were wise indeed, could we discern truly the signs of our own time; and, by knowledge of its wants and advantages, wisely adjust our own position in it. Let us then, instead of gazing idly into the obscure distance, look calmly around us, for a little, on the perplexed scene where we stand. Perhaps, on a more serious inspection, something of its perplexity will disappear, some of its distinctive characters, and deeper tendencies, more clearly reveal themselves; whereby our own relations to it, our own true aims and endeavours in it, may also become clearer.

Were we required to characterise this age of ours by any single epithet, we should be tempted to call it, not an Heroical, Devotional, Philosophical, or Moral Age, but, above all others, the Mechanical Age. It is the Age of Machinery, in every outward and inward sense of that word; the age which, with its whole undivided might, forwards, teaches and practises the great art of adapting means to ends. Nothing is now done directly, or by hand; all is by rule and calculated contrivance. For the simplest operation, some helps and accompaniments, some cunning, abbreviating process is in readiness. Our old modes of exertion are all discredited, and thrown aside. On every hand, the living artisan is driven from his workshop, to make room for a speedier, inanimate one. The shuttle drops from the fingers of the weaver, and falls into iron fingers that ply it faster.[13] The sailor furls his sail, and lays down his oar, and bids a strong, unwearied servant, on vaporous wings, bear him through the waters. Men have crossed oceans by steam; the Birmingham Fire-king has visited the fabulous East; and the genius of the Cape, were there any Camoens now to sing it, has again been alarmed, and with far stranger thunders than Gamas.[14] There is no end to machinery. Even the horse is stripped of his

---

11 The Evangelical Revival in the protestant churches in Britain in the early nineteenth century included a strong millenarian element: that is, a belief that Christ's return, followed by the end of the world, was imminent. The Book of Revelation mentions a Fifth Monarchy that would rule at this period (following on from the four empires of the ancient world) and a book with seven seals, the breaking of which in turn constitute a count-down to the Final Judgement. Carlyle parallels this with the considerably more rational thought of the political philosophers Jeremy Bentham (1743–1832) and James Mill (1773–1836). They had argued (Mill in a series of articles in the *Edinburgh Review*) that government policy should be determined by 'the greatest happiness of the greatest number' of its subjects, a doctrine known as Utilitarianism.

12 Delphic: prophetic, like the classical Greek oracle at Delphi.

13 Steam-powered looms for weaving cloth had been multiplying and improving since the start of the century: in 1829 they accounted for about half the cloth produced in Britain, and in the following decades would replace the hand-loom completely, and wipe out the cottage-based hand-loom weavers as a class.

14 The first commercial steamship began taking passengers from Glasgow to Greenock in 1812; by 1829 ocean-going ships were using steam-engines to supplement sails on Atlantic crossings, and one made it round Cape Horn to Calcutta in 1825. This sea-route to India was pioneered by the Portuguese sailor Vasco de Gama in 1497–9; he is celebrated, alongside other Portuguese heroes of the period, in the epic poem *The Lusiads* (1573) by Luís de Camões

harness, and finds a fleet fire-horse yoked in his stead.[15] Nay, we have an artist that hatches chickens by steam — the very brood-hen is to be superseded! For all earthly, and for some unearthly purposes, we have machines and mechanic furtherances; for mincing our cabbages; for casting us into magnetic sleep. We remove mountains, and make seas our smooth highway; nothing can resist us. We war with rude nature; and, by our resistless engines, come off always victorious, and loaded with spoils.

What wonderful accessions have thus been made, and are still making, to the physical power of mankind; how much better fed, clothed, lodged, and, in all outward respects, accommodated, men now are, or might be, by a given quantity of labour, is a grateful reflection which forces itself on every one. What changes, too, this addition of power is introducing into the social system; how wealth has more and more increased, and at the same time gathered itself more and more into masses, strangely altering the old relations, and increasing the distance between the rich and the poor, will be a question for Political Economists — and a much more complex and important one than any they have yet engaged with. But leaving these matters for the present, let us observe how the mechanical genius of our time has diffused itself into quite other provinces. Not the external and physical alone is now managed by machinery, but the internal and spiritual also. Here, too, nothing follows its spontaneous course, nothing is left to be accomplished by old, natural methods. Every thing has its cunningly devised implements, its pre-established apparatus; it is not done by hand, but by machinery. Thus we have machines for Education: Lancastrian machines; Hamiltonian machines — monitors, maps and emblems.[16] Instruction, that mysterious communing of Wisdom with Ignorance, is no longer an indefinable tentative process, requiring a study of individual aptitudes, and a perpetual variation of means and methods, to attain the same end; but a secure, universal, straightforward business, to be conducted in the gross, by proper mechanism, with such intellect as comes to hand. Then, we have Religious machines, of all imaginable varieties — the Bible Society, professing a far higher and heavenly structure, is found, on enquiry, to be altogether an earthly contrivance,[17] supported by collection of monies, by fomenting of vanities, by puffing, intrigue and chicane — and yet, in effect, a very excellent machine for converting the heathen. It is the same in all other departments. Has any man, or any society of men, a truth to speak, a piece of spiritual work to do, they can nowise proceed at once, and with the mere natural organs, but must first call a public meeting, appoint committees, issue prospectuses, eat a public dinner; in a word, construct or borrow machinery, wherewith to speak it and do it. Without machinery they were hopeless, helpless — a colony of Hindoo weavers squatting in the heart of Lancashire.[18] Then every machine must have its moving power, in some of the great currents of society: Every

---

(known as Camoens in English). Birmingham appears here as a hotbed of engineering innovation.

15 At the time of Carlyle's writing in 1829, steam locomotives were already used to pull coal and ore from mines to ironworks. The first passenger railway, the Liverpool and Manchester, opened the following year.

16 Carlyle alludes to two educational reformers: Joseph Lancaster (1778–1838), whose methods included the teaching of younger by older pupils (monitors), and James Hamilton (1769–1831), who developed a new method of teaching languages.

17 The British and Foreign Bible Society, an Evangelical missionary organisation, was founded in 1804.

18 As an image of irrelevance, this has a particular poignancy. The Bengali textile industry had expanded vastly since the mid 17th century to meet demand from Britain; it was wiped out by the cheaper produce of steam-powered production in, above all, Lancashire.

little sect among us, Unitarians, Utilitarians, Anabaptists, Phrenologists,[19] must each have its periodical, its monthly or quarterly magazine—hanging out, like its windmill, into the *popularis aura*,[20] to grind meal for the society.

With individuals, in like manner, natural strength avails little. No individual now hopes to accomplish the poorest enterprise single-handed, and without mechanical aids; he must make interest with some existing corporation, and till his field with their oxen. In these days, more emphatically than ever, 'to live, signifies to unite with a party, or to make one.' Philosophy, Science, Art, Literature, all depend on machinery. No Newton, by silent meditation, now discovers the system of the world from the falling of an apple; but some quite other than Newton stands in his Museum, his Scientific Institution, and behind whole batteries of retorts, digesters, and galvanic piles, imperatively 'interrogates Nature,'[21]—who, however, shows no haste to answer. In defect of Raphaels, and Angelos, and Mozarts, we have Royal Academies of Painting, Sculpture, Music;[22] whereby the languishing spirit of Art may be strengthened by the more generous diet of a Public Kitchen. Literature, too, has its Paternoster-row mechanism,[23] its Trade-dinners, its Editorial conclaves, and huge subterranean, puffing bellows; so that books are not only printed, but, in a great measure, written and sold, by machinery. National culture, spiritual benefit of all sorts, is under the same management. No Queen Christina, in these times, needs to send for her Descartes; no King Frederick for his Voltaire,[24] and painfully nourish him with pensions and flattery: But any sovereign of taste, who wishes to enlighten his people, has only to impose a new tax, and with the proceeds establish Philosophic Institutes. Hence the Royal and Imperial Societies, the Bibliothèques, Glypcothèques,[25] Technothèques, which front us in all capital cities, like so many well-finished hives, to which it is expected the stray agencies of Wisdom will swarm of their own accord, and hive and make honey. In like manner, among ourselves, when it is thought that religion is declining, we have only to vote half-a-million's worth of bricks and mortar, and build new churches. In Ireland, it seems they have gone still farther—having actually established a 'Penny-a-week Purgatory Society!' Thus does the Genius of Mechanism stand by to help us in all difficulties and emergencies; and, with his iron back, bears all our burdens.

---

19 The 'sects' mentioned here are a heterogeneous bunch: the Anabaptists are a very old Protestant sect, the Unitarians, as a denomination, a fairly new one. Phrenology was a pseudo-science which held that the shape of the skull was a guide to personality.

20 *Popularis aura*: public opinion.

21 Isaac Newton (1643–1727), mathematician and discoverer of universal laws of motion. 'Galvanic piles' are what we would now call electric batteries.

22 In defect of: 'in default of, for want of' (*OED*). In Britain, the Royal Academy of Arts was founded in 1768; of Music in 1822. In France, the Royal Academy of Painting and Sculpture dates back to 1648.

23 Paternoster Row was a centre of the London publishing trade. The following reference to bellows depends on the colloquial expression for promoting books through good reviews, 'puffing'. The *Edinburgh Review* saw itself as above all that kind of thing.

24 The paradigm cases of Enlightenment thinkers receiving patronage from 'enlightened' absolutist rulers: Queen Christina of Sweden invited Descartes (see below) to her court in 1649 (the Baltic winter killed him within six months); Voltaire (1694–1778) lasted three years (1750–52) with Frederick the Great of Prussia before falling out with his people and fleeing back to France.

25 A bibliothèque is a library: Carlyle invents the two following words analogously with it. Glypcothèques: in ancient Greek, *glyphikos* means 'to do with carving', so Carlyle might be thinking of a sculpture gallery in coining this word.

These things, which we state lightly enough here, are yet of deep import, and indicate a mighty change in our whole manner of existence. For the same habit regulates, not our modes of action alone, but our modes of thought and feeling. Men are grown mechanical in head and in heart, as well as in hand. They have lost faith in individual endeavour, and in natural force, of any kind. Not for internal perfection, but for external combinations and arrangements, for institutions, constitutions — for Mechanism of one sort or other, do they hope and struggle. Their whole efforts, attachments, opinions, turn on mechanism, and are of a mechanical character.

We may trace this tendency, we think, very distinctly, in all the great manifestations of our time; in its intellectual aspect, the studies it most favours, and its manner of conducting them; in its practical aspects, its politics, arts, religion, morals; in the whole sources, and throughout the whole currents, of its spiritual, no less than its material activity.

Consider, for example, the state of Science generally, in Europe, at this period. It is admitted, on all sides, that the Metaphysical and Moral Sciences are falling into decay, while the Physical are engrossing, every day, more respect and attention. In most of the European nations there is now no such thing as a Science of Mind; only more or less advancement in the general science, or the special sciences, of matter. The French were the first to desert this school of Metaphysics; and though they have lately affected to revive it, it has yet no signs of vitality. The land of Malebranche, Pascal, Descartes, and Fenelon, has now only its Cousins and Villemains;[26] while, in the department of Physics, it reckons far other names. Among ourselves, the Philosophy of Mind, after a rickety infancy, which never reached the vigour of manhood, fell suddenly into decay, languished, and finally died out, with its last amiable cultivator, Professor Stewart.[27] In no nation but Germany has any decisive effort been made in psychological science; not to speak of any decisive result.[28] The science of the age, in short, is physical, chemical, physiological, and, in all shapes, mechanical. Our favourite Mathematics, the highly prized exponent of all these other sciences, has also become more and more mechanical. Excellence, in what is called its higher departments, depends less on natural genius, than on acquired expertness in wielding its machinery. Without undervaluing the wonderful results which a Lagrange, or Laplace, educes by means of it,[29] we may remark, that its calculus, differential and integral, is little else than a more cunningly-constructed arithmetical mill, where the factors being put in, are, as it were, ground into the true product, under cover, and without other effort on our part, than steady turning of the handle. We have more Mathematics certainly than ever; but

---

26 Nicolas Malebranche (1638–1715) and Blaise Pascal (1623–62) both combined pioneering work in rationalist philosophy and mathematics with religious piety; René Descartes (1596–1650), whose rationalist philosophy included an attempt to prove the existence of God; François Fénelon (1651–1715), Catholic theologian and critic of the French monarchy. Carlyle contrasts these giants of early modern French thought with the more derivative work of contemporary French writers like philosopher Victor Cousin (1792–1867) and literary historian Abel-François Villemain (1790–1870).

27 Dugald Stewart (1753–1828), influential professor of Moral Philosophy at Edinburgh 1785–1810, but a populariser of the Scottish tradition in philosophy rather than one of its innovators.

28 Carlyle has in mind German idealism, to which his own thinking owes a great deal; especially Immanuel Kant (1724 –1804) and G.W.F. Hegel (1770–1831).

29 Joseph-Louis Lagrange (1736 –1813), pioneer of calculus in its application to mechanics; Pierre-Simon Laplace, author of *Mécanique Céleste* (1799–1825) which applied similar ideas to the solar system.

less Mathesis.[30] Archimedes and Plato could not have read the *Méchanique Céleste*; but neither would the whole French Institute see aught in that saying, 'God geometrises!' but a sentimental rodomontade.[31]

From Locke's time downwards, our whole Metaphysics have been physical; not a spiritual Philosophy, but a material one. The singular estimation in which his Essay was so long held as a scientific work, (for the character of the man entitled all he said to veneration,) will one day be thought a curious indication of the spirit of these times.[32] His whole doctrine is mechanical, in its aim and origin, in its method and its results. It is a mere discussion concerning the origin of our consciousness, or ideas, or whatever else they are called; a genetic history of what we see *in* the mind. But the grand secrets of Necessity and Freewill, of the mind's vital or non-vital dependence on matter, of our mysterious relations to Time and Space, to God, to the universe, are not, in the faintest degree, touched on in their enquiries; and seem not to have the smallest connexion with them.

The last class of our Scotch Metaphysicians had a dim notion that much of this was wrong; but they knew not how to right it. The school of Reid had also from the first taken a mechanical course, not seeing any other. The singular conclusions at which Hume, setting out from their admitted premises, was arriving, brought this school into being; they let loose Instinct, as an undiscriminating bandog, to guard them against these conclusions—they tugged lustily at the logical chain by which Hume was so coldly towing them and the world into bottomless abysses of Atheism and Fatalism.[33] But the chain somehow snapped between them; and the issue has been that nobody now cares about either—any more than about Hartley's, Darwin's, or Priestley's contemporaneous doings in England.[34] Hartley's vibrations and vibratiuncles one would think were material and mechanical enough; but our continental neighbours have gone still farther. One of their philosophers has lately discovered, that 'as the liver secretes bile, so does the brain secrete thought;' which astonishing discovery Dr. Cabanis, more lately still, in his *Rapports du Physique el du Morale de l'Homme*, has pushed into its minutest developements.[35] The metaphysical philosophy of this last enquirer is certainly no shadowy or unsubstantial one. He fairly lays open our moral structure with

---

30 *Mathesis* in Greek means the *action* of learning (*OED*).
31 The phrase is attributed to Plato by the Roman historian Plutarch; the Greek philosopher does equate geometry with a knowledge of the divine in his surviving writings. Rodomontade: 'a vainglorious brag or boast' (*OED*).
32 The English philosopher John Locke (1632–1704) published *An Essay Concerning Human Understanding* in 1690. Where Descartes and his followers ground truth on the operation of reason on its own, Locke finds the origin of knowledge in the world as we experience it through our senses, from which we ultimately derive all the ideas with which we think (empiricism).
33 David Hume (1711–76) in *A Treatise of Human Nature* (1739–40) argued that, on Locke's definition of knowledge, we cannot *know* the existence of the self, or of the world, or of relations of cause and effect. Thomas Reid (1710–1796) attempted to refute Hume's scepticism with a 'Common Sense' school of epistemology. Hume was also a notorious atheist.
34 David Hartley (1705–57) and Joseph Priestley (1733–1804), both, among their various other work, tended to understand human thought and experience in material terms, as a movement of particles, or an analogous 'association of ideas'. Erasmus Darwin (1731–1802) explored the way in which living organisms adapt themselves to their environments: perhaps another instance, for Carlyle, of life being determined by mere material circumstances.
35 Pierre Jean George Cabanis (1757–1808). *On the Relation between the Physical and Moral Aspects of Man* (1802) tries to reduce psychology to a branch of physiology.

his dissecting-knives and real metal probes; and exhibits it to the inspection of mankind, by Leuwenhoek microscopes and inflation with the anatomical blowpipe.[36] Thought, he is inclined to hold, is still secreted by the brain; but then Poetry and Religion (and it is really worth knowing) are 'a product of the smaller intestines!' We have the greatest admiration for this learned doctor: with what scientific stoicism he walks through the land of wonders, unwondering—like a wise man through some huge, gaudy, imposing Vauxhall, whose fire-works, cascades, and symphonies, the vulgar may enjoy and believe in—but where he finds nothing real but the saltpetre, pasteboard and catgut.[37] His book may be regarded as the ultimatum of mechanical metaphysics in our time: a remarkable realisation of what in Martinus Scriblerus was still only an idea, that 'as the jack had a meat-roasting quality, so had the body a thinking quality,'—upon the strength of which the Nurembergers were to build a wood and leather man, 'who should reason as well as most country parsons.'[38] Vaucanson did indeed make a wooden duck, that seemed to eat and digest; but that bold scheme of the Nurembergers remained for a more modern virtuoso.[39]

This condition of the two great departments of knowledge; the outward, cultivated exclusively on mechanical principles—the inward finally abandoned, because, cultivated on such principles, it is found to yield no result— sufficiently indicates the intellectual bias of our time, its all-pervading disposition towards that line of inquiry. In fact, an inward persuasion has long been diffusing itself, and now and then even comes to utterance. That, except the external, there are no true sciences; that to the inward world (if there be any) our only conceivable road is through the outward; that, in short, what cannot be investigated and understood mechanically, cannot be investigated and understood at all. We advert the more particularly to these intellectual propensities, as to prominent symptoms of our age; because Opinion is at all times doubly related to Action, first as cause, then as effect; and the speculative tendency of any age, will therefore give us, on the whole, the best indications of its practical tendency.

Nowhere, for example, is the deep, almost exclusive faith, we have in Mechanism, more visible than in the Politics of this time. Civil government does, by its nature, include much that is mechanical, and must be treated accordingly. We term it indeed, in ordinary language, the Machine of Society, and talk of it as the grand working wheel from which all private machines must derive, or to which they must adapt, their movements. Considered merely as a metaphor, all this is well enough; but here, as in so many other cases, the 'foam hardens itself into a shell,' and the shadow we have wantonly evoked stands terrible before us, and will not depart at our bidding. Government includes much also that is not mechanical, and cannot be treated mechanically; of which latter truth, as appears to us, the political speculations and exertions of our time are taking less and less cognisance.

36 Antony van Leuwenhoek (1632 –1723) was the first microbiologist.
37 Vauxhall was a pleasure garden on the south bank of the Thames in London, which put on the kinds of entertainments mentioned here. Saltpetre is an ingredient in gunpowder (in the fireworks); pasteboard is used to construct stage scenery; and catgut provided the strings for musical instruments.
38 A jack is a machine for turning a spit. *Memoirs of Martinus Scriblerus* (1741) was a satirical pseudo-autobiography written by a group of writers including Jonathan Swift and Alexander Pope. It includes a description of an attempt, at Nuremberg, to construct a mechanical man capable of thought.
39 Virtuoso: here, scientist or scholar. The eighteenth century was fascinated by clockwork automatons: Jacques de Vaucanson (1709–1782) made the most sophisticated ones, including the duck mentioned here.

Nay, in the very outset, we might note the mighty interest taken in *mere political arrangements,* as itself the sign of a mechanical age. The whole discontent of Europe takes this direction. The deep, strong cry of all civilised nations—a cry which, every one now sees, must and will be answered, is, Give us a reform of Government! A good structure of legislation—a proper check upon the executive—a wise arrangement of the judiciary, is *all* that is wanting for human happiness. The Philosopher of this age is not a Socrates, a Plato, a Hooker, or Taylor,[40] who inculcates on men the necessity and infinite worth of moral goodness, the great truth that our happiness depends on the mind which is within us, and not on the circumstances which are without us; but a Smith, a De Lolme,[41] a Bentham, who chiefly inculcates the reverse of this—that our happiness depends entirely on external circumstances; nay that the strength and dignity of the mind within us is itself the creature and consequence of these. Were the laws, the government, in good order, all were well with us; the rest would care for itself! Dissentients from this opinion, expressed or implied, are now rarely to he met with; widely and angrily as men differ in its application, the principle is admitted by all.

Equally mechanical, and of equal simplicity, are the methods proposed by both parties for completing or securing this all-sufficient perfection of arrangement. It is no longer the moral, religious, spiritual condition of the people that is our concern, but their physical, practical, economical condition, as regulated by public laws. Thus is the Body-politic more than ever worshipped and tended: But the Soul-politic less than ever. Love of country, in any high or generous sense, in any other than an almost animal sense, or mere habit, has little importance attached to it in such reforms, or in the opposition shown them. Men are to be guided only by their self-interests. Good government is a good balancing of these: and, except a keen eye and appetite for self-interest, requires no virtue in any quarter. To both parties it is emphatically a machine: to the discontented, a 'taxing-machine;' to the contented, a 'machine for securing property.' Its duties and its faults are not those of a father, but of an active parish constable.[42]

Thus it is by the mere condition of the machine; by preserving it untouched, or else by re-constructing it, and oiling it anew, that man's salvation as a social being is to be insured and indefinitely promoted. Contrive the fabric of law aright, and without farther effort on your part, that divine spirit of freedom which all hearts venerate and long for, will of herself come to inhabit it; and under her healing wings every noxious influence will wither, every good and salutary one more and more expand. Nay, so devoted are we to this principle, and at the same time so curiously mechanical, that a new trade, specially grounded on it, has arisen among us, under the name of 'Codification,' or code-making in the abstract;[43] whereby any people, for a reasonable consideration, may be accommodated with a patent code—more easily than curious individuals with patent breeches, for the people does *not* need to be measured first.

To us who live in the midst of all this, and see continually the faith, hope and practice of every one founded on Mechanism of one kind or other, it is apt to seem quite natural, and as if it could never have been otherwise. Nevertheless, if we recollect or reflect a

---

40 Richard Hooker (1554–1653), Anglican theologian; I cannot find a likely candidate for 'Taylor'.

41 Adam Smith (1723–1790), moral philosopher and political economist; Jean-Louis de Lolme (1741–1804), political theorist, who in 1775 advocated recasting the French constitution along British lines.

42 Carlyle is describing one version of the 'liberal' state, in which government's duties extend no further than to protect property and enforce contracts; often referred to a the 'night watchman' version of the state.

43 'Code' here meaning, of course, *legal* code or constitution.

little, we shall find both that it has been, and might again be otherwise. The domain of Mechanism, — meaning thereby political, ecclesiastical or other outward establishments, — was once considered as embracing, and we are persuaded can at any time embrace, but a limited portion of man's interests, and by no means the highest portion.

To speak a little pedantically, there is a science of *Dynamics* in man's fortunes and nature, as well as of *Mechanics*. There is a science which treats of, and practically addresses, the primary, unmodified forces and energies of man, the mysterious springs of Love, and Fear, and Wonder, of Enthusiasm, Poetry, Religion, all which have a truly vital and *infinite* character; as well as a science which practically addresses the finite, modified developments of these, when they take the shape of immediate 'motives,' as hope of reward, or as fear of punishment.

Now it is certain, that in former times the wise men, the enlightened lovers of their kind, who appeared generally as Moralists, Poets or Priests, did, without neglecting the Mechanical province, deal chiefly with the Dynamical; applying themselves chiefly to regulate, increase and purify the inward primary powers of man; and fancying that herein lay the main difficulty, and the best service they could undertake. But a wide difference is manifest in our age. For the wise men, who now appear as Political Philosophers, deal exclusively with the Mechanical province; and occupying themselves in counting-up and estimating men's motives, strive by curious checking and balancing, and other adjustments of Profit and Loss, to guide them to their true advantage: while, unfortunately, those same 'motives' are so innumerable, and so variable in every individual, that no really useful conclusion can ever be drawn from their enumeration. But though Mechanism, wisely contrived, has done much for man, in a social and moral point of view, we cannot be persuaded that it has ever been the chief source of his worth or happiness. Consider the great elements of human enjoyment, the attainments and possessions that exalt man's life to its present height, and see what part of these he owes to institutions, to Mechanism of any kind; and what to the instinctive, unbounded force, which Nature herself lent him, and still continues to him. Shall we say, for example, that Science and Art are indebted principally to the founders of Schools and Universities? Did not Science originate rather, and gain advancement, in the obscure closets of the Roger Bacons, Keplers, Newtons;[44] in the workshops of the Fausts and the Watts;[45] — wherever, and in what guise soever Nature, from the first times downwards, had sent a gifted spirit upon the earth? Again, were Homer and Shakspeare members of any beneficed guild, or made Poets by means of it? Was Painting and Sculpture created by forethought, brought into the world by institutions for that end? No; Science and Art have, from first to last, been the free gift of Nature; an unsolicited, unexpected gift — often even a fatal one. These things rose up, as it were, by spontaneous growth, in the free soil and sunshine of Nature. They were not planted or grafted, nor even greatly multiplied or improved by the culture or manuring of institutions. Generally speaking, they have derived only partial help from these; often enough have suffered damage. They made constitutions for themselves. They originated in the Dynamical nature of man, not in his Mechanical nature.

Or, to take an infinitely higher instance, that of the Christian Religion, which, under every theory of it, in the believing or unbelieving mind, must ever be regarded

---

44 Roger Bacon (d.1294), Franciscan friar and one of the first to promulgate the scientific knowledge of the Islamic world in the west; Johannes Kepler (1571-1630), discoverer of the laws of planetary motion.

45 An odd conjunction of the fictional and the contemporary: Faust is the frustrated polymath of the 16th-century German legend who sells his soul to the devil in exchange for knowledge; James Watt (1736–1819) the engineer who first developed practicable steam engines.

as the crowning glory, or rather the life and soul, of our whole modern culture: How did Christianity arise and spread abroad among men? Was it by institutions, and establishments, and well-arranged systems of mechanism? Not so; on the contrary, in all past and existing institutions for those ends, its divine spirit has invariably been found to languish and decay. It arose in the mystic deeps of man's soul; and was spread abroad by the 'preaching of the word,' by simple, altogether natural and individual efforts; and flew, like hallowed fire, from heart to heart, till all were purified and illuminated by it; and its heavenly light shone, as it still shines, and as sun or star will ever shine, through the whole dark destinies of man. Here again was no Mechanism; man's highest attainment was accomplished, Dynamically, not Mechanically. Nay, we will venture to say, that no high attainment, not even any far-extending movement among men, was ever accomplished otherwise. Strange as it may seem, if we read History with any degree of thoughtfulness, we shall find that the checks and balances of Profit and Loss have never been the grand agents with men; that they have never been roused into deep, thorough, all-pervading efforts by any computable prospect of Profit and Loss, for any visible, finite object; but always for some invisible and infinite one. The Crusades took their rise in Religion; their visible object was, commercially speaking, worth nothing. It was the boundless, Invisible world that was laid bare in the imaginations of those men; and in its burning light, the visible shrunk as a scroll. Not mechanical, nor produced by mechanical means, was this vast movement. No dining at Freemasons' Tavern,[46] with the other long train of modern machinery; no cunning reconciliation of 'vested interests,' was required here: only the passionate voice of one man, the rapt soul looking through the eyes of one man;[47] and rugged, steel-clad Europe trembled beneath his words, and followed him whither he listed. In later ages, it was still the same. The Reformation had an invisible, mystic, and ideal aim; the result was indeed to be embodied in external things; but its spirit, its worth, was internal, invisible, infinite. Our English Revolution, too, originated in Religion.[48] Men did battle, even in those days, not for Purse sake, but for Conscience sake. Nay, in our own days, it is no way different. The French Revolution itself had something higher in it than cheap bread and a Habeas-corpus act.[49] Here too was an Idea; a Dynamic, not a Mechanic force. It was a struggle, though a blind and at last an insane one, for the infinite, divine nature of Right, of Freedom, of Country.

Thus does man, in every age, vindicate, consciously or unconsciously, his celestial birthright. Thus does Nature hold on her wondrous, unquestionable course; and all our systems and theories are but so many froth-eddies or sand-banks, which from time to time she casts up and washes away. When we can drain the Ocean into mill-ponds, and bottle up the Force of Gravity, to be sold by retail, in our gas-jars; then may we hope to comprehend the infinitudes of man's soul under formulas of Profit and Loss; and rule over this too, as over a patent engine, by checks, and valves, and balances.

Nay, even with regard to Government itself, can it be necessary to remind any one that Freedom, without which indeed all spiritual life is impossible, depends on

---

46 This was the regular meeting place of a debating society in London.
47 The 'one man' is presumably Pope Urban II, who organised the First Crusade in 1095; but the 'rapt' and 'passionate' voice might more plausibly belong to St. Bernard of Clairvaux, zealous promoter of the Second Crusade in 1146-7.
48 Carlyle is probably thinking of the accession of William III in 1688, commonly referred to as 'the Revolution' in his time. But this was, in England at least, a peaceful process; unlike the Civil Wars of the 1640s, which gave more opportunity for giving 'battle' in the literal sense.
49 'Habeas Corpus' names the right, originating in English Common Law, to freedom from arbitrary detention by the state.

infinitely more complex influences than either the extension or the curtailment of the 'democratic interest?' Who is there that 'taking the high *priori* road,' shall point out what these influences are;[50] what deep, subtle, inextricably entangled influences they have been, and may be? For man is not the creature and product of Mechanism; but, in a far truer sense, its creator and producer: it is the noble people that makes the noble Government; rather than conversely. On the whole, Institutions are much; but they are not all. The freest and highest spirits of the world have often been found under strange outward circumstances: Saint Paul and his brother Apostles were politically slaves; Epictetus was personally one.[51] Again, forget the influences of Chivalry and Religion, and ask, — what countries produced Columbus and Las Casas? Or, descending from virtue and heroism to mere energy and spiritual talent: Cortes, Pizarro, Alba, Ximenes?[52] The Spaniards of the sixteenth century were indisputably the noblest nation of Europe; yet they had the Inquisition and Philip II. They have the same government at this day; and are the lowest nation. The Dutch, too, have retained their old constitution; but no Siege of Leyden, no William the Silent, not even an Egmont or De Witt, any longer appears among them.[53] With ourselves, also, where much has changed, effect has nowise followed cause, as it should have done: two centuries ago, the Commons' Speaker addressed Queen Elizabeth on bended knees, happy that the virago's foot did not even smite him; yet the people were then governed, not by a Castlereagh, but by a Burghley; they had their Shakspeare and Philip Sidney, where we have our Sheridan Knowles and Beau Brummel.[54]

These and the like facts are so familiar, the truths which they preach so obvious, and have in all past times been so universally believed and acted on, that we should almost feel ashamed for repeating them; were it not that, on every hand, the memory of them seems to have passed away, or at best died into a faint tradition, of no value as a practical principle. To judge by the loud clamour of our Constitution-builders,

50 An '*a priori*' argument is one from first principles. Carlyle is quoting Pope's couplet on philosophical scepticism in *The Dunciad* book IV ll.471–2: 'We nobly take the high Priori road/And reason downward, till we doubt of God.'
51 Epictetus (55 –135), Greek Stoic philosopher. The Apostle Paul was in fact a Roman citizen.
52 'Alba' is Fernando, duke of Alba, Spain's ruthless enforcer against the rebels in the Low Countries from 1567. The others are all men involved in the Spanish crown's conquests in the Americas in the 16th Century: Christopher Columbus (d.1506), their Genoese admiral; Hernán Cortes (d.1547) and Francisco Pizarro (d.1541), conquistador generals; Fortún Ximenes (d.1533), first European settler in Baja California. The odd one out is Bartolomé de las Casas (1484–1566), the Dominican priest who campaigned to stop the slaughter and enslavement of the native people.
53 William I, Prince of Orange (d.1584), leader of the Dutch revolt against Spanish rule in the 1560s; Lamoral, Count of Egmont (d.1568), Flemish statesman whose execution by the Duke of Alba helped spark the revolt; Johan de Witt (d.1672), prime minister presiding over the rise of the now independent United Provinces to imperial wealth, involving several wars with England. Leiden held out heroically against a Spanish siege in 1573–4.
54 William Cecil, Baron Burghley (d.1598), one of Elizabeth I's closest ministers for nearly 40 years; Robert Stewart, Viscount Castlereagh, was Secretary of State for War and the Colonies during the conflict with Napoleon, and influential in the post-war reconstruction of the European order, but committed suicide in 1822 by cutting his throat. James Sheridan Knowles (1759-1840) was a successful actor and playwright in the 1820s and 30s. Sir Philip Sidney (1554-86) is best known now as a poet, but figures here as an ideal type of the English gentleman (also a courtier and soldier, he died fighting against the Spanish in the Low Countries), in contrast to George 'Beau' Brummell (d.1840), the quintessential Regency gambler and dandy.

Statists, Economists, directors, creators, reformers of Public Societies; in a word, all manner of Mechanists, from the Cartwright up to the Code-maker; and by the nearly total silence of all Preachers and Teachers who should give a voice to Poetry, Religion and Morality, we might fancy either that man's Dynamical nature was, to all spiritual intents, extinct—or else so perfected, that nothing more was to be made of it by the old means; and henceforth only in his Mechanical contrivances did any hope exist for him.

To define the limits of these two departments of man's activity, which work into one another, and by means of one another, so intricately and inseparably, were by its nature an impossible attempt. Their relative importance, even to the wisest mind, will vary in different times, according to the special wants and dispositions of those times. Meanwhile, it seems clear enough that only in the right co-ordination of the two, and the vigorous forwarding of *both*, does our true line of action lie. Undue cultivation of the inward or Dynamical province leads to idle, visionary, impracticable courses, and, especially in rude eras, to Superstition and Fanaticism, with their long train of baleful and well-known evils. Undue cultivation of the outward, again, though less immediately prejudicial, and even for the time productive of many palpable benefits, must, in the long-run, by destroying Moral Force, which is the parent of all other Force, prove not less certainly, and perhaps still more hopelessly, pernicious. This, we take it, is the grand characteristic of our age. By our skill in Mechanism, it has come to pass that, in the management of external things we excel all other ages; while in whatever respects the pure moral nature, in true dignity of soul and character, we are perhaps inferior to most civilised ages.

In fact, if we look deeper, we shall find that this faith in Mechanism has now struck its roots down into man's most intimate, primary sources of conviction; and is thence sending up, over his whole life and activity, innumerable stems—fruit-bearing and poison-bearing. The truth is, men have lost their belief in the Invisible, and believe, and hope, and work only in the Visible; or, to speak it in other words, This is not a Religious age. Only the material, the immediately practical, not the divine and spiritual, is important to us. The infinite, absolute character of Virtue has passed into a finite, conditional one; it is no longer a worship of the Beautiful and Good; but a calculation of the Profitable. Worship, indeed, in any sense, is not recognised among us, or is mechanically explained into Fear of pain, or Hope of pleasure. Our true Deity is Mechanism. It has subdued external Nature for us, and, we think, it will do all other things. We are Giants in physical power: in a deeper than metaphorical sense, we are Titans,[55] that strive, by heaping mountain on mountain, to conquer Heaven also.

The strong mechanical character, so visible in the spiritual pursuits and methods of this age, may be traced much farther into the condition and prevailing disposition of our spiritual nature itself. Consider, for example, the general fashion of Intellect in this era. Intellect, the power man has of knowing and believing, is now nearly synonymous with Logic, or the mere power of arranging and communicating. Its implement is not Meditation, but Argument. 'Cause and effect' is almost the only category under which we look at, and work with, all Nature. Our first question with regard to any object is not, What is it? but, How is it? We are no longer instinctively driven to apprehend, and lay to heart, what is Good and Lovely, but rather to enquire, as onlookers, how it is produced, whence it comes, whither it goes? Our favourite Philosophers have no love and no hatred; they stand among us not to do, nor to create any thing, but as a sort of Logic-mills, to grind out the true causes and effects of all that is done and created. To

---

55 The Titans, in Greek mythology, were the original gods, against whom the gods of Mount Olympus went to war.

the eye of a Smith, a Hume or a Constant, all is well that works quietly.[56] An Order of Ignatius Loyola, a Presbyterianism of John Knox, a Wickliffe, or a Henry the Eighth,[57] are simply so many mechanical phenomena, caused or causing.

The *Euphuist* of our day differs much from his pleasant predecessors.[58] An intellectual dapperling of these times boasts chiefly of his irresistible perspicacity, his 'dwelling in the daylight of truth,' and so forth; which, on examination, turns out to be a dwelling in the *rush*-light of 'closet-logic,'[59] and a deep unconsciousness that there is any other light to dwell in; or any other objects to survey with it. Wonder, indeed, is, on all hands, dying out: it is the sign of uncultivation to wonder. Speak to any small man of a high, majestic Reformation, of a high, majestic Luther; and forthwith he sets about 'accounting' for it! how the 'circumstances of the time' called for such a character, and found him, we suppose, standing girt and road-ready, to do its errand; how the 'circumstances of the time' created, fashioned, floated him quietly along into the result; how, in short, this small man, had he been there, could have performed the like himself! For it is the 'force of circumstances' that does everything; the force of one man can do nothing. Now all this is grounded on little more than a metaphor. We figure Society as a 'Machine,' and that mind is opposed to mind, as body is to body; whereby two, or at most ten, little minds must be stronger than one great mind. Notable absurdity! For the plain truth, very plain, we think is, that minds are opposed to minds in quite a different way; and *one* man that has a higher Wisdom, a hitherto unknown spiritual Truth in him, is stronger, not than ten men that have it not, or than ten thousand, but than *all* men that have it not; and stands among them with a quite ethereal, angelic power, as with a sword out of Heaven's own armoury, sky-tempered, which no buckler, and no tower of brass, will finally withstand.

But to us, in these times, such considerations rarely occur. We enjoy, we see nothing by direct vision; but only by reflexion, and in anatomical dismemberment. Like Sir Hudibras,[60] for every Why we must have a Wherefore. We have our little *theory* on all human and divine things. Poetry, the workings of genius itself, which in all times, with one or another meaning, has been called Inspiration, and held to be mysterious and inscrutable, is no longer without its scientific exposition. The building of the lofty rhyme is like any other masonry or bricklaying: we have theories of its rise, height, decline and fall — which latter, it would seem, is now near, among all people.[61] Of our 'Theories of Taste,' as they are called, wherein the deep, infinite, unspeakable Love

56 Benjamin Constant (1767–1830), French liberal political philosopher. What Constant has in common with Smith and Hume is a belief that the commercial basis of modern society makes its politics completely different from previous historical models: liberty now consists in the secure enjoyment of private goods (family or business) rather that in rights of participation in public politics that must be noisily, often violently, defended (as in the ancient Roman Republic and its French imitator in the 1790s).

57 Ignatius Loyola (1491–1556), founder of the Jesuit order as an intellectual counter-force to the Protestant reformation; John Knox (c.1510–1572), preacher and leader of the Scottish Reformation; John Wycliffe (c.1325–1384), first translator of the Bible into English and critic of the medieval church; Henry VIII of England (1491–1547), the king who forced the English church to split from Rome.

58 A euphuist is 16th-century verbal show-off, delighting in similes and alliteration.

59 Lighting in the homes of the poor consisted in a metal lamp full of oil, with a rush as a wick.

60 The hero of the mock-heroic narrative poem *Hudibras* (1663–4, 1678) by Samuel Butler, who answers every question by asking another one.

61 Carlyle might be thinking of Thomas Love Peacock's *Four Ages of Poetry* (1820) which takes something like this view.

of Wisdom and Beauty, which dwells in all men, is 'explained,' made mechanically visible, from 'Association,' and the like, why should we say anything?[62] Hume has written us a 'Natural History of Religion;'[63] in which one Natural History, all the rest are included. Strangely, too, does the general feeling coincide with Hume's in this wonderful problem; for whether his 'Natural History' be the right one or not, that Religion must have a Natural History, all of us, cleric and laic, seem to be agreed. He indeed regards it as a Disease, we again as Health; so far there is a difference; but in our first principle we are at one.

To what extent theological Unbelief, we mean intellectual dissent from the Church, in its view of Holy Writ, prevails at this day, would be a highly important, were it not, under any circumstances, an almost impossible inquiry. But the Unbelief, which is of a still more fundamental character, every man may see prevailing, with scarcely any but the faintest contradiction, all around him; even in the Pulpit itself. Religion, in most countries, more or less in every country, is no longer what it was, and should be — a thousand-voiced psalm from the heart of Man to his invisible Father, the fountain of all Goodness, Beauty, Truth, and revealed in every revelation of these; but for the most part, a wise prudential feeling grounded on mere calculation; a matter, as all others now are, of Expediency and Utility; whereby some smaller quantum of earthly enjoyment may be exchanged for a far larger quantum of celestial enjoyment. Thus Religion, too, is Profit; a working for wages; not Reverence, but vulgar Hope or Fear. Many, we know, very many, we hope, are still religious in a far different sense; were it not so, our case were too desperate: but to witness that such is the temper of the times, we take any calm observant man, who agrees or disagrees in our feeling on the matter, and ask him whether our *view* of it is not in general well-founded.

Literature, too, if we consider it, gives similar testimony. At no former era has Literature, the printed communication of Thought, been of such importance as it is now. We often hear that the Church is in danger; and truly so it is — in a danger it seems not to know of: For, with its tithes in the most perfect safety,[64] its functions are becoming more and more superseded. The true Church of England, at this moment, lies in the Editors of its Newspapers. These preach to the people daily, weekly; admonishing kings themselves; advising peace or war, with an authority which only the first Reformers, and a long-past class of Popes, were possessed of; inflicting moral censure; imparting moral encouragement, consolation, edification; in all ways, diligently 'administering the Discipline of the Church.' It may be said, too, that in private disposition, the new Preachers somewhat resemble the Mendicant Friars of old times:[65] outwardly full of holy zeal; inwardly not without stratagem, and hunger for terrestrial things. But omitting this class, and the boundless host of watery personages who pipe, as they are able, on so many scrannel straws,[66] let us look at the higher regions of Literature, where, if anywhere, the pure melodies of Poesy and Wisdom should be heard. Of natural talent there is no deficiency: one or two richly-endowed

---

62 The 'association of ideas', a concept long current in philosophy of mind, appears as a basis for poetry in Wordsworth's 1800 'Preface' to *Lyrical Ballads*.

63 This essay was published in 1757 in *Four Dissertations*. It discusses the development of religious belief through history as the product of human nature, putting to one side the possibility of divine agency in the world.

64 Tithes were the proportion of a parish's agricultural produce that went to support the church.

65 Mendicant: that is, one of the orders who lived entirely on charitable donations.

66 Scrannel: thin, meagre. Here, an echo of Milton, *Lycidas* (1637), complaining of other poets that 'their lean and flashy songs / Grate on their scrannel pipes of wretched straw' (ll.123–4).

individuals even give us a superiority in this respect. But what is the song they sing? Is it a tone of the Memnon Statue, breathing music as the *light* first touches it?[67] A 'liquid wisdom,' disclosing to our sense the deep, infinite harmonies of Nature and man's soul? Alas, no! It is not a matin or vesper hymn to the Spirit of Beauty, but a fierce clashing of cymbals, and shouting of multitudes, as children pass through the fire to Moloch![68] Poetry itself has no eye for the Invisible. Beauty is no longer the god it worships, but some brute image of Strength; which we may call an idol, for true Strength is one and the same with Beauty, and its worship also is a hymn. The meek, silent Light can mould, create and purify all nature; but the loud Whirlwind, the sign and product of Disunion, of Weakness, passes on, and is forgotten. How widely this veneration for the physically Strongest has spread itself through Literature, any one may judge, who reads either criticism or poem. We praise a work, not as 'true,' but as 'strong;' our highest praise is that it has 'affected' us, has 'terrified' us. All this, it has been well observed, is the 'maximum of the Barbarous,' the symptom, not of vigorous refinement, but of luxurious corruption. It speaks much, too, for men's indestructible love of truth, that nothing of this kind will abide with them; that even the talent of a Byron cannot permanently seduce us into idol-worship; that he, too, with all his wild syren charming, already begins to be disregarded and forgotten.[69]

Again, with respect to our Moral condition: here also, he who runs may read that the same physical, mechanical influences are everywhere busy. For the 'superior morality,' of which we hear so much, we, too, would desire to be thankful: at the same time, it were but blindness to deny that this 'superior morality' is properly rather an 'inferior criminality,' produced not by greater love of Virtue, but by greater perfection of Police; and of that far subtler and stronger Police, called Public Opinion. This last watches over us with its Argus eyes more keenly than ever;[70] but the 'inward eye' seems heavy with sleep. Of any belief in invisible, divine things, we find as few traces in our Morality as elsewhere. It is by tangible, material considerations that we are guided, not by inward and spiritual. Self-denial, the parent of all virtue, in any true sense of that word, has perhaps seldom been rarer: so rare is it, that the most, even in their abstract speculations, regard its existence as a chimera. Virtue is Pleasure, is Profit; no celestial, but an earthly thing. Virtuous men, Philanthropists, Martyrs, are happy accidents; their 'taste' lies the right way! In all senses, we worship and follow after Power; which may be called a physical pursuit. No man now loves Truth, as Truth must be loved, with an infinite love; but only with a finite love, and as it were *par amours*.[71] Nay, properly speaking, he does not *believe* and know it, but only '*thinks*' it, and that 'there is every probability!' He preaches it aloud, and rushes courageously forth with it—if there is a multitude huzzaing at his back! yet ever keeps looking over his shoulder, and the instant the huzzaing languishes, he too stops short. In fact, what morality we have takes the shape of Ambition, of Honour: beyond money and money's worth, our only rational blessedness is Popularity. It were but a fool's trick to die for conscience. Only for 'character,' by duel, or, in case of extremity, by suicide, is the wise

---

67 In Roman times, one of the colossi at Memnon on the Nile was reputed to issue a musical sound at dawn.

68 Moloch (in the King James bible, Molech) is an idol to whom God bans the Isrealites from giving child sacrifice: see e.g. Leviticus 20.2–5.

69 Byron, by far the most celebrated poet in English of his age, had died in 1824.

70 In Greek myth, Argus is a giant with a hundred eyes.

71 *Par amours*: that is, as a mistress, rather than a wife.

man bound to die.[72] By arguing on the 'force of circumstances,' we have argued away all force from ourselves; and stand leashed together, uniform in dress and movement, like the rowers of some boundless galley. This and that may be right and true; *but we must not do it*. Wonderful 'Force of Public Opinion!' We must act and walk in all points as it prescribes; follow the traffic it bids us, realise the sum of money, the degree of 'influence' it expects of us, *or* we shall be lightly esteemed; certain mouthfuls of articulate wind will be blown at us, and this what mortal courage can front? Thus, while civil Liberty is more and more secured to us, our moral Liberty is all but lost. Practically considered, our creed is Fatalism; and, free in hand and foot, we are shackled in heart and soul, with far straiter than feudal chains. Truly may we say, with the Philosopher, 'the deep meaning of the Laws of Mechanism lies heavy on us;'[73] and in the closet, in the marketplace, in the temple, by the social hearth, encumbers the whole movements of our mind, and over our noblest faculties is spreading a nightmare sleep.

These dark features, we are aware, belong more or less to other ages, as well as to ours. This faith in Mechanism, in the all-importance of physical things, is in every age the common refuge of Weakness and blind Discontent; of all who believe, as many will ever do, that man's true good lies without him, not within. We are aware also, that, as applied to ourselves in all their aggravation, they form but half a picture; that in the whole picture there are bright lights as well as gloomy shadows. If we here dwell chiefly on the latter, let us not be blamed: it is in general more profitable to reckon up our defects than to boast of our attainments.

Neither, with all these evils more or less clearly before us, have we at any time despaired of the fortunes of society. Despair, or even despondency, in that respect, appears to us, in all cases, a groundless feeling. We have a faith in the imperishable dignity of man; in the high vocation to which, throughout this his earthly history, he has been appointed. However it may be with individual nations, whatever melancholic speculators may assert, it seems a well-ascertained fact that, in all times, reckoning even from those of the Heraclides and Pelasgi,[74] the happiness and greatness of mankind at large have been continually progressive. Doubtless this age also is advancing. Its very unrest, its ceaseless activity, its discontent, contains matter of promise. Knowledge, education, are opening the eyes of the humblest — are increasing the number of thinking minds without limit. This is as it should be; for, not in turning back, not in resting, but only in resolutely struggling forward, does our life consist. Nay, after all, our spiritual maladies are but of Opinion; we are but fettered by chains of our own forging, and which ourselves also can rend asunder. This deep, paralysed subjection to physical objects comes not from nature, but from our own unwise mode of *viewing* Nature. Neither can we understand that man wants, at this hour, any faculty of heart, soul or body, that ever belonged to him. 'He who has been born, has been a First Man;' has had lying before his young eyes, and as yet unhardened into scientific shapes, a world

---

72 In this sentence, 'character' means a person's public reputation, rather than their true essence. Duelling was very rare but still occasionally resorted to by aristocratic men to uphold their 'honour'. The Prime Minister, the Duke of Wellington, had fought one earlier in 1829, against the Earl of Winchilsea, who had accused him of 'treacherously plotting the destruction of the Protestant constitution' by enacting Catholic emancipation. It didn't come to much: Wellington shot wide, and Winchilsea held his fire, and later wrote an apology.

73 As often in Carlyle, what appears to be a quote from another writer is just more Carlyle.

74 *Pelasgoí* is used by some ancient Greek writers to name the people who were in Greece before the Greeks arrived. The Dorian Greeks imagined themselves to be descended from the hero Heracles, with ancestors called the Heraclides providing the link.

as plastic, infinite, divine, as lay before the eyes of Adam himself. If Mechanism, like some glass bell, encircles and imprisons us, if the soul looks forth on a fair heavenly country which it cannot reach, and pines, and in its scanty atmosphere is ready to perish—yet the bell is but of glass; 'one bold stroke to break the bell in pieces, and thou art delivered!' Not the invisible world is wanting, for it dwells in man's soul, and this last is still here. Are the solemn temples, in which the Divinity was once visibly revealed among us, crumbling away? We can repair them, we can rebuild them. The wisdom, the heroic worth of our forefathers, which we have lost, we can recover. That admiration of old nobleness, which now so often shows itself as a faint *dilettantism,* will one day become a generous emulation, and man may again be all that he has been, and more than he has been. Nor are these the mere daydreams of fancy—they are clear possibilities; nay, in this time they are even assuming the character of hopes. Indications we do see, in other countries and in our own, signs infinitely cheering to us, that Mechanism is not always to be our hard taskmaster, but one day to be our pliant, all-ministering servant; that a new and brighter spiritual era is slowly evolving itself for all men. But on these things our present course forbids us to enter.

Meanwhile, that great outward changes are in progress can be doubtful to no one. The time is sick and out of joint. Many things have reached their height; and it is a wise adage that tells us, 'the darkest hour is nearest the dawn.' Whenever we can gather indication of the public thought, whether from printed books, as in France or Germany, or from Carbonari rebellions and other political tumults,[75] as in Spain, Portugal, Italy and Greece, the voice it utters is the same. The thinking minds of all nations call for change. There is a deep-lying struggle in the whole fabric of society; a boundless grinding collision of the New with the Old. The French Revolution, as is now visible enough, was not the parent of this mighty movement, but its offspring. Those two hostile influences, which always exist in human things, and on the constant intercommunion of which depends their health and safety, had lain in separate masses, accumulating through generations, and France was the scene of their fiercest explosion; but the final issue was not unfolded in that country: nay, it is not yet anywhere unfolded. Political freedom is hitherto the object of these efforts; but they will not and cannot stop there. It is towards a higher freedom than mere freedom from oppression by his fellow-mortal, that man dimly aims. Of this higher, heavenly freedom, which is 'man's reasonable service,' all his noble institutions, his faithful endeavours and loftiest attainments, are but the body, and more and more approximated emblem.

On the whole, as this wondrous planet, Earth, is journeying with its fellows through infinite Space, so are the wondrous destinies embarked on it journeying through infinite time, under a higher guidance than ours. For the present, as our Astronomy informs us, its path lies towards *Hercules,* the constellation of *Physical Power:* but that is not our most pressing concern. Go where it will, the deep HEAVEN will be around it. Therein let us have hope and sure faith. To reform a world, to reform a nation, no wise man will undertake; and all but foolish men know, that the only solid, though a far slower reformation, is what each begins and perfects on *himself.*

---

75 The Carbonari were an underground liberal nationalist movement in Italy, which in 1820–21 had risen against the various monarchies and empires that divided up the peninsula between them. They were defeated. Similar movements existed in other Mediterranean countries, perpetuating a sense of national identity fostered during the Napoleonic period.

Lightning Source UK Ltd.
Milton Keynes UK
UKOW021805020912

198348UK00003B/6/P